DATE DUE

JA 8 '93		AP 7 '03	
JE 22 '93		AP 23 '03	
JY 30 '93	DE 19 97	JE 9 '04	
JA 14 '94	MR 18 '98		
MR 4 '94	AP 8 '98		
JE 23 '94	MY 20 '98		
AP 7 '95	MY 18 '98		
MY 26 '95	MY 30 '98		
JE 15 '95			
FE 23 '96	SE 14 '98		
	MR 19 '99		
MY 10 '96	MY 27 '99		
DE 3 '96			
AP 14 '97	NO 9 '00		
OC 8 '97	NO 30 '00		
NO 25 '97	JE 4 '01		
DE 5 '97			

DRUG TESTING AT WORK
A Guide for Employers & Employees

DRUG TESTING AT WORK

A Guide for Employers & Employees

by Beverly Potter, Ph.D.
and Sebastian Orfali, M.A.

Ronin Publishing, Inc.
Post Office Box 1035, Berkeley CA 94701

iii

Published by
Ronin Publishing, Inc.
Post Office Box 1035
Berkeley, California 94701

Drug Testing at Work: A Guide for Employers and Employees
ISBN: 0-914171-32-1
Copyright © 1990 by Beverly Potter and Sebastian Orfali

Printed in the United States of America
First printing 1990

9 8 7 6 5 4 3 2 1

Project Editors: Sebastian Orfali and Beverly Potter
Copy Editors: Aiden Kelley, Nancy Crompton, Lora Koehler
Research: Nancy Krompotich, Nancy Freedom
Word Processing: Julie O'Ryan, Vikki Barron
Typography: Beverly Potter, Sebastian Orfali
Index: Nancy Freedom, Beverly Potter

The material herein is presented for reference and informational purposes only, not as legal or medical advice. The author and publisher advise readers to consult an attorney regarding legal matters and a physician regarding medical matters.

U.S. Library of Congress Cataloging in Publication Data
Sebastian Orfali and Beverly Potter
   Drug Testing at Work: A guide for Employers and Employees
   Includes appendix, bibliography & index
   1. Business. 2. Controlled Substances.3. Drug laws
   4. Employee Assistance Programs. I. Title.

Acknowledgements

We are grateful to the many people who helped us in researching, writing, editing and producing this book, and to the companies who gave us information about their services and products.

Special thanks to the following people for giving us help and materials:

Michael Aldrich, Ph.D.; David Smith, M.D.; of the Haight Ashbury Free Medical Clinic; Alexander T. Shulgin, Ph.D.; Aiden Kelley, Ph.D.; Barbara Lang Rutkowski, Ed.D., and Arthur D. Rutkowski, J.D., of the newsletter, *Employment Law Update;* William Adams, Esq., of Orrick, Herrington, and Sutcliffe; John True, Esq., of the Employment Law Center; Daphne Macklin of the American Civil Liberties Union; Peter Strom of the California Department of Personnel Administration; Chuck Flacks, aide to California Senator Lockyear; Gene Peterson of MARCOM at Hewlett Packard; and Clary Nelson of the Picture Group.

Special thanks to the following organizations for information regarding their products and services:

Roche Diagnostic Systems, a Division of Hoffmann-LaRoche Inc., Keystone Medical Corporation, Marion Scientific, a division of Marion Labs, Inc., Hewlett Packard Company, Inc., Luckey Laboratories, Inc., PharmChem Laboratories, Inc., Rutkowski and Associates, Inc., The American Civil Liberties Association, and the Haight Ashbury Free Medical Clinic, Inc.

Contents

Part 4 Guidelines For Employers

Part 5 Guidelines For Employees

Appendices

FOREWORD

When in presenting his administration's National Drug Control Strategy, President Bush stated that the federal government has a responsibility to taken an active role in comprehensive drug-free workplace policies. He encouraged both public and private sector employers to train supervisors on how to identify employees who use drugs, including drug testing where appropriate, and to educate employees about the established plan.

Drug Testing At Work: A Guide For Employers and Employees is a comprehensive guide to accomplishing both objectives.

The book begins with a social history of drugs including alcohol and their impact on the workplace. It correctly emphasizes that legal drugs such as alcohol and nicotine cost industry more money than do highly, publicized illicit drugs such as cocaine.

A comprehensive review of drug testing methodology is presented followed by a discussion of the legal issues of drug testing including employer liability and the right to privacy. This is a particularly important section for employers who are rushing to implement low cost programs which do not include adequate input from all sectors of the complicated workplace environment.

The section guidelines for employers including deciding on a drug program and establishing a drug testing policy provides a framework for making such decisions. I was also happy to see a strong component on setting up employee assistance programs and preventing drug use without testing.

In this era of drug testing and discipline it should be emphasized that demand reduction prevention and employee assistance are vital elements to a comprehensive strategy aimed at reducing substance abuse in the workplace.

This excellent book provides such a comprehensive view and will be of benefit to both employers and employees.

David E. Smith, M.D.
Founder and Medical Director
Haight Ashbury Free Clinics, Inc.
Research Director of Merritt Peralta Institute
Associate Clinical Professor of Occupational Medicine
     and Clinical Toxicology

Advertisement for Coca Cola™ from 1887, a time when the beverage contained cocaine. At the turn of the century Americans consumed cocaine in a variety of elixirs, tonics, medicines and just plain soda pop commonly available at the grocery store

The Drug Society

Chapter 1
Drug Usage Past And Present

People have been using drugs for a long time. As early as 2000 B.C. opium was used in Greece and Cyprus for rituals. Ololiuqui, which is similar to LSD, peyote, and marijuana, was used by the ancient Aztecs. Witches supposedly rubbed their bodies with hallucinogenic ointments in the Middle Ages. Historians believe that George Washington used hemp because of tooth and gum pains. President Ulysses Grant used cocaine while writing his memoirs.

After the Civil War doctors prescribed opium-based remedies for common maladies such as headache and skin rashes. Narcotic potions, such as Mrs. Winslow's Soothing Syrup and Hooper's Anodyne, the Infant's Friend, were commonly used by Victorian ladies to calm their babies. At the turn of the century, heroin and morphine derivatives were sold legally in drugstores and by mail-order catalogues.

Cocaine had also entered American culture by this period. The Peruvian Indians in the Andes have been using coca leaves for over 5,000 years, and their mild stimulation and appetite-depressing effect has been an important part of their culture. Coca was central in the Inca Indian's culture where they used the leaves as money. But it was not until 1860, when the cocaine alkaloid was extracted from the coca leaf, that the health hazards in cocaine became known.

From Cure-All To Menace

When cocaine, the drug, became commercially available in a pure form in 1884, its many useful qualities were hailed worldwide by doctors. Because it worked simultaneously as a painkiller and vasoconstrictor, cocaine became a popular anesthetic for procedures, such as eye and throat surgery, in which clearing away blood was difficult. It anesthetizes the body, but keeps the mind sharp; so doctors prescribed it for the terminally ill. Cocaine was used in cough medicines, hemorrhoid balms, nasal sprays and wine. Vin Mariani, the popular coca wine, bore the endorsements of President William McKinley, Thomas Edison, and Pope Leo XIII. And, of course, cocaine was once the major ingredient in Coca-Cola®. In 1884 Sigmund Freud wrote, "Absolutely no craving for further use of cocaine appears after the first or repeated, taking of the drug."

> *"Ironically, the common use of alcohol as a mainstay of the workplace was the ground in which the first roots of job-based alcohol rehab programs took hold. Throughout much of the first half of the nineteenth century, workers in practically all occupations drank on the job, frequently at the employer's expense, and often during specific times set aside for imbibing. In the Southern United States, for example, men often took off from work for 'eleveners,' a whiskey and brandy version of the coffee break. In England, dockworkers during this period, and on into the twentieth century, typically had at least four or five drinking breaks with 'practically no restrictions in the workers' access to liquor during the hours of labor.' These practices were even more evident in eighteenth century England. In London during this century it was commonplace for workers in many trades to be directly dependent upon tavern keepers, since taverns were the employment agencies of that period. In one extreme instance, men who worked on coal-carrying ships were almost required to drink specific amounts each day; the cost of the assigned amount was taken from their wages — whether it was drunk or not. Other employers sold drinks in the workplace and frequently charged the cost of these against wages."*
> Harrison Trice & Mona Schonbrunn[115]

In the late nineteenth century, an estimated one in 400 Americans used opiates regularly. Parke-Davis Pharmaceuticals manufactured many products containing cocaine, including cigarettes, cheroots, coca skin salve, and face powder. By 1900, America had developed a population of opiate and cocaine addicts estimated at 250,000. Deaths, sickness, and crime caused by drugs became commonplace. By the turn of the century public opinion began to change violently. Despite the opposition of U.S. drug companies, many states passed laws regulating cocaine and opiates. In 1909, the import of opium was banned. In 1914, the Harrison Narcotics Act made numerous drugs illegal under Federal law. By the 1920s, cocaine, heroin, and morphine use had declined dramatically.

Once widely regarded as a harmless cure-all, cocaine became America's most feared and loathed drug. Coke and opium quickly went underground, and "decent" Americans steered clear of them. Most Americans in the years after World War I indulged in bootleg gin. However, some jazz-band musicians and avant-garde actors and artists still used cocaine.

A Nation Forgets

Over the decades that followed most people forgot the nation's earlier brush with opiates and cocaine. Almost all that remained in popular memory were such cultural artifacts as Eugene O'Neill's *Long Day's Journey Into Night* set in 1920, which depicts the crushing effects on a family of a mother's drug addiction.

The nation's attention turned to marijuana. Mexican immigrants, who came north looking for jobs in the twenties and thirties, brought marijuana with them. During prohibition, the popularity of marijuana grew. *Reefer Madness*, a 1936 film, warned that smoking the "killer weed" would lead to insanity, and hell. In fact, social attitudes about drugs are revealed in films of the period. *Cocaine Fiends and Reefer Madness: The History of Drugs in the Movies* by Michael Starks is an excellent chronicle of this phenomenon.

Drugs stayed on the fringe of society throughout the fifties. Beat Generation artists began enhancing their perceptions with pot, and later with more mind-bending hallucinogens. LSD's hallucinogenic qualities were discovered by Albert Hoffman, a chemist who accidentally swallowed it in 1943. In the early sixties, Harvard professor Timothy Leary gave his students LSD and told them to "turn on, tune in, and drop out." Fired by Harvard, he promptly became a counter-cultural hero. The baby boom provided the drug-culture priest with ready-made disciples. "By 1960, there was a whole generation who knew nothing about drugs or their dangers, and what little they did know came from people who didn't know anything about drugs either," said historian Musto. "When people found out that marijuana didn't drive you wild and mad, the government lost what little credibility it had."

In an age of youth rebellion, the fact that parents were shocked by drugs was all the more reason for young people to take them. Hollywood and Broadway, ever-sensitive to changing mores, romanticized the drug culture with pot-smoking anti-heroes in *Easy Rider* (1969) and let-it-all-hang-out hippies in *Hair* (1968). "In the 1960s, the baby boomers got fooled into thinking, just like the people in the 1890s, that you could use drugs recreationally and not get addicted to them," said Dr. Mark Gold of the National Cocaine Hotline. "Marijuana had a meaning beyond just getting high. It was a source of shared identity among people who had a common point of view, notably that their parents were stupid, the government was immoral, and the war in Vietnam was wrong."

History Repeats

Slowly the dark side emerged. San Francisco's Haight-Ashbury, which spawned "Flower Power," became a seedy slum of strung-out addicts. Heroin sent urban crime soaring as addicts stole to sustain their habits. In spite of bad LSD trips, social drug use had become so deeply entrenched that it continued to permeate all levels of society, particularly the youth culture. Although still illegal, drugs became socially acceptable in many quarters. Marijuana was smoked as openly as tobacco while police looked the other way. Man-made chemicals like phenylcyclidine, better known as "angel dust" or PCP, drove users into violent frenzies, making the myth of wild-eyed drug fiends, which had been scoffed at by the sixties college student, a horrifying reality.

Cocaine was the perfect drug for the "Me Generation." The mid-seventies marked the second coming of cocaine. "The new morality of young Americans is success, the high-performance ethic," says university professor Ralph Whitehead. "Pot bred passivity. On alcohol you can't perform. You smell. People can tell when you've been drinking. But cocaine fits the new value system. It feeds it and confounds it. Young adults walk a tight line between high performance and self-indulgence, and cocaine puts the two together."

In show business and in chic society, dinner guests were offered crisp white lines of cocaine along with their demi-tasse. Cute silver spoons worn as jewerly began to adorn the hip and rich. Coke became a workplace pick-me-up, like coffee, only "trippier." Says Dr. Wesley Westman, Chief of the Alcohol and Drug Dependency Center at the Veteran's Administration Hospital in Miami, "Cocaine is the drug of choice by people who are into the American Dream. `I love my job, I am successful' — except that they don't and they're not."

Cocaine use has increased dramatically as the availability increased and the price went down during the 1980s. By the end of the decade there was a tremendous increase in the use of crack, a form of freebase cocaine. David Smith, the Director of the Haight-Ashbury Free clinic, said that crack is "like a MacDonald's hamburger. If you had to go through all the problems preparing the hamburger, you might not eat it. If you had to get a freebase kit and convert the cocaine yourself, you might not smoke it. This is cocaine that's ready to smoke. It's already prepared in freebase form."

Crack is actually more expensive than powdered coke, but is sold in amounts that make it more available to people. For example, in San Francisco, one-tenth of a gram of smokeable cocaine cost about $30 in the late 1980s, compared with cocaine powder, which cost between $100 and $120 a gram. After crack came "ice," a smokeable form of methamphetamine or speed, which was introduced in 1989 in Hawaii and quickly spread to the

West Coast. The dangers of ice surpass those of crack because the high is longer lasting and it is easier and cheaper to manufacture.

Therapeutic And Recreational Use Of Psychoactive Drugs

Psychoactive drugs are often self-prescribed to relieve pain or stress, achieve psychological insight, or to get "high." Many drugs that began in a therapeutic context evolved into recreational drugs. Nitrous oxide, for example, was an anesthetic that became widely used recreationally. Quaaludes (methaqualone), another therapeutic drug, were very popular as a recreational drug in the late seventies. But drug use for therapeutic and religious purposes goes back historically to the use of such drugs as peyote, and, more recently, to their use by philosophers such as Aldous Huxley, who used mescaline as a drug for insight. Later LSD and MDMA were used for philosophical and moral insight.

A popular recreational drug of the 1980s was MDMA, or "Ecstasy," as it is commonly called. Users claim it has the power to make people more trusting, to banish jealousy, and to break down barriers separating lover from lover, parent from child, therapist from patient. Yet, unlike LSD, it does not impair one's ability to distinguish between reality and fantasy. Bruce Eisner's book, *Ecstasy: The MDMA Story*, chronicles the history, use and dangers of MDMA. MDMA, methylenedioxymethamphetamine, is related to both amphetamines and mescaline. It began to be used in the seventies as a therapeutic drug.

Drug Use Among Youth

Use of drugs among adolescents and college students continues at alarmingly high levels. Among teenagers, ten risk factors have been identified: poor academic achievement (low grades), low religiosity (low religious commitment), early alcohol use, poor self-esteem or self-acceptance, psychopathology (largely depression), poor relationship with parents, deviance (law-breaking), sensation-seeking, peer drug use, and adult drug use.[5] A survey of 16,502 teenagers conducted in 1986 showed that 17 percent of them had already tried cocaine, an increase of more than 10 percent in a single year.[10]

A study by the National Institute on Drug Abuse surveyed the number of people who said that they had used cocaine in the preceding 12 months. They found cocaine use was highest among 18-25 year olds, peaking in 1979 at over 19 percent.

Questionnaire surveys of 4171 students, carried out in 1970, 1973, 1976, 1980, and 1984 at five American universities, showed an increase in the use of cocaine, cannabis, hallucinogens, sedatives, amphetamines, and alcohol. Cocaine use increased from 2.7 percent in 1970 to 30 percent in 1974, and cannabis use almost doubled during that period. The surveys found that intercollegiate athletes used significantly more anabolic steroids than nonathletes, but did not differ significantly from the nonathletic students in use of other substances.[6]

Table 1.1
Number Of People Who Said They Used Drugs In The Previous Month

Alcohol	113.1
Marijuana	18.2
Cocaine	5.8
Stimulants	2.7
Analgesics	2.5
Tranquilizers*	2.2
Sedatives*	1.7
Hallucinogens	1.0

*non-medical use
from 1985 National Institute on Drug Abuse survey[58]

Estimated number of people, in millions, who said they used each drug. Alcohol and marijuana are the most frequently cited as drugs used. Alcohol use is six times that of marijuana in 1985. By the late 1980s cocaine use increases dramatically.

Public Outcry

According to a report by Charles Schuster, Director of the National Institute on Drug and Alcohol Abuse, since 1979 people have been backing away from almost all drugs. Long feared as the "gateway drug," marijuana declined in use among younger people in the 1980s. In 1978, according to government surveys, 10 percent of all high-school seniors smoked marijuana everyday, whereas by the late 1980s, the percentage dropped to about 5 percent.

By the mid-1980s, there was a new toughness on drugs, reflected in the sharp increase in public support for treating even possession of small amounts of marijuana as a crime. The Gallup/Newsweek poll conducted by telephone in 1986, found that most Americans favored testing all workers for drug use, emphasized the need for treatment, and saw education as the key area of government action.

Even the San Francisco Bay Area, which has always been exceptionally tolerant of recreational drug use, began witnessing a change in attitude. A study by the *San Francisco Chronicle* in the summer of 1986 polled 740 adults by phone. The *Chronicle* study found that fewer people in the Bay Area support the legalization of marijuana than did so in 1983; that a third of the population is turning away from alcohol; that less than a third still smoke tobacco; and that four out of five believe it is wrong to drink or get high on the job.

The anti-drug crusade reflects public opinion that the sale and use of narcotics is one of the most important problems facing the United States, and that it is of compelling national urgency. In a Time/CBS survey conducted in 1986, 57 percent of those questioned believed possession of even small amounts of marijuana should be treated as a criminal offense, as opposed to 41 percent who believed it should be decriminalized in 1977. An amazing 72 percent of full-time workers said they would be willing to be tested for recent use of illegal drugs. One out of every 10 full-time workers (and almost 25 percent of full-time factory workers) reported that some colleague used illegal drugs in the workplace. Among full-time office workers, drug use at work was reported by 5 percent.

But employers can't afford to forget about an older and even more prevalent problem: alcoholism among workers. According to the National Institute on Alcohol Abuse and Alcoholism the number of people who are addicted to alcohol has increased by 8 percent to 12 million. More than any other factor, alcoholism causes absenteeism, high medical bills and reduced work quality. Estimates by Triangle Research Institute in North Carolina put the cost to the U.S. economy at $117 billion in 1983.

When faced with higher taxes to build more prisons, an overwhelming majority of taxpayers said they would pay a hundred dollars a year more in taxes in order to give stiffer sentences. According to the Time/CBS poll, 16 percent said people convicted of selling cocaine or crack for the first time should be sentenced to 30 days in jail; 22 percent favored a year in jail; and 42 percent recommended more than a year in jail for first-time cocaine sellers.

Widely publicized instances of drug abuse among talented and superbly conditioned athletes, including the deaths in the late 1980s of University of Maryland basketball star Len Bias and Cleveland Browns' football player Don Rogers, created a demand that young people's sports models should police their own ranks and submit to urine tests when required. People started to feel that it was reasonable to expect strict compliance with the anti-drug laws from professionals responsible for the safety of other people, such as airline pilots, air-traffic controllers, surgeons, and police officers.

By 1980, Miami had become the major port for smuggling dope into the U.S.A. No one really knows how much is actually smuggled in, but the conventional wisdom is that about 90 percent gets through. That would suggest that over a hundred tons of cocaine and two million pounds of marijuana entered south Florida in 1985. The official estimates are more modest — 85 tons of coke and 30 million pounds of marijuana for the entire United States. But even official estimates mean that upwards of 82,000 pounds of marijuana is consumed in the U.S. daily. On February 28, 1982, President Reagan established the South Corridor Task Force to reduce the flow of illegal drugs coming to the United States through Florida by greatly increasing air, sea, and land interdiction efforts, and by "arresting and convicting smugglers apprehended during these activities," according to Charles F. Rinkevich, the Task Force coordinator.

When marijuana became regarded as a "soft drug," like alcohol and tobacco, lots of people began using it. Some states, not wanting to imprison members of the younger generation, decriminalized marijuana. Eventually, 11 states decriminalized, and one legalized marijuana, and 29 others made possession of small amounts of marijuana a misdemeanor. Some 20 million to 30 million people or more were smoking grass.

War On Drugs

President Reagan declared "war on drugs" and created a network of 12 Organized Crime Drug Enforcement Task Forces across the country. The battle was on. In response to lobbying by parents, revision of the 1878 Posse Comitatus Act, which prohibited the military from entering civilian affairs, made it possible for the military to play a limited role in the war on drugs. The Reagan Administration's strategy, a five-pronged program that attacked the problem from every important angle, sounded like a winner, at least in theory. It took into consideration the fact that any war on drugs must pursue both law enforcement and education programs to be successful. In the words of Dr. Carlton Turner, the Reagan's chief adviser on drug policy, its goal was "to take the customers away from the dealers as well as to take the dealers away from the customers." The money spent on the war on drugs rose dramatically in the middle eighties, reaching 1.2 billion dollars in 1985.

Federal spending on radar, tracking aircraft and other measures to detect airborne smugglers increased dramatically, to nearly $205 million in 1989 fiscal year from about $18 million in 1982, the year Reagan declared war on drugs. Nonetheless, the General Accounting Office (GOA), the investigative arm of Congress, found in an 18 month study that the detection technology did not work. They estimated that only about 10 percent of airborne anti-smuggling missions resulted in seizure of drugs.[208]

Many consider Ronald Reagan's "war on drugs" to have been a dismal failure. Despite the changes in social attitudes and a moderate decline in the use of marijuana, use of the much more dangerous crack cocaine skyrocketed during his administration. Some fault Reagan for failing to address one of the major causes of the rise of crack, black urban poverty. Others allege there was a cynical cooperation between intelligence operatives and big-time drug lords.

The major form of the war on drugs in northern California is CAMP, the Campaign Against Marijuana Planting. Each summer, state officials working with federal funds hire local police and sheriffs backed with helicopters in a major campaign to eradicate marijuana growing. They have the power to confiscate property on which marijuana is growing.

In spite of CAMP and other law-enforcement attempts to eradicate it, nearly 2,000 tons of high-quality American-grown marijuana is reported to be available for sale each year. In countries like Columbia, drug cartels have become the most powerful internal political forces, able to exert control through bribes and open assassinations of top government officials. Simultaneously, in the United States marijuana is the largest cash crop after corn, according to NORML, the National Organization for Reform of Marijuana Laws which reported that growing marijuana was a $16.6 billion-a-year industry in 1987.

Drugs were a major issue during the 1988 political campaign. Despite its strong anti-drug stance, the Reagan Administration lost some credibility due to dealings with reputed narco-dictator Manuel Noriega, the alleged Contra-cocaine connection, and the dramatic rise in the use of crack and related violent crime. Congress took the initiative and passed the 1988 Omnibus Drug Bill, appropriating billions of dollars and mandating fines of $10,000 for possession of even small amounts of marijuana. President Bush, during his early months in office, made his first TV address to the nation on the war on drugs, urging increased enforcement and interdiction efforts.

William Bennett, former Secretary of Education, was appointed by Bush as "Drug Czar" to coordinate the federal anti-drug efforts. Bennett launched a comprehensive anti-drug strategy with specific goals of lowering drug use in the U.S. Bennett brought a new balance between "supply-side" strategies of law enforcement and interdictim and "demand-side" strategies of prevention, treatment, and education.

While the U.S. may finally be trying to kick its habit, other countries around the world are just getting hooked. Like blue jeans and rock-and-roll, America's drug culture has been exported to Europe and Asia. Although statistics are hard to come by, drug use seems to be expanding worldwide, especially in the countries that export drugs to the U.S. When the Soviet invasion of Afghanistan and the overthrow of the Shah of Iran drove the Asian drug trade through Pakistan, the number of heroin addicts there went from virtually nil in 1980 to 650,000 by the end of the decade. The U.S.S.R. has not escaped the global epidemic, either. Soviet soldiers in Afghanistan were reported trading their weapons for opium and hashish.

On the other side of the world, along the spine of the Andes in Bolivia, Peru, Colombia, and Ecuador, both the lower and the middle classes began smoking coca paste, a potent and addictive form of cocaine that costs only pennies a cigarette. "These countries have never had a problem like this before," says Manuel Gallardo, Chief of the Department of State's Bureau of International Narcotics Matters. "Their people are getting strung out right and left from all social classes, and the governments don't know what to do." In 1989, drug dealers in Colombia gunned down an anti-drug presidential candidate, triggering a massive crackdown on the drug cartels. Cartel leader went into hiding and retaliated with killings and bombings.

Many argue that a nation will drink more alcohol, smoke more cigarettes, or abuse more opiates if the relevant drug is made more available. The key to reducing drug- and alcohol-related problems, they argue, lies in controlling production, marketing, retailing, and distribution. The fact is that drugs constitute a very big business throughout the world. In Zimbabwe, tobacco production is the largest industry. In Malawi, 100,000 families rely on cash from tobacco, while in the Indian state of Uttar Pradesh, tobacco provides a living for 75,000 farmers, and about two million other workers are engaged in curing, packing, and shipping it.

Soaring consumption of alcohol in Third World countries has just begun to worry health workers at a time when some economists see it as a sign of improving living standards and growing industrialization. Spectacular growth rates in beer production have been achieved in countries as varied as Japan, Bulgaria, the Netherlands, and Yugoslavia. In the past 20 years, Nigeria, Mexico, and Brazil have become major beer producers by world standards, and have joined such traditional producers as the Federal Republic of Germany and the United Kingdom at the top of the league. The situation is little different for illicit drugs. Ever since the opium market was opened in Southeast Asia in the nineteenth century by the United Kingdom and other European imperialist powers, there has been a massive increase in the cultivation and distribution of opiates and related substances in exchange for guns and other European specialties.

Chapter 2
The Social Costs
Of Drug Abuse

Estimates of the costs of drug use in the U.S. vary widely. A 1980 study by the Triangle Research Institute of North Carolina calculated the toll to the nation at 47 billion dollars as a result of lost productivity and related deaths, crime, and medical treatment.[58] The literature contains references to the cost of drug abuse to American industry but most of these are estimates, extrapolations, and projections. The cost estimates tend to be derived from a set of seldom questioned but surely questionable assumptions.

There is a common belief that drug use always results in reduced performance and lessened cognitive and intellectual abilities. There is the assumption that a dysfunctional work or life history is *caused* by use or preference for a drug, and that those who use drugs will soon malfunction like the drug abusers seen in treatment programs.[33] However, some drugs seem to improve performance on tests of conceptual ability, rapid visuomotor, scanning, tracking, and set-shifting, abstracting abilities, and other kinds of intellectual and verbal functioning.

Laurence Miller of Fair Oaks Hospital in Summit, New Jersey, researched the presence of neuropsychological impairment in chronic users of CNS depressants, including alcohol, opiates, and cocaine.[33] He found in his review of the literature, and in his own research on alcohol, that neither total lifetime consumption nor current frequency of drinking was related to cognitive performance. Rather, "there was a significant association between current quantity of alcohol consumed per drinking occasion and impairment on neuropsychological tasks. Most seriously affected were the processes of abstraction, adaptive abilities, and concept formation." Curiously enough, and contrary to common assumptions, the neuropsychological studies of marijuana users have generally failed to document any permanent impairment in cognitive functioning as a result of marijuana use alone. Of course, marijuana is a drug that is rarely used alone.

The "marijuana question" was the object of a lot of interest in the middle 1970s. In the permissive social climate of that time many scientists were able to research the question without compromising their reputations. In 1977, Carlin and Trupin[35] compared daily marijuana smokers who denied that use with a control group of abstainers. The marijuana smokers performed significantly faster than the nonsmokers on tests of rapid visuomotor, scanning, tracking, and set-shifting.

Grant's[35] research group studied heavy use of marijuana in 1978. They found that better performance on certain tasks actually correlated with heavy use, replicating the findings of Carlin and Trupin. Bruhn and Maage[35] compared four groups of subjects in 1975 on an variety of intellectual and cognitive tests. The groups were non-drug users, marijuana and hallucinogen users, hallucinogen and amphetamine users, and marijuana, hallucinogen, amphetamine, and heroin users. Their results showed that use of these drugs had no significant effect on neurocognitive functioning, alone or in combination. However, Bruhn and Maage's results were disputed by Helen Jones in *The Marijuana Question*, where she presented a great deal of data indicating mental impairment from regular marijuana consumption. What this research highlights is that the social costs of drug use are complex and difficult to assess.

"In terms of sheer numbers our worst problem drugs are the legal recreational drugs, alcohol and tobacco. Out of a total population of 240 million Americans, more than 100 million use alcohol, and 10 to 13 million are probably addicted to it. Roughly 56 million American are addicted to tobacco. Almost all users are addicts.

"Among illegal drugs, marijuana is still the most popular. According to the U.S. government, 20 million Americans smoke marijuana occasionally. My own studies, based on government data, suggest that the number of marijuana users — people who smoke at least once a year — is probably between 35 and 40 million. Of these perhaps three million smoke it everyday, which is one definition (among many) of an addict. But my guess is that no more than 1.5 million are compulsive users — smokers who would suffer great discomfort if forced to suddenly stop using the

drug. So I suspect that roughly one in every 20 pot users is totally addicted, while roughly 1 in 10 alcohol users is.

"Cocaine now has become the second most popular illegal drug. Somewhere between 12 and 15 million Americans probably use cocaine at least once a year. Of those, perhaps 500,000 to 750,000 use it every day. Another 3 to 5 million may use heroin at least once a year, and about 300,000 to 500,000 are addicts. Finally, a couple of million Americans are addicted to valium and other more obscure drugs that aren't much talked about." [20]

Arnold S. Trebach
Professor of Justice, American University

Drugs And Crime

It is clear that crime is directly fueled by drug abuse. "I believe the crime problem in America today is the drug problem," declared New York City Police Commissioner Ward. The sheer dollar volume of narcotics traffic is immense, estimated between $27 billion and $100 billion a year. A study released in 1986 of the link between drugs and street crime in New York and Washington found that 56 percent of suspects tested were using drugs at the time of arrest. [19]

The use of alcohol and other drugs has long been suspected as a risk factor for homicide victimization. Alcohol use can lead to an increased risk of being killed. Usage increases the likelihood that the users will engage in risk-taking and provocative behavior. Alcohol, being a CNS depressant, may release inhibitory control mechanisms, and thereby permit expression of aggressive or violent behavior. Also, being "drunk" or "stoned" makes people easier targets for robberies and other types of crimes. [63]

Richard A. Goodman [63] studied the blood-alcohol levels in homicide victims who were killed between 1970 and 1979 in Los Angeles, and found that alcohol consumption was common. Wolfgang [63] found that alcohol use prior to the homicide had been reported for 50 percent of the victims in Pennsylvania, and that in nearly 44 percent of all homicides, alcohol use had been reported for both the victim and the offender. Voss and Hepburn [63] reported a history of alcohol use for 54 percent of all homicides in Chicago. The results clearly indicate that an increased use of alcohol is associated with more homicides. Most of the results reported are very modest, because information about alcohol use is not routinely collected during police investigations, and can only be indirectly inferred from autopsy reports.

"We've always been a drug-ridden society. There were probably as many psychoactive drugs in use 100 years ago, but there was no crime associated with drugs. Most of the crime associated with drugs has to do with their enormously inflated price, which is a direct consequence of their illegalization, so that people have to get the money to afford them, which often

involves committing crimes. But the pharmacological effects of many drugs are against violence. That's certainly true with heroin and probably with marijuana."

Dr. Andrew Weil
From Chocolate to Morphine

"It's a sad commentary on our times that the `Not as bad as alcohol and tobacco' test has become so relevant. For one thing, it shows that two extremely dangerous drugs have become the standard of acceptability. Yet it is hard to imagine anything much worse than alcohol and tobacco. These two drugs account for 30 percent of all premature deaths — some 525,000 — in the United States annually. That's almost as many as the 650,000 Americans who have died in combat in all the wars that we have ever fought, including the American Revolution. Each year, 325,000 Americans die from the effects of smoking, but only 29,557 Americans died fighting in World War II.

"But it isn't just the loss of life that takes a toll. The economic loss to society due to alcohol — including health care costs, accidents, and work loss — runs $120 billion annually. For tobacco the figure is $65 billion a year."[14]

The War On Drugs: Fighting To Lose
The Coming Revolution

About 25 percent of the convicted jail inmates in 1983 were under the influence of one or more drugs just prior to their offense. Nearly half had been drinking, according to data released by the U.S. Justice Department. Three-fourths of all jail inmates reported using illegal drugs at some time in their lives.

Alcohol contributes to as many as 200,000 deaths annually in the United States.[18] Tobacco contributes to another 250,000. There are no comparable figures on the long-term lethal effects of cocaine abuse, but some comparative data does exist on "crisis deaths." The NIDA (National Institute on Drug Abuse) maintains a Drug Abuse Warning Network (DAWN), which collects information on drug overdoses from emergency rooms and medical examiners in 26 metropolitan areas. The data are sketchy, but they do give some indication of the relative dangers of the various drugs. In 1984, cocaine was implicated in 604 deaths, and was third on the list behind heroin and morphine, which caused 1,072 deaths, and alcohol use in combination with other drugs, which led to 1,131 deaths.

An alarming statistic is the rate at which the number of cocaine deaths is increasing. Between 1980 and 1985, the number of deaths reported to DAWN in which cocaine was implicated increased by 324 percent. The rise of cocaine use increased dramatically in the 1980s. Between 1981 and 1986 the number nearly tripled. Yet, as late as 1986 cocaine deaths were still relatively infrequent. For example, more people (570) died from appendicitis in 1986 than from cocaine abuse (563). The death toll from cocaine is minute compared with the number of fatalities attributed in 1980 to alcohol (98,186) and tobacco (some 300,000 annually). By 1988 the number of deaths attributed to cocaine rose to 1,582 according to a NIDA report.[207]

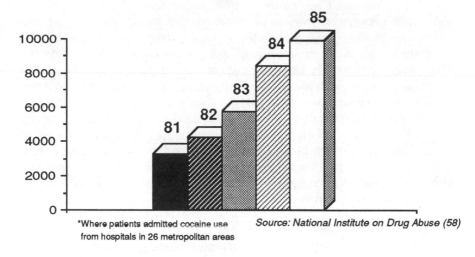

*Where patients admitted cocaine use from hospitals in 26 metropolitan areas

Source: National Institute on Drug Abuse (58)

Fig. 2.1 Cocaine And Emergency Room Visits*

The health cost of drug abuse was estimated by one National Center for Health Statistics study at $59.7 billion in 1983, but the medical bill for alcohol abuse was $116.7 billion. "There is no question that alcoholism in terms of social costs remains our number-one problem. We can't lose sight of that because of our emphasis on drugs," said the NIDA's Schuster.

A similar paradox exists with marijuana. Mark Kleiman, past Director of Policy Management Analysis at the Criminal Divison of the Justice Department, said, "Marijuana is certainly not a purely benign drug, at least for the 2 or 3 million Americans who smoke five joints a day. But it's hard to prove that Saturday-night marijuana use does much damage. The scientific evidence is just not that impressive. Assume the worst about the evidence linking it to lung cancer, and the danger is still small compared with that of tobacco smoking. The studies linking marijuana to drops in IQ just don't hold up. Evidence that it weakens the immune system is interesting but inconclusive."[20]

Dr. Phillip W. Landfield of Wake Forest University in Winston-Salem, North Carolina, said in a report to the Associated Press in September, 1986 that animal research indicated that THC might affect the structure of the brain in the same way as aging. He said that THC, the psychoactive ingredient in marijuana, might act like a steroid hormone, reducing the density of the brain cells in the hippocampus of the brain by 20 percent. The decreased number of cells is similar to that seen in aging animals in this part of the brain, he said. There is speculation that a drug-induced loss of brain cells of 20 to 30 percent, combined with a similar loss due to normal aging, might cause conditions similar to Parkinson's disease at an early age.[7]

On the other hand, physiological psychologists Bruhn and Maage in 1975, and Grant and his group in 1978, failed to find evidence of any significant neuropsychological impairment as a result of persistent amphetamine abuse or marijuana use. Marijuana use was not found to be associated with any impairment in mental capability.[35] However, *The Marijuana Question* by Helen Jones and Paul Lovinger, describes hundreds of studies of marijuana and presents the most convincing data about the hazards of marijuana use.

Some medical doctors speculate that the repeated use of cocaine, even in small doses, can eventually trigger seizures like the one suspected of killing baseball star Len Bias. Government scientists reported that a "kindling" process gradually leaves the brain more vulnerable to cocaine toxic effects, probably by altering neurological systems that govern emotion and the body's motor functions.[11]

The "kindling" phenomenon, according to Dr. Robert Post of the Health and Human Services Department, occurs because cocaine is a "dirty drug" that combines stimulant properties with local anesthetic properties. This could explain some of cocaine's exceedingly unpredictable behavioral effects, such as panic attacks. Dr. David Smith, Director of the Haight-Ashbury Free Clinic, warns, "Smoking a dangerous drug is even more hazardous. A heart can be perfectly healthy and still stop working, because the electrical rhythm is disturbed by smoking cocaine. The healthiest person in the world can die of a cocaine overdose."[16]

Andrew Weil, M.D., comments, "The government continues to subsidize tobacco addiction, and cigarettes are the worst form of drug abuse in this culture, the greatest public-health problem that we have, and the most flagrant example of drug pushing, since most of it is pushed on teenagers, who are lured by advertising into thinking it's cool to smoke. If you want to talk about death penalties for drug pushers, start with the executives of tobacco companies. I think there is no illegal drug that comes near alcohol in dangerousness. All you have to do is ask law enforcement agencies about the association of alcohol and violent crime."[8]

Designer Drugs

Designer drugs are chemical variations on federally controlled synthetic drugs that mimic the effects of classic narcotics, stimulants, and hallucinogens and pose severe health hazards. By slightly altering the molecular structures, black-market chemists create new, untested legal drugs. The term "designer drugs" also refers to new street drugs, such as crack, which are concentrated forms of already existing drugs, uniquely marketed for a target income group. As the variety of designer drugs began to flourish on the black market, there was a sudden rise in overdose deaths and neurodengenerative diseases with Parkinson-like symptoms. Two of the most obvious risks are clear. First, many of the designer drugs are new drugs not tested before, whose potency and selective action are unknown. Second, because they are produced illicitly by phantom chemists practicing no quality control, many of the substances are contaminated by impurities and dangerously toxic by-products.[66]

Many of the synthetic narcotics are not detected by routine chemical analysis. So they are attractive to parolees, prison populations, and the growing number of white-collar workers who are fearful of mandatory drug testing. According to the National Institute of Mental Health, many heroin users are beginning to show symptoms of Parkinson's disease, because a heroin synthetic analog is being used that contains MPTP, a by-product which was created by a faulty chemical procedure. MPTP has been linked with symptoms of Parkinson's disease.

Lethal mistakes can be made during the simple process of mixing the active ingredient with a common cut or dilutent. Because the fentanyl derivatives, used as a substitute for heroin, are so potent, the actual dose may be as little as a microgram — less that a grain of salt. Dealers along the way attempt to dilute the product, a technique requiring skill and sophistication, which most street dealers don't have.

Illicit synthetic narcotics have spread dramatically. The drugs can be disguised to look like whatever organic heroin is currently being sold on the street, or sold as cocaine or methamphetamine to unsuspecting users. They are made to look, taste, and feel like the real thing. The chances have sky-rocketed for both addicts, recreational users and first-time experimenters.

Chapter 3
Drug Use On The Job

⌊Drug use on the job isn't a new issue. Nonetheless alcohol, the most commonly abused drug, has only recently been recognized as a problem. It is estimated that 10 percent of the workforce is alcoholic, and that nearly half of all industrial injuries can be linked to alcohol abuse. But other drugs, as they become more available, are becoming more of a problem. Peter B. Bensinger, former head of the Federal Drug Enforcement Administration, estimates that within any given month, seven million people abuse prescription drugs, such as stimulants, barbiturates, and tranquilizers. Increasingly, workers are bringing prescribed tranquilizers and sedatives into the workplace.[2] ⌋

A study of drug abuse in the general population conducted by the New York State Narcotic Addiction Control Commission in 1971 was based on a statewide representative sample of 7,500 persons.[4] A special analysis was prepared using a subset of employed respondents. As would be expected, a primary finding was that drug use among employed persons parallels drug-use patterns in the overall population. The rate of regular use of certain drugs such as marijuana, barbiturates, major tranquilizers, and heroin was in fact slightly higher than in the general population. Although many of the drugs listed in Table 3.1 are of the legitimate prescription type, the surveys reveal that approximately one out of every eight workers in New York was a regular user of one or more of these drugs. Note that cocaine, at the time of the study, was not included as a separate category because cocaine use was so low. By the 1980s cocaine became one of the drugs most frequently used on the job.

Table 3.1
Drug Use On The Job*

| Drug | Regular Use** | | Ever Used | |
	Total Population	Employed	Total Population	Employed
Tranquilizers	4.3	3.9	23.2	22.7
Sedatives	4.0	3.8	28.7	27.5
Marijuana	3.5	4.0	10.5	12.1
Speed	2.7	2.4	19.9	19.1
LSD	0.3	0.3	2.4	2.6
Heroin	0.2	0.5	1.0	1.3
Other Narcotics	0.1	0.3	7.5	6.9

Source: New York State Narcotic Contol Commission, 1971 (4)
*Percentage of total population and employeed persons in New York households over 14 years old
** Used six or more times per month

CONSAD Research Corporation conducted a survey of industrial drug use in 1975, using a nationwide sample of 197 firms. About 35 percent of the firms indicated the existence of a drug problem, although most of them characterized it as a small problem, and about 10 percent described the problem as ranging from moderate to severe.[4]

Most employed users are young and have limited seniority. When older workers experience drug problems, the drugs involved are usually alcohol, barbiturates, or amphetamines. Although the hiring of inner-city minorities is frequently cited in the literature as a cause of company drug-abuse problems, one study conducted by Halpern and reported to the American Management Association involving over 230 companies found no relationship between minority-group employment and an increased incidence of drug abuse. Drug abuse now seems to cut across ethnic, racial, educational, and class lines.

The second phase of the CONSAD study involved gathering detailed data on use from 20 of the 197 firms, and 2,500 employees were interviewed. The survey revealed that 17 percent of these employees, or one of out every six, had experience with or were currently using illegal or nonmedical drugs. Nearly 7 percent indicated current use of illegal or nonmedical drugs. The substances more frequently cited were marijuana, amphetamines, and barbiturates. The reasons most frequently cited for using drugs were "experimentation" and "kicks," with very few citing job-related reasons, such as coping with the job or peer pressure.

Bobby Guinn, a professor of Health Studies at the Pan-American University, studied job satisfaction and amphetamine use among long-distance truck drivers. She found that more than 62 percent of the drivers reported at least occasional use of drugs while driving, but their reason for doing so was not for recreation, unlike the workers described in other studies. The truckers believed that using drugs was essential to meeting a delivery schedule. This does not indicate dissatisfaction with the job, but rather reflects a perceived necessity for the use of amphetamines in order to do one's job.[61]

During the 1980s American workers rediscovered the use of cocaine as a stimulant to improve performance. Early in the use of cocaine, all the positive effects of cocaine are experienced. But as use continues, the negative effects become evident.

The temptation to use drugs while working can be seen among athletes performing for endurance, and musicians, actors, speakers, people on TV, and anchorpersons who have to lose their inhibitions and project charisma. Cocaine is used much as caffeine is, except that cocaine is euphoric and, at first, engenders conviviality and a feeling that you can succeed at anything; a feeling of omnipotence. Drugs might also be used in order to bear stress or pain by individuals who have to perform difficult tasks such as shiftwork, or endure long periods of loneliness or combat. Probably the greatest use of drugs sanctioned in recent history was during World War II, when many major military operatives had a chain of distribution of stimulant drugs, which included cocaine, dexedrine, or methedrine. These gave the ordinary soldier a feeling of invincibility, and enabled him to go out into battle.

Ironically, cocaine appeals to those who would never think of using alcohol on the job, because it gives a sense of enhanced intellectual capabilities and doesn't interfere with motor functioning.

Who Uses Drugs On The Job

People who use drugs on the job tend to be 20 to 40 years old, and of limited seniority, but use cuts across ethnic, race, educational, and class lines. Use on the job parallels overall drug use in the population.

There is a sharp contrast between the profile of drug abusers in 1977 and that in 1985. In 1977, the average clients in treatment centers were addicted to heroin, were black adult males from the ghetto, and used mostly one drug. By 1984, abusers were predominantly lower-to middle-class whites, whose drug use seemed to stem from a recreational motive instead of escapism. By the mid-1980s, many people entering treatment were polydrug abusers, using more than one drug. Their willingness to use whatever drug available was a symptom of the "let's party" syndrome.[23]

On-the-job users who used cocaine during the 1980s were usually middle class. One 1985 survey of callers to the 800 cocaine national hotline found the average caller to be 30 years old, with more than 14 years of schooling. Of those surveyed, 33 percent earned more than $25,000 a year. Increasingly, drug users include women. From 1982 to 1983 only 18 percent of the patients at Cokenders, a San Francisco area treatment program, were women. By 1985 that percentage had nearly doubled to 36 percent. When the 800 Cocaine hotline was started in 1983, one of every four callers was a woman. By the mid-1980s women made up nearly half of the line's 900 to 1,500 daily calls.

Drug use at work includes street drugs, such as marijuana and amphetamines, and most of all, cocaine. The reasons are relatively simple. Generations that grew up experimenting with illegal drugs now make up a large percentage of the workforce. The National Institute on Drug Abuse recently estimated that nearly two-thirds of those now entering the workforce have used illegal drugs at least once.[2]

In a random sample of calls to 800 Cocaine in two months in 1985, 75 percent of callers said they used drugs on the job; 25 percent used them daily; and nearly half had sold or distributed drugs while at work.

Some professions and types of jobs are especially prone to drug use. One is "shift work," or work between 5 p.m. and 8 a.m. Another is any particularly boring or tedious work. The professionals most likely to use drugs on the job are in the health professions. Health workers, especially nurses, doctors, and anesthesiologists, are commonly identified as being in danger of drug use on the job, because of such factors as access to drugs, shift work, and stress.

Researchers at the Harvard School of Public Health studied 500 physicians and 504 medical students in Massachusetts about their experiences with drugs, excluding alcohol.[26] According to the responses, 59 percent of the doctors and 78 percent of the students said they had used psychoactive substances at least once in their lives. Recreational use was most prevalent among students and physicians under the age of 40, and most often involved marijuana and cocaine. There was a significant increase in cocaine use among medical students during early 1980s. Another problem that doctors have with drugs is self-treatment, usually with tranquilizers and opiates such as fentanyl, which are very hard to detect in urine analysis. How does drug use by doctors affect the welfare of patients? In the survey 3.3 percent of physicians and 5.2 percent of students declared that they had become dependent on drugs, but only 1.8 percent of the doctors reported that drug use had caused them to give poor care.

Reasons For Drug Use At Work

Motivation for most drug use in the workplace can be categorized as any of the following: (1) performance facilitation; (2) relief of boredom; (3) physical and psychological pain; (4) drug addiction, or self-medication of side-effects such as hangover or nervousness from other drugs.

Performance Facilitation

Some drug use is an attempt by the employee to work harder or to be more productive. Most commonly the drug is a stimulant of some form to combat fatigue. Piece workers may take amphetamines or opiates to enable them to work longer or faster without intolerable discomfort. Executives may use cocaine to allow them to work past their usual fatigue limit. Writers may use alcohol or cocaine to loosen up in an attempt to enhance their creative output.

Stimulants, primarily amphetamines, are used extensively in the trucking industry, where individuals must stay awake and alert for extended periods of time. There has been a tremendous concern that fatigue in the truck drivers might override the drug's effects and result in accidents. However, two separate governmental investigations (the Surgeon General's Report On Health Promotion And Disease Prevention in 1979, and the President's Commission On Law Enforcement And Administration Of Justice of 1967) have reported no evidence of a causal relationship between amphetamine use and accidents.

Relief Of Boredom

Many jobs are inherently routine and offer only rare opportunities for challenge. For example, watchdog jobs are structured to have a person available to take action if there is equipment malfunction or an atypical condition. With increasing automation of routine tasks by computers, the number of jobs having a watchdog function will increase. Watchdog jobs are extremely vulnerable to drug abuse. The employee's impairment may not be apparent until an emergency condition arises that may require high-judgment performance by the employee to divert disaster.

Self-Medication Of Side Effects Of Other Drugs

With high-dose recreational drug use of alcohol or cocaine and other stimulants, users may have hangovers, depression, and nervousness that persists throughout the next day. They may attempt to offset these adverse effects by the use of tranquilizers or other medications.

Abuse Of Prescription Drugs

The National Institute for Drug Abuse estimates that abuse of prescription drugs causes 60 percent of hospital emergency-room admissions for drug overdoses, and 70 percent of all drug-related deaths. Usually drug abuse of prescribed medications occurs in one of two ways: prescribed medication comes to be used for recreation, or dependency develops from therapeutic treatment.

Patients may visit a physician claiming symptoms of nonexistent illnesses, or exaggerate symptoms of real illnesses, in order to convince the physician to prescribe the medication that the patient plans to use recreationally.

Therapeutic use of medication can result in addiction. Medication may have been initially prescribed for an indicated condition, but the patient discovers that the medication produces euphoria, and continues to use it for that purpose after the condition for which it was prescribed has been cleared up.

Decline In Productivity Caused By Drug Abuse

The decline in American productivity has continued for more than a decade. The causes of this decline in productivity growth and decline are complex, interdependent, and rooted in all forms of economic activity.[3]

The cost of employee drug abuse takes many forms, and can sometimes be substantial. It has been estimated that dysfunctional drug-abusing employees lose three times as much time from the job as do other employees. In addition to absenteeism, other evidences of dysfunctional employee drug abuse are lessened productivity, safety problems, theft, and increased turnover. Also, drug use often seems to spread after it is introduced into a work unit.

The cost to our society of alcohol and drug abuse in both financial and social terms is devastating. More than 100 million people are currently employed in the U.S. Between 5 and 10 percent of the workforce suffers from alcoholism. Estimates of the nature and extent of drug abuse among American workers are more difficult to pinpoint, because general unawareness of the signs and symptoms allow many drug users to filter undetected through most personnel procedures. It is estimated that 3 to 7 percent of the employed population use some form of illicit drugs on the job, ranging from marijuana to heroin, on a daily basis. Marijuana appears to be the principal substance used, and accounts for 90 percent of current users. Amphetamines are used 34 percent of the time, barbiturates 21 percent, and heroin 5 percent.

The use of alcohol and drugs in the work site presents a clear and present danger. But alcohol and drug consumption off the job can also impair work performance, since alcohol and many drugs remain active in the body for differing periods of time. The danger to the public safety is clearly evident when drugs are used by pilots, air-traffic controllers, bus, taxi, and train drivers, nuclear-plant operators, and military personnel. Employees with a drinking or drug problem are absent 16 times more than the average employee, have an accident rate that is 4 times greater, use a third more sickness benefits, and have five times more compensation claims while on the job; 40 percent of industrial fatalities and 74 percent of industrial injuries can be traced to alcohol abuse.

Drugs may make the worker feel more productive. The problem is that the stoned assembly-line worker and coked-up executive or typist are not necessarily working well.

Drug-related work impairment shows up as a reduction in work quality, capacity, or creativity. The amount of tolerable impairment depends on the work task and on whether situations might arise that require peak performance. A commercial airline pilot's impairment due to a hangover, for example, may not be apparent during routine flight condition, but may be disastrous if the aircraft has an equipment malfunction, for example.

Drug-related work impairment can also result when chronic use of alcohol, marijuana, or cocaine causes brain dysfunction persisting beyond the period of intoxication. Drug use away from work can result in family discord or personal problems that preoccupy the employee's mental activity while at work.

Researchers Parker, Parker, Brody, and Schoenberg did a study on a representative sample of 1,367 employed men and women in Detroit.[62] The subjects responded to questions about their drinking practices, and then completed cognitive tests that measured abstraction abilities. Abstraction tested while respondents were sober decreased significantly as the reported quantity of alcohol usually consumed per drinking occasion increased. Additionally, the study investigated consumption during the previous 24 hours, and found that the impact of recent drinking on cognitive processes lasted longer than 24 hours.

Unfortunately, the drug testing technology usually used by employers will only detect recent alcohol consumption, even though alcohol continues to impair cognitive performance.

Security And Drugs

Alcohol and drug abuse can create many security problems in the workplace, ranging from theft or destruction of company property to the compromising of individuals in sensitive positions.[3]

Thefts are a plaguing problem associated with industrial drug abuse, and have tended to be primarily attributable to heroin-dependent persons. A heroin addict's habit may cost from $50 to $150 a day. Common company theft targets of addicts are tools, small office machinery, company products, uncashed pay checks, and petty-cash boxes.[4] However, the increase of cocaine abuse may be contributing to on the-job-thefts.

Abuse of illicit drugs may result in additional problems for the employer. Some examples include: (1) theft or misuse of company resources to purchase drugs; (2) vulnerability of the employee to blackmail because of the fact of drug use; (3) association of the employee with criminals during the procurement of drugs.[27]

Theft of company property and embezzlement of company funds are common ways in which users support drug habits. Alarm systems, locks, and other security measures are therefore included in the estimated costs of substance abuse. The American Society for Industrial Security reported that in 1982, 25 percent of undercover assignments for police and private security agents were drug-related.[65]

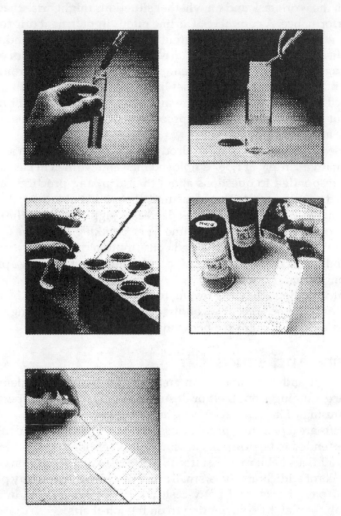

From top-to-bottom. *Extraction:* Urine sample is mixed with extraction solvent and centrifuged. *Concentration:* Sample with solvent is placed in concentration cups containing "standard," "control" and "sample" testing disks, which are small dots of paper, and evaporated. *Inoculation:* Testing disks are placed on the chromatography strip. *Development:* The chromatography strip is placed into a developing jar with a dye marker which migrates with the solvent up the front of the strip. *Detection:* The chromatography strip is dipped into the reagent, then dried. The dry chromatography strip is placed against a light source and inspected for the presence of the drug in question by comparing the migrations of the sample to that of the standard. Samples displaying the same color characteristics and position on the chromatography strip as the standard indicates the presence of the drug. (From product literature of Analytical Systems, Division of Marion Laboratories, Inc., Kansas City, Missouri.)

Drug Testing In Theory And Practice

Chapter 4
Reasons For Drug Testing

There are many reasons why an employer will set up a drug testing program. Let us survey them.

Investigating Accidents

Testing for drugs is very common following an industrial accident. Drug testing after accidents has been successfully used by Southern Pacific Transportation Company. They found that drug testing after accidents substantially reduced the number of accidents. In the 24 months preceding the initiation of their testing program, there were 15,082 accidents. In the 24 months following the introduction of drug testing, the number of accidents dropped dramatically, to 4,865, a reduction of 69 percent. Personal injuries dropped 24 percent after the implementing of drug testing.

There are two considerations to note with post-accident testing. If the person has been receiving psychotropic medication under prescription, that medication or its metabolites will appear in the urine, and impairment may be inferred when none existed. Second, drug metabolites can be detected in the urine long after the period of intoxication or impairment. This occurs most often when the employee has smoked marijuana a day or two before, but not the day of, the accident; yet the presence of cannabinoids in the urine can be construed as marijuana intoxication, and claimed as a contributor to the accident.

Work Fitness

Testing for drug use may determine if a person is fit to work. For example, pilots might blow into a breathalyzer, which records alcohol vapor on the flight recorder, before assuming flight command. If measurable levels of alcohol are present, that fact will be displayed to both the intoxicated pilot and the crew members. Recording the breathalyzer results assures that crew members will not be tempted to cover for an intoxicated pilot.

Mass Screening

The military and many corporations randomly screen employees to detect drug using individuals and to assess the need for drug prevention. Personnel to be screened are selected at random and not because there is any reason to suspect drug use. People included in mass screenings are usually pulled from all positions and levels of the organization and not solely from high risk, safety or security jobs. Urine is generally first "screened" with an inexpensive and easy-to-analyze test.

Many experts argue that random testing is the most effective deterrent to drug use because each employee has some chance of being tested on any given day. Proponents argue that it is fair because there is no stigma or accusation attached to a particular employee who is selected for testing and because the decision to test is not influenced by supervisor biases. Civil rights attorneys Edward Chen and John True reject this argument. They assert that random testing "reverses the presumption of innocence upon which much of our jurisprudence is built, and violates the strong prohibition of dragnet searches sweeping in the many who are innocent in order to find the few who are guilty which is the hallmark of a free and democratic society.[225]

Experts favoring drug testing at work argue that random testing is the most effective deterrent to drug use because each employee has some chance of being tested on any given day. It is fair because there is not stigma or accusation attached to a particular employee who is selected for testing and because the decision to test is not influenced by supervisor biases.

Mass screening programs have drawn the most criticism and have been the main source of legal attacks on drug testing program. People who have no history of drug use resent being treated with suspicion. People using prescription drugs and over-the-counter drugs often test positive and must defend themselves, proving innocence. And it's in mass screening programs that most of the instances of false positives and inappropriate confirmation testing have occurred.

Pre-Employment Screening

Screening applicants' urines to detect drug use in order to avoid hiring drug users is a common use of drug testing. However, there is a great danger that people with false positives will be denied jobs even though they are not drug users, or only occasionally use drugs off the job with no work impairment.

Presumptive Testing

A presumptive situation is one in which there is some strong reason to suspect a person is using drugs: a test is administered to detect or confirm the usage. For example, a supervisor might notice that the person smells of alcohol and walks with a staggering gate; or a person might display signs of barbituate use such as lethargy. In such cases the supervisor might request drug testing.

Controlling Abuse

Rear Admiral Paul J. Mulloy told the Senate Subcommittees on Defense Manpower and Personnel and Defense Preparedness in 1983 that urinalysis is the most effective element in the Navy's "war on drugs." He said that implementation of urinalysis resulted in a decrease of detectable drug use among enlisted Navy personnel. Positive tests dropped from 48 percent in 1980 to 21 percent in 1982. Marijuana was the most common drug detected. However, he glossed over the finding that, following implementation of urinalysis for drug use, there was a notable shift to increased alcohol use.

Southern Pacific Transportation Company reported a decline in positive tests after implementing their drug testing program. In the first testing, they found 23 percent of those tested were reported positive: 60 percent were positive for marijuana; 20 percent for cocaine; 14 percent for alcohol; and 6 percent for other drugs. In comparison testings two years later, only 6.5 percent came up with positive results. Proponents of testing argue that using drug testing as a way to control drug use is legitimate, because after frequent urinalysis is implemented and well-known among the population being tested, continued positive tests occur only in drug abusers who have lost control of their drug use.

Proof Of Abstinence

Drug tests can be a positive indicator for a person who wants to prove that "I have been drug-free." This can provide substantial legal protection for both a recovering drug abuser as well as the employer. For example, an anesthesiologist recovering from chemical dependency would give a urine specimen following any operation with anesthetic complications. If a lawsuit were filed and the plaintiff's attorney discovered the anesthesiologist's history of drug abuse, the attorney would probably claim that the mishap occurred because the anesthesiologist was intoxicated. A negative result on the drug test helps document that the complication did not result from drug use by the anesthesiologist.

As An Adjunct To Treatment

Often a drug abuser will make a contract to be tested for drug use regularly as a condition of treatment. Such testing is a valuable adjunct to treatment. Users fail in their program most commonly when they attempt to return to controlled use of the drug, which typically occurs in the first 3 to 6 months. Drug testing can catch use before the person returns to an abusive level. In short, regular testing helps the individual to break the habit and avoid the drug.

Millicent Buxton, recovery maintenance and re-entry coordinator for Ross General Hospital in Kentfield, California, believes drug testing is a positive tool for monitoring recovery of the chemically dependent. She uses urine testing to monitor treatment contracts for re-entry nurses, doctors, veterinarians, pharmacists, anesthesiologists, and other health professionals recovering from drug abuse. She sometimes jokingly calls her program "the-pay-to-pee program" or "the golden showers project."

Chet Pelton of the California State Board of Medical Quality Assurance also uses urine testing in his recovery program for chemically dependent doctors. Here the purpose of testing is to protect the public. Doctors in the program are actively practicing medicine. Drug testing helps doctors in recovery by identifying a relapse at the earliest possible time. Samples are taken unannounced, by a compliance officer, group facilitators, or a condition monitor. Urine collection is observed. Pelton says that even though tests are unscheduled in his program, scheduled tests are also effective. People who abuse drugs are out of control and cannot refrain from using drugs even though they know they will be tested. The testing helps them to develop self-control.

To Confirm A Positive Test Result

Confirmatory tests are used to confirm the results of the presumptive test. They yield fewer false positives, and are more elaborate and expensive. Samples that test positive are retested or "confirmed" with a more powerful and expensive method.

Whether the confirmatory step is necessary depends on the intended use of the results. For therapeutic monitoring in a drug treatment program, where the goal is detection of early relapse, and a positive result has no disciplinary consequences, screening methods alone are adequate and confirmation is not necessary. Instead, the person is confronted with the positive results and usually acknowledges use. On the other hand, in situations in which a single positive urine test could result in discipline, termination of employment, or loss of professional license, "forensic" or legal standards of testing positives using a different confirmatory method are essential.

Chapter 5
What Is Tested

Drug tests can be applied to many different kinds of samples and materials, and their validity can range from excellent to nil, depending on just what is being tested and what tests are performed. Here we will survey these substances and the consequences of the results of testing for them.

Urine

Urine is most commonly tested, because of the ease of getting a sample, the speed of conducting the analysis, and the low cost. The major drawback of testing urine is that presence of drug metabolites in urine *does not indicate whether the person was actually under the influence of the drug at the time* the sample was given. The drug may have been used in the past, but not be actively affecting functioning. This is particularly common with marijuana, which can lead to positive test results two or three weeks or longer after use.

EMIT ST® tests are easy to perform. The urine sample is compared to a reference solution — the calibrator — that contains a known amount of the drug being tested for. Each test vial contains all the materials needed for a test. The operator uses the EMIT ST® diluter to transfer a small, fixed amount of calibrator into one test vial and an equal amount of the urine

*sample into another vial, and then places the vials into the EMIT ST®
photometer. The photometer measures and compares the speed of the
chemical reactions in the vials and within 90 seconds prints the test result.
If the reaction in the sample vial is as fast or faster than that in the calibrator vial, the photometer prints a "+," meaning that the sample contains a
detectable drug; if the reaction in the sample vial is slower than that in the
calibrator vial, the photometer prints a "-," meaning that the sample does
not contain a detectable drug.*

Breath

Breath testing is common for alcohol. It has the advantage of being
nonintrusive, inexpensive, and almost instantaneous. A positive breath test
indicates the percentage of alcohol in the blood, which is a positive indication of intoxication.

Disposable breath analyzers for motorists have become a competitive
business." BreathScan" from Prescott Technologies is a 3-inch tube filled
with yellow crystals. The driver exhales into the tube, and the crystals turn
blue-green if he is too drunk to drive. BreathScan® sells for $1.59 per test, and
is available to the general public.[57]

Saliva

Testing saliva for marijuana can determine recent use, whereas use of
marijuana as long as two months in the past will sometimes cause a positive
urine test in regular users.

Intravenously administered THC or tetrahydrocannabinol, the primary psychoactive ingredient in marijuana, does not appear in human
saliva. Thus cannibinoids that are detected in saliva must result from recent
smoking or ingestion. Because THC metabolites can be detected in urine
several days and sometimes weeks after marijuana has been smoked, a
saliva test is a useful alternative to document recent marijuana use. In a
study using a RIA (Radio Immunoassay) test, cannibinoids were detected
in saliva 4 to 10 hours after subjects smoked a single marijuana cigarette.

Blood

Blood testing measures the actual presence of the drug or its metabolite
in the blood at the time of testing. Blood-test results are the best indicator of
intoxication. However, blood testing, which requires trained medical skill,
is an expensive and intrusive method.

The most accurate confirmation of drugs is a blood test. A blood
sample can be collected at the time of the initial test and later used to confirm
an initial positive result. This is especially important in accident investigations. A positive test can be confirmed by a Gas Chromatography (GC)
blood test to detect whether or not the drug was present in the blood at the
time the sample was taken. This gives a much greater indication of impaired

function and intoxication than does urine testing, which indicates drug use in the past, but not present intoxication. Blood tests can indicate recent drug use with greater accuracy, especially with marijuana. In confirmation by a replication of the test, it is important that the sample be frozen, since drug metabolites deteriorate. Marijuana can be detected up to six hours after consumption by testing blood. After that, concentration falls rapidly, and marijuana is not detectable in blood after 22 hours.

Hair

Testing hair can reveal past drug use, but can not indicate dysfunction or intoxication. At about $15 per substance analyzed, hair testing is claimed to be evasion proof and capable of distinguishing extent of use.[238] Doctor Ron Siegel of UCLA analyzed strands of hair of John Keats, the nineteenth-century romantic English poet, and proved that Keats was, indeed, an opium smoker.[99]

Behavior

Observation of behavior is not commonly thought of as a drug test; yet most people do observe behavior to decide whether people are under the influence of a drug. We do this instinctively.

Behavior is often a better indication of intoxication than chemical analysis. Observation of performance, such as the ability to walk a straight line or maintain balance on one leg, is valuable. Slurred speech, unsteady gait, mood changes, and irritability are good indicators of drug intoxication. Quick-reflex tests include walking the line, eye-hand coordination, balance, and standing on one leg. Reports of the subject's behavior from spouse, friends, work supervisors, or other individuals are another type of behavior assessment. Recent needle marks would be a presumptive indicator of intravenous drug use, for example.

Physiological Signs

The diameter of the pupils is a quick indicator of recent opiate use. Normal pupils are between 3 and 6 mm in diameter. However, following opiate use, pupils are constricted to 1 to 2 mm. This is called "pinned." Pupillary constriction is a useful sign even in daily users, because tolerance to pupillary constriction does not evolve with continued opiate use. Observations should be made under low-light conditions. Although opiate use is the most common reason for pinned pupils, medications used in the treatment of glaucoma, a disease that causes increased pressure inside the eye, also produces marked pupillary constriction under low-light conditions.

In an opiate overdose producing unconsciousness, pupils may be dilated, because lack of oxygen in the brain, hypoxia, produces pupillary dilation which overrides pupillary constriction induced by the opiate.

Nystagmus, a persistent 1 to 2 mm back-and-forth eye movement when looking to the extreme left or right, is another sign of intoxication. To test for nystagmus, the person is asked to hold his or her head in a fixed position while tracking the examiner's finger, pen, or small flashlight with the eyes. The object to be tracked is moved across the visual field 12 to 20 cm from the face. It is easier to observe nystagmus if there is a light source diagonal to the subject's eye that reflects a small point of light from the sclera, or white portion, of the subject's eyes.

The back-and-forth movement can be seen by watching a circle of light reflected from a point on the sclera. Eye movement is characterized by a quick movement to the side of the gaze and a slow return movement toward the nose after the eye has moved to the extreme lateral position. When sober, most people's eyes will have one to three cycles of nystagmus and them stop. When people are intoxicated with alcohol or sedative hypnotics, the back-and-forth eye movements persist. This is called *sustained horizontal nystagmus,* and is strong evidence for alcohol or sedative hypnotic intoxication.

Vertical nystagmus is a similar disturbance in eye movement occurring in extreme vertical gaze. There may be a slight rotation of the eyes, called *rotary nystagmus.* PCP (phencyclidine) intoxication produces *central nystagmus,* severe back-and-forth eye movement when the person is looking straight ahead. Because sustained nystagmus is not under voluntary control, it is an objective, reproducible, and strong test for intoxication.

Table 5.1
Pupil Size Reveals Drug Use

Drug	Pupil Size	Nystagmus
Stimulants	Large	No
Marijuana	Large	No
Opiates		
Intoxication	Pinned	No
Withdrawal	Large	No
Alcohol & Sedatives		
Intoxication	Variable	Yes, horizontal
Withdrawal	Large	No
Phencyclidines (PCP)	Large	Yes, central & horizontal

Source: David Smith & Donald Wesson, *Substance Abuse In The Workplace*, 1984 (27)

Chapter 6
Testing Methods

Drug tests depend on various modern chemical techniques. We need to understand these techniques in order to evaluate their reliability. Testing methods vary greatly in their cost, accuracy, time required for analysis, selectivity, and sensitivity. Typically, laboratories use a low-cost screening procedure first, then confirm positive results with an expensive but highly accurate method. The most popular screening methods are immunochemical tests called *immunoassays* and *thin-layer chromatography* (TLC).

Immunoassay

The immunoassay operates on the principle of antigen-antibody interaction. The basic principle is similar to the rabbit test for pregnancy. Drugs of interest are coupled to large molecules and injected into rabbits or sheep. The animal's immunologic system produces antibodies against the specific drug and competing drug molecules. Competition exists for available antibody binding sites between the tagged drug in the test and the drug in the unknown sample. Reliability depends upon how specific and sensitive the antibodies are to a given compound.

Immunoassay tests have many limitations, however. Drug-specific immunoassay can discriminate only between the presence and absence of the suspected drug. They are at best semiquantitative, that is, they can yield only an estimate of the quantity of drug in an individual's system. Cross-reactivity, in which nondrug substances and over-the-counter drugs bind with the antibodies, is a serious shortcoming of this method and causes lower specificity and false positives.

How Enzyme Immunoassay Tests Work

Antibody preparation: *Haptens of low molecular weight (e.g., most drugs) will not generally elicit an immune response in an animal. Specific antibodies to drugs are therefore made by attaching the compound to be assayed to a protein carrier, most commonly bovine serum albumin (BSA), to produce a larger antigen. Animals are immunized with this new antigen. After several months, the antibody-bearing gamma globulin fraction of the animal's blood is isolated. An antibody will bind to the specific shape of molecules for which it is designed, leaving unbound the variety of other biochemical compounds present in the sample.*

Enzyme-labeled drug: *The choice of the enzyme label to be used in the EMIT® immunoassay depends on several criteria: it should possess a high specific activity at a pH that does not impair antigen-antibody binding; it should be readily available in highly purified, soluble, and stable form at reasonable cost; it should be simply and very sensitively detectable; it should be present in biological fluids; it should not be inhibited by substances present in biological fluids; it should possess reactive groups through which it can be linked to other molecules without significantly impairing either the enzyme activity or antigen-antibody binding.*

John Miller, PhD[54]
Lab 78: Laboratory Medicine for Practicians Physicians

The EMIT® Test

The Enzyme Multiplied Immunoassay Test (EMIT®) manufactured by Syva Corporation in Palo Alto relies on modifying an enzyme's ability to act on its substrate, lysozyme. An animal is injected with the drug or a drug metabolite, usually in combination with other chemicals. The injection provokes the animal to produce specific immune chemicals, called antigens, that will bind to the drug. These antigens are then harvested by extracting and purifying certain proteins (gamma globulins) from the animal's blood. The lysozymes or other enzymes are bound to the drug or metabolite of interest, such as morphine, amphetamine, or methadone. This drug-enzyme complex is inactivated as a functional enzyme when the drug antibody is placed in the same solution. If, however, an added urine sample contains the drug in question, the antibody will bind less of the drug-enzyme complex, because the antibody will also bind to the free drug. Any unbound drug enzyme is active and lyses the bacterial suspension from *micrococcus luteus*, clearing the solution. This clearing is measured as a change in absorption of light by using a spectrophotometer.

EMIT® assays are available in a variety of kits for screening urine for amphetamine, barbiturates, benzodiazephines, cocaine metabolites, methadone, PCP, morphine, proposyphene, ethanol, and urinary cannabinoids. The EMIT® method can utilize several different enzyme systems available in different assay products.

How The EMIT®Test Works

EMIT ®principle: *The drug to be assayed (e.g., throphylline) is contained in a solution, such as serum or plasma. Antibodies specific to the theophylline are added to the solution, along with an enzyme substrate and NAD. Enzyme-labeled throphylline is then added to the mixture. Competition for the antibody binding sites occurs between throphylline in the person's sample, and the enzyme-labeled theophylline. When the enzymne-labeled theophylline binds to the antibody, enzyme activity is significantly reduced due to steric exclusion of the substrate by the antibody. Only the free enzyme-labeled theorphylline can act on the substrate, converting NAD to NADH in the process. Enzyme activity, which is directly proportional to concentration of theophylline in the sample, is measured spectrophotometrically at 340 nm.*

John Miller, PhD[54]
Lab 78: Laboratory Medicine for Practicians Physicians

The RIA Test

The radioimmunoassay (RIA) marketed under the name Abuscreen® by Hoffman-LaRoche, Inc., uses similar technology to the EMIT® test. The RIA also used specially produced antibodies, but differs from the EMIT® by using radioactive isotopes to label and measure the results. The U.S. Department of Defense relies on the RIA as its primary method of urine screening, conducting over 10 million RIA screenings a year.

RIA is considered more accurate than EMIT®, but is somewhat more costly and requires more sophisticated laboratories due to the use of radioactive isotopes. Since EMIT® and RIA are both immunoassay techniques, one should not be used as a back-up or confirming test for the other. Instead, a positive test result should be confirmed by a nonimmunological procedure such as gas chromatograph.

The most important weakness of immunoassays in general is their lack of specificity, because there are few antisera that are specific for a single compound.[33] A more sensitive and more specific technique, fluorescent polarization immunoassy (FPIA) was developed by Abbott Labs and extended to testing drugs of abuse in 1986.

Thin-Layer Chromatography

With all forms of chromatography, the urine is first extracted with a reagent, and the extract is then subjected to a procedure that causes the components to separate. With thin-layer chromatography (TLC), results are created by the reproducible migration pattern of a drug on a thin layer of absorbant, usually a silica-coated glass plate. The plate is sprayed with a solution that reacts differently with different drugs, producing colored spots, that represent different drugs.

The sample is "spotted" by putting a drop of urine extract on the TLC plate, which is put in a solvent which runs up the plate by capillary action, carrying with it the drugs present in the extract. A specific drug will always migrate to the same spot. After drying, the plate is analyzed for the position of drugs of interest. If cocaine is present in the sample, for example, the visualization solution is sprayed and reveals a specific spot on the plate that indicates where the cocaine has traveled. The spot location is identified by an "Rf" number which is a ratio of the distance traveled by the drug in questionto the distance traveled by the solvent from the origin, where the sample was originally spotted. The plate can be illuminated by ultraviolet lights. Identical molecules are expected to migrate to the same Rf zone, and to give identical color reactions. TLC can produce false positives, that is, certain over-the-counter and prescription drugs will travel to approximately the same spot as illegal substances. Therefore, results of TLC must be interpreted by a skilled technician and positive results must be confirmed by a more reliable testing method.

TLC is used most often in drug detoxification clinics, methadone maintenance programs, testing of parolees and prison inmates, and industrial screening.

Problems With TLC Tests

Results from thin-layer chromography tests are qualitative, giving either a positive or negative result. Positive results can not be quantified. TLC is far less sensitive than other tests. Low levels of substance abuse are not readily detected by TLC so the meaning of screenings by TLC is confusing. Whether a sample is called positive or negative often depends on the concentration of the drug in the sample or the sensitivity cutoff of the test. The sensitivity cutoff of most TLC tests is between 1,000 and 2,000 nanograms per millileter (ng/ml). Most drugs are detectable only when they reach a concentration of more than 2,000 ng/ml, which makes many drugs difficult to detect. A negative TLC result may simply mean that the method is not sensitive enough to detect the drug in the sample. TLC suffers from low specificity. TLC is used as a broad screen for drugs because it is fast, inexpensive, and does not require sophisticated instrumentation.

TLC is often used in medical settings to detect recent high-dose drug abuse and toxic levels of drugs. It is an ideal test for an emergency room, where the drugs taken are unknown and quick measurement of toxic levels is necessary.

A TLC "street test" for morphine in the urine was developed in 1984 by Henneberg, Woznik, Brodzineska, and Wencel. It uses a thin layer of resin-coated plastic rods. The method was specific enough to differentiate morphine from synthetic opiates, such as pethidine. Sensitivity is claimed to be down to 1.0 ng/ml for morphine and 0.1 ng/ml for petidine. The portability of the rods makes it possible to detect opiates in urine samples on the spot, e.g., the street corner, and to easily transport the coated rods to the labs for subsequent analysis.

Some studies have shown that the TLC technique is a practical, inexpensive, and reliable way to confirm EMIT® and RIA positives (EMIT® and RIA are discussed earlier). This becomes critical when the initial test indicates cannibinoids could be in the system, even though the person hasn't smoked in several days or even weeks, and was not intoxicated at the time of testing.[44]

Muraby and Mullay confirm that BPA-TLC, or bonded-phase-absorption/thin-layer chromatography, is a reliable technique for confirming EMIT® and RIA. These results indicate that use of the more expensive and more accurate GC/MS or GLC may not be required.[42]

Table 6.1
Drugs Included In Simple Screen Tests

Tests typically included	Other tests available
Alcohol (Ethanol)	Other Benzodiazepines
Codeine	Dilantin (Diphenyihydantoin)
Morphine (for Heroin)	Placidyl (Ethchlorvynal)
Dilaudid (Hydromorphone)	Quaalude (Methaqualone)
Amphetamine	Ritalin (Methylphenidate)
Methamphetamine	Percodan (Oxycodone)
Benzoylecgonine (for Cocaine)	Quinine
Cannabinoids (Marijuana)	Preludin (Phenmetrazine)
Amobarbital	
Butabarbital	
Pentobarbital	
Phenobarbital	
Secobarbital (PCP)	
Valium (Diazepam)	

from product literature for the drug testing services offered by PharmChem, a respected lab located in Palo Alto, California (46)

Gas Chromatography

Gas chromatography (GC) separates molecules by use of a glass or metal tube that is packed with material of a particular polarity. The sample to be tested is vaporized at the injection port, and carried through the column by a steady flow of gas. Gas-liquid chromatography (GLC) may also be used on samples not suitable for vaporization. Identical compounds travel through the column at the same speed, since their interaction with the column packing is identical. The column terminates at a detector that permits recording and quantification. The time from injection until a response is observed at the recorder is referred to as the "retention time." Identical retention time of substances run on two different columns is strong evidence that the substances are identical.

Gas Chromatography/Mass Spectrometry

Chromatographs are typically fitted with one or more detectors that identify various chemical properties by means of thermal conductivity, flame, ionization, electron capture, or nytrin/phosphorus analysis. When one of the detectors is a mass spectrometer or a mass selective detector, the characteristic mass spectra of the ions of the compounds under examination can be directly monitored and recorded. Computerized data bases can then be searched to find a positive spectral match. Gas chromatography with a mass spectrometry detector (GC/MS) is the most sensitive and specific procedure commonly used for drug identification. It is used primarily for confirmatory tests and for tests that must meet forensic (courtroom) standards.

The sample is first separated into components by gas chromatography, and then mass spectrometry is used to identify the substances emerging from the gas chromatograph. The mass spectrometer subjects the components to an electron beam that breaks them into fragments and accelerates them through a magnetic field. A molecule of a drug always breaks into the same fragments, known as its mass spectrum. A mass spectrum for each drug is unique, like a finger print. Information on the fragmentation pattern is compared to a computer library, which lists that mass of the parent compound and its most likely fragments. A perfect match is considered absolute confirmation of the presence of the compound.

Detection by GC/MS is highly specific, but the equipment for GC/MS is costly, and requires great technical expertise to interpret the analysis of the results. GC/MS devices provide state-of-the-art accuracy and are widely used in forensic, pharmaceutical, clinical, and industrial service laboratories.

The use of GC/MS has been out of the reach of most laboratories because of the cost and the technical expertise needed for operation. However, advances in computerization, automated samples, and analytic technology have placed GC/MS capability within the reach of most labs.

GC/MS technique can be used both quantitatively and qualitatively. Depending on the drug measured, sensitivity can be measured between nanograms and picagrams. GC/MS is more specific and 100 to 1,000 times more sensitive than the TLC system. Commonly abused drugs such as marijuana, cocaine, and heroin, are readily identified. Infrared spectroscopy is a new device that puts a third test on top of the GC/MS system.[238] Bob Fogerson of PharmChemsays that there is a technique in development that puts two mass spectrometers together to give better test results and allow use with high numbers of samples.[238]

GC/MS, GLC, PHLC, and some RIA methodologies can be applied effectively to all biological fluids, including serum or blood. Blood levels of PCP, amphetamine, and other drugs are important because only these levels indicate *actual levels of intoxication*, a fact that could have great legal significance.

Dr. Werner Baumgartner, Scientific Director for Psychemedics Corporation, pioneered radioimmunoassay of hair (RIAH), which is different from nutritional hair analysis. He says RIAH promises to be particularily useful for legal proceedings because he claims it is evasion proof. That is, while employees may try to flush their biological systems or to adulterate the sample, drug metabolites can not be removed from the hair. Hair analysis can determine the extent of use, i.e., light, medium or heavy. A hair test has not yet been developed for detecting alcohol use, but it can detect polydrug use.[238]

Table 6.2
Sensitivity Of Commonly Used
Urine Analysis Methods

| Drug Group | Chromatography | | | Immunoassay | |
	TLC	GLC	GC/MS	EMIT®	RIA*
Amphetamine	0.5 mcg	0.7 mcg	10.0 ng	0.7 mcg	1.0 mcg
Barbiturates	0.5 mcg	0.5 mcg	0.5 ng	0.5 mcg	0.1 mcg
Benzodiazepines			0.5 mcg	0.5 mcg	
Cannabinoids			1.0 ng	100.0 ng	100.0 ng
Cocaine	2.0 mcg	.75 mcg	5.0 ng	.75 mcg	5.0 mcg
Methadone	1.0 mcg	0.5 mcg	5.0 ng	0.5 ng	
Heroin/Morpine	0.5 mcg		0.5 mcg	0.5 mcg	25.0 ng
Phencyclidine (PCP)	0.5 mcg	150.0 ng	5.0 ng	150.0 ng	100.0 ng

Source: David Smith & David Wesson, *Substance Abuse in the Workplace (27)*
Values are either micrograms (mcg) or nanograms (ng) per milliliter. The values listed are not precise because many variables alter the sensitivity of the test in a particular laboratory
*RIA levels listed are the lower limit of detection

Do-It-Yourself Drug Testing

In 1987, at-home drug tests began to appear on the market. One kit called AWARE® was developed by American Drug Screens of Dallas. The kit, complete with specimen bottles and mailing tubes, is geared toward parents who fear their children are using drugs. Samples are mailed to a processing lab, and results are returned within two weeks.

Rapid Eye Check® is a video course with a special pen light that instructs parents in how to examine their children's eyes for drugs.[209] The eye test is essentially the same as the basic eye examination doctors use to gauge pupil size, response to light, and the eyes' ability to follow a moving object, all of which can be affected by drugs. Highway patrol use a similar roadside eye test for determining the sobriety of drivers.

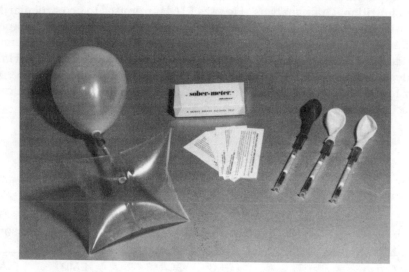

The low cost MOBAT Sober-Meter ™ sobriety screening tester from Luckey Laboratories, Inc. shows whether or not alcohol is present and gives an approximation of the amount. Screening tubes turn from yellow to green in the presence of ethyl alcohol. Results are read by observing how far the green color extends. (From product literature of Luckey Laboratories, Inc.)

Chapter 7
Drug Testing Basics

The goal of drug testing may be to detect drug use in the past or to detect current dysfunction. Pre-employment mass screenings, for example, are oriented toward detecting drug use in the past rather than current use, and thus the tests are less accurate and less expensive, as opposed to drug screenings in a criminal context, where accuracy and forensic or legal standards are required.

Terminology

Drug testing is a highly technical field, involving complex issues in both law and chemistry. Hence it is important to understand precisely what some of the commonly used phrases mean.

Chain Of Custody

Chain of custody is a monitoring process to prevent tampering with the sample or the results. Chain of custody begins with collection of the urine, and continues through the final reporting of test results to clients. Sealing of sample containers, transport and control of samples, receipt of samples by the laboratory, and supervision of lab tests remain under strict discipline throughout the chain of custody. Authorized signatures are required at each step. Laboratory results can be effectively challenged in court if there are weak links in the chain.

There are standards regulating the handling, analysis, and collection of samples that are intended to be admissible in a court of law. Transfer of urine, blood, or saliva from the subject to the container must be witnessed. For example, if a person is taken to a physician for a blood sample, the physician becomes the first link in the chain of custody. Few physicians understand the legal chain of custody procedures. Unless otherwise instructed, they will usually follow clinical laboratory standards, which will not stand up to challenge by a knowledgeable attorney. The person collecting the blood sample must be able to testify regarding the collection procedure. Likewise, the person collecting the sample must be able to testify to the accuracy of the container label, including the subject's name and other identifying information, such as date, time of the collection, and type of collection receptacle. The chain of custody must be maintained until the specimen reaches the laboratory.

Observation

In order to meet chain of custody requirements, observation of the urine collection is required. Without observation one cannot be sure the urine has not been tampered with to create a false negative, or that it is the person's urine at all. Until recently, observed collection was rare except in criminal justice situations. Whenever observation has been used in the workplace, there has been a loud outcry. People feel humiliated and degraded by the process.

Dedicated Bathroom

A "dedicated bathroom" is one solution to the observation problem. This is a bathroom with all water supply cut off, so that urine cannot be diluted. Before entering, the person giving the sample leaves behind coats, purses, and any other obvious hiding places. Such precautions increase the probability that the sample cannot be altered. However, the person can still wear a colostomy bag containing foreign urine or hide contaminating substances under the fingernails.

Confirmation Of Positive Results

All urine samples reported positive should be analyzed a second time by a different testing method. Both tests must give a positive result before a positive report is made. This process is called confirmation.

Detection Period

The length of time a drug or metabolite can be found in bodily fluids is known as the detection period. Detection periods vary widely according to the inherent physical and chemical properties of the drug itself, the person's history of use, and characteristics such as age, sex, body weight, and health. For example, the cocaine detection period is very short (12 to 48 hours) whereas marijuana has a long detection period, depending on drug-use history. Casual marijuana use can be detected from 2 to 7 days later; with chronic use, detection may be possible 2 months after the last use.

To avoid detection on most screening tests, a drug user generally must abstain from most drugs for a week or even less. Chronic marijuana users, on the other hand, will probably need to abstain for up to four weeks to avoid detection, since cannabinoids will still be detectable for this length of time.

Table 7.1
Approximate Detection Times Of Drugs In Urine*

Drug	Approximate Detection Time	
	hours	days
Alcohol	12.0	0.5
Barbiturates		
Phenobarbital	900.0	37.5
Benzodiazepines		
Oxazepam	72.0	3.0
Cocaine		
as Benzoylecgoine	18.0-144**	.75-6**
Heroin	24.0	1.0
Propoxyphene	48.0	2.0
Marijuana		
single dose	120.0	5.0
daily use	240.0	10.0
chronic daily use	336.0-720	14.0-30
Methaqualone	112.0-570	4.67-23.75
Phencyclidine	200.0	8.34

Source: Smith & Wesson, *Substance Abuse in the Workplace (27)*
*Detection times vary from individual to individual depending upon fluid and food intake, metabolic rates, kidney function, amount of drug used, mode and duration of use, other drugs used simultaneously and the sensitivity of the test used.
** Different studies yields different times.

Drug Urinalysis

Urine drug screening is an analytical tool for detecting the presence of drugs and their metabolites in urine. The technology for performing urinalysis varies, and can be designed to meet the specific needs of individual clients.

A major limitation of urinary drug tests is their lack of specificity or inability to detect *when the drug was taken.* There is considerable individual variability in detection limits. Diet, urine flow, and dose dependency can alter the test results. Some people test positive at lower doses than others, for example.

False Positives And False Negatives

"False positive" means that a drug-free sample was reported positive for drugs. Clerical and laboratory errors can be made anywhere in the process from collection, identification of the sample, to reporting of the results. "False negative" means that a sample containing drugs was reported as drug-free.

Metabolite And Metabolism

After a drug is swallowed, smoked, injected, or snorted, it is distributed throughout the bloodstream. As the blood repeatedly passes through the liver and other parts of the body, the drug encounters numerous enzyme systems, which convert most of the drug into one or more end products called *metabolites.* How long it takes for this to occur depends on metabolism, and the length of time the metabolites stay in the system is called *detection time.*

Sensitivity And Specificity

Test sensitivity is a measure of the smallest amount of the drug that can be detected in the urine sample. Specificity of a test is its ability to distinguish one drug from another. Sensitivity of the screening test should be set appropriately for the goals of the test.

Cut-Off Level And Detection Limit

Cut-off level and detection limit are two factors influencing a test's sensitivity. Cut-off level refers to the concentration of a drug necessary to indicate a positive reading on the test. Detection limit of the test is the concentration below which a particular drug is undetectable by the method.

Typically the first test given is for broad screening and is inexpensive. These include the EMIT®, TLC, or RIA. These are relatively sensitive, and can detect most drugs or metabolites in the system. They give an on-off, positive or negative result. If there is a positive, it should be confirmed by a different test. The most credible confirmation is GC/MS, which may cost from $100 to $200 per test. The confirmation test used should be more specific in its results.

Chapter 8
Drug Testing Problems

The appeal of drug testing at work is that it appears to be objective and scientific. But there are many serious problems arising from tests, and results should never be taken as established "proof" of drug use.

Validity

There are many reasons to be skeptical about the validity of test results. For one thing, drug testing is far from perfect. The Center for Disease Control (CDC) evaluated the performance of 13 laboratories conducting tests for methadone treatment facilities.[38] The CDC prepared samples containing known quantities of barbiturates, amphetamines, methadone, cocaine, codeine, and morphine. The prepared samples were sent through as though they were patient samples, so that the labs did not know they were being evaluated. The results varied widely. The CDC reported error rates of 0 to 94 percent in false negatives (labs unable to detect drugs present in the samples) and 0 to 66 percent in false positive errors (drugs detected by the labs not present in the samples).

High Level Of False Positives

The high level of false negatives showed that labs are often unable to detect drugs at the low concentrations called for by their contracts. The most

sult of this study was the astonishingly high level of false
labs reported 152 false positives in 106 of the 160 samples.
incredible 66.5 percent false-positive error rate! Commenting on
CDC study, David Smith, Director of the Haight Ashbury Free Clinic
said, "in many cases the labs would have done a better job if they had poured

Table 8.1
Error Rates For The 13 Labs In The CDC Study

Drug Tested	False Negatives	False Positives
Barbituates	11-94%	0-6%
Amphetamines	19-100%	0-37%
Methadone	0-33%	6-66%
Cocaine	0-100%	0-6%
Codeine	0-100%	0-7%
Morphine	5-100%	0-10%

Source: Center For Disease Control, 1985 (38)

the urine down the drain and flipped a coin." On the other hand, Bob
Fogerson, Quality Assurance Manager at PharmChem, argues that "it is not
valid to conclude drug testing can not be done accurately just because it has
not been done accurately." The CDC blind proficiency evaluation study
suggests that patients' samples may result in a great number of false positives.

Problems of laboratory performance, faulty confirmation, legal action, and carelessness began appearing in mass-screenings of enlisted
military personnel for drugs during the early 1980s. In 1984, the Army and
Air Force began reviewing the results of 100,000 urinary drug tests administered between April 1982 and November 1983. At that time, the American
Civil Liberties Union estimated that as many as 30,000 military personnel
might be eligible to have disciplinary charges against them dismissed. The
Navy suffered similar problems. In 1982, the Navy began a massive screening program. In some months as many 10,000 tests were conducted.
However, the frequent occurrence of positive drug reports brought questions from Naval Commanders, who insisted on closer study. 6,000 positive
urines were reexamined. The Navy found that 2,000 of these could not be
"scientifically substantiated as positive." An additional 2,000 test results
were of questionable validity because documentation was missing. One of

the investigators, Lt. Commander Debrah Durnette, said that the use of the same test for both the finding and the confirmation made many of the Navy's tests invalid. The Navy labs used the EMIT® as a backup test to the RIA. This strategy is of questionable validity since the two tests are generally of the same type, both being immunoassays. Confirmation should be made by a different method, such as GC/MS. The Navy subsequently announced that it would discontinue the use of EMIT® as a confirmation.

The Army stopped using the Navy labs in 1982 because over 1,000 Army personnel had been affected by these lab problems. However, the Army also had problems at its own Fort Mead lab. A civilian lawyer aggressively defended soldiers disciplined for marijuana use as a result of drug tests, and the problems came to light. Many court-martials were dropped because lab records could not stand scrutiny.[33]

The Einsel Commission, an investigative commission of the Department of Defense, released a report in March, 1984, showing a devastating error rate. High percentages of false positive were reported from the labs at Forts Mead (97%), Brooks (60%), Wiesbaden (75%), and at Trippler (20%). These error rates demonstrated a "basis for argumentation as to the legal and technical credibility or sufficiency of the testing process." The Army and Air Force were conducting 800,000 tests per year at these facilities. During the 20 months in question, approximately 1,320,000 tests were performed. Positive reports were more higher 10 percent. According to the Einsel Commission report, most errors were related to poor management, inadequate personnel, broken chain of custody, faulty maintenance, and faulty transmissions of reports and records, rather than to the tests themselves.

A former commander of the Brooks lab said that the contamination of glassware with positive urine caused a false positive rate of 3 to 5 percent. The military had conducted about 13,000,000 RIA screens in nine laboratories prior to these investigations. In spite of these problems the Navy continued to conduct at least 30,000 EMIT® tests per month.

Human Error

Manufacturers of drug tests say that their instruments are 95 to 99 percent accurate at detecting traces of drugs in urine, when their own lab employees operate the machines while closely watched for proficiency. Manufacturers claim that the gas chromatography/mass spectrometry is nearly 100 percent accurate. But these high accuracy rates hold only when the lab operators are extremely proficient and diligent. Such ideal conditions virtually never exist in practice. Commercial drug test manufacturers sell and lease their instruments to private labs and hospitals. There is no government or industry agency responsible for monitoring the quality of work done at these labs. The reality is that the machines are only as reliable as the people operating them. Careless, overworked, or incompetent operators can misuse the machines in innumerable ways, yielding false positive results on clean urine specimens.

Regulation Needed

At a California State Senate Hearing to evaluate the need for lab regulations, David Smith was adamant in pointing out that "in a random or mass testing, without probable cause, error is inevitable." Because the methods used in mass testing are less sophisticated, clerks are often trained to get the samples. Typically, the cheapest tests are used. These give only a positive or a negative result, and are subject to substantial error. Consequently, wrong interpretation of the results in mass testing is inevitable. Smith points out that many employers are not adequately informed by the manufacturers or companies selling the testing programs. Often the lab technicians themselves do not understand the testing process or how data is to be interpreted.

Causes Of False Positives

✦ *Improper laboratory procedures*

✦ *Samples getting mixed up*

✦ *Paperwork being lost or messed up*

✦ *Passive inhalation*

✦ *Cross-reactivity with other, legal drugs*

✦ *Tampering with samples*

✦ *Unknown reasons*

False Positives

Positives may occur on the EMIT® because equipment was contaminated or because the operator did not clean glassware properly. Of course, operator error is present to some degree in all technologies, but in drug testing it is common to have nonspecialist personnel carrying out on-site specimen collection at private companies.

A high false-positive rate is of lesser importance in research, drug abuse treatment programs, or nonpunitive situations. On the other hand, in a screening program directed at probationers, pre-employment or prepromotion examinations, or job-fitness evaluations, reporting a positive urine test takes on great social significance. The potential repercussions of a positive drug test result in an employment context can be catastrophic to the person tested positive.

As with most politically important terms, the definition of false positive is subject to tedious argument. In fact, some call them "unconfirmed positives," which implies that, although the positive result has not been confirmed, it still may be a positive. For this reason, it is necessary to confirm all positives, because EMIT® and other immunoassays are not specific in their results. Positives should be confirmed by using a test that is more sensitive than the initial screen and is based on *a different methodology*. That is, a chromatography test should be used to confirm immunoassay test results, because they utilize a different method, whereas *EMIT® and RIA should never be used to confirm other immunoassays*. Using TLC to confirm an RIA result is valid because it is of the chromatography group. There are other considerations in using TLC, however. The TLC is ordinarily a first step or screening test, and subject to more error than the GC or GC/MS. If confirmation of a positive can have a significant impact on the person tested, then the most accurate test available should be used. This would call for the GC/MS, and sometimes a drug test on a blood sample would be indicated.

Cross-Reactivity

Cross-reactivity was studied by Allen and Stiles, who tested 161 prescription and over-the-counter drugs with the EMIT®-d.a.u. screens for opiates, amphetamines, barbiturates, benzodiazepines, methadone, propoxyphene, and cocaine metabolite. They found that 65 of the prescription drugs and over-the-counter products caused false positives. Fortunately, most of the positives occurred at concentrations that are not achievable in human urine and do not present practical problems.

Some people argue that tonic water containing quinine can cause false positives for heroin use. Appedrine diet pills tested positive for amphetamines. Ibuprofen, the anti-inflammatory agent in Advil® and Nuprin®, is reported to produce false positives when testing for marijuana. About 150 legal over-the-counter medications, especially those containing synthetic compounds like phenylpropanolamine, have been reported as causing false positives in amphetamine tests, and can also cause a false positive in a methedrine test. Some sources claim that the cocaine EMIT® test can yield a positive if the person being tested drank large quantities of tea. Antihistamines may cause a false positive for PCP. Melanin, steroids, and mebuprotin may also cause false positives. Melanin, the substance responsible for pigmentation of the skin, may cause a false positive on an THC test. This is potentially problematic to black people. Blacks with renal disease will have marked secretion of maldehydrogen in their urine, which can register as positive on some EMIT® tests.

Syva and Roche, which manufacture the EMIT® and Abuscreen® tests, say they inform labs purchasing machines from them that the tests are "class assays," designed to detect broad categories for drug-like substances in the urine. For example, the heroin screen looks for substances *similar* in basic structure to morphine, the basic opiate molecule. Syva explains that opioid substances include dextromethorphan, a nonintoxicating cough suppressant found in common, uncontrolled, drugstore nostrums like Nyquil®, Doco Children's Cough Syrup®, Comtrex®, Peda-care®, and Benylin®. EMIT® and Abuscreen® both yield amphetamine positives on phenylpropanolamine or PPA, a mild decongestant which is an active ingredient in dozens of drugstore medications, including Alka-Selzer Plus®, as well as popular weight-reduction preparations like Dexatrim® and Dietac®, Syva reported that ephedrine cross-reacts with amphetamines on both the EMIT® and the Abuscreen®. Ephedrine is a decongestant in common over-the-counter medicines.

Table 8.2
Cross-Reactivity With EMIT® At ≥100 MG/ML

Generic name	Brand name*	Cross-reactivity
Amitriptyline HCl	Elavil	Methadone
Carisoprodol	Soma	Methadone
Clindinium bromide	Quarzan	Benzodiazepine
Cloxacillin Na	Tegopen	Benzodiazepine
Diphenhydramine HCl	Benadry	Methadone
Imipramine HCl	Tofranil	Methadone
Isoxuprine HCl	Vasodilan	Amphetamine
Orphenadrine citrate	Norflex	Methadone
Perphenazine	Trilafon	Benzodiazepine
Promethazine HCl	Phenergan	Methadone & Opiate
Thiethylperzine maleate	Torecan	Methadone
Tripelennamine HCl	Pyribenzamine	Benzodiazepine & Methadone

* All brand name drugs listed are ® Registered. Values are equal to or greater than 100 micrograms per milliliter. Source: Allen & Stiles, 1981 (33)

Table 8.2 shows the over-the-counter medicines that often cause cross-reactivity on EMIT® tests. This is serious because the medicines are widely used for common ailments such as the flu or colds. People who do not abuse drugs can come up with positive results on a drug test which can result in suspicion and inconvenience. Cross-reactivity is a problem that has not been solved and is misunderstood by many companies that have drug testing programs.

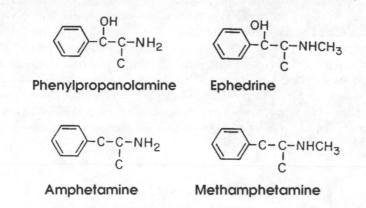

Fig. 8.1 The molecular diagram showing the sensitivity between phenylpropanolamine and ephedrine which are found in many over-the-counter medicines and amphetamine and methamphetamine. These similarities are the reason that many over-the-counter medicines cause cross-reactivity and false positives. (From John P. Morgan, M.D., "Problems of Mass Urine Screening of Misused Drugs," pg. 26 *Substance Abuse in the Workplace*.)[33]

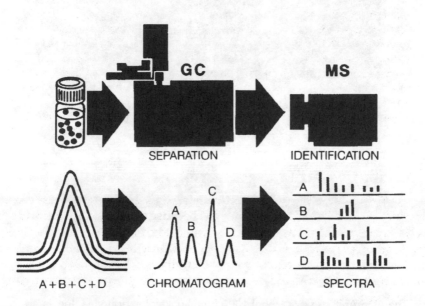

Fig. 8.2 How GC/MS works. Left-to-right, the sample is separated into its components by the gas chromatograph and then the components are ionized and identified by the characteristic spectra produced by the mass spectrometer. (From product literature for Hewlett Packard's GC/MS systems for drug confirmation.)

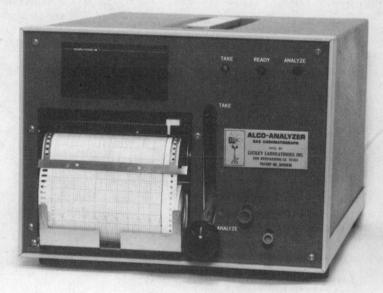

The Alco-Analyzer GC Model 1000 from Luckey Laboratories, Inc. is an electronic gas chromatography instrument that analyzes breath, blood and urine samples for ethyl alcohol. The results appear on a digital LED readout and printed on a paper chart with the levels of blood alcohol content (BAC) in gms%. The chart is intended for use as evidence for driving while intoxicated (DWI) convictions. (Photo supplied by Luckey Laboratories, Inc.)

Legal Issues Of Drug Testing

Chapter 9
Employer Liability

Employers have always been concerned about the behavior of employees. An employee with impaired functioning diminishes productivity and hurts the business. It is not just a matter of economics and productivity, but also a matter of public safety if there is potential for accidents in which citizens could be injured. Where safety is involved, such as a surgeon performing an operation or a pilot flying hundreds of passengers, the company has a great deal at stake in avoiding accidents and being able to certify that employees are fit for duty.

An employee acting on the job can be considered legally to be an extension of the employer. This means that the employer can become liable for accidents caused by employees. An accident could be caused by diminished capacity due to drug abuse. Consequently, employers need to detect and eliminate drug use in order to reduce exposure to liability.

Employer's Liability

Employers can be held directly responsible for negligence in screening and hiring applicants, and in supervising or retraining incompetent or dangerous employees.[53] Because the behavior of drug and alcohol abusers can present serious problems to co-workers and to the public, an employer must pay particular attention to any sign that an applicant or current employee may present such a danger. An employer who does not act reasonably when such information is available *or could have been available* is exposed to substantial liability.

There have been some dramatic cases. For example, in Texas, in *Otis Engineering Corp.* v. *Clark,* a wrongful death action against the employer was permitted when a supervisor sent a seemingly intoxicated employee home, and, on the way, the employee caused an automobile accident that killed two people. In another case, *Brockett* v. *Kitchen Boyd Motor Company,* cause of action for an automobile accident was permitted against the employer when an intoxicated employee left a prolonged company Christmas party and caused an accident. As these cases demonstrate, employers can be held liable even when the accident is caused by an employee after leaving the plant.

Employers Must Be Proactive

Lack of information is not a good defense, because employers are expected to be proactive in getting information about the potential diminished capacity of employees. It is not surprising that employers have felt the need to do drug testing in order to protect themselves and the public safety. The greatest liability results from inaction by an employer who is aware of a drug abuse problem, if this inaction results in the drug abuser harming another employee or a member of the public while in the service of the employer. For this reason employers are under tremendous pressure to detect drug use on the job.

Pitfalls Of Observation

Traditionally, drug use was detected through observation of behavior and other work-related factors. However, employers have run into problems with this approach, as illustrated by the experience of the Southern Pacific Transportation Company. Bob Taggard, Director of Public Affairs, gave the example of a supervisor who observed that an employee seemed to have been absent often, was very irritable on the job, and had a constantly runny nose, all of which would suggest cocaine abuse. However, when the supervisor pulled the person off the job and wrote up a reprimand, it came before the arbitration board. When asked the reason for the symptoms, the employee said, "I don't use cocaine. I had the flu. So of course I was absent and had a runny nose. And I was irritable because I had an argument with my wife!" As the example illustrates, the company may have a hard time proving that employees are actually using drugs; so they are sent back to the job. Drug testing attempts to alleviate this problem.

Drug testing helps employers avoid many of the legal problems that could arise from observation of on-the-job performance problems by supervising personnel. The word "test" implies an objective measurement of fluids and of the amount of drugs or drug metabolites in the body. Drug test results are much easier to use in court or arbitration than a supervisor's speculations. For reasons such as these many companies have embraced drug testing.

Carrying out drug testing is an action which shows that the employer is taking responsibility in an objective way. This can be a legal defense that the employer is making every reasonable effort to detect and prevent drug use on the job.

Public Relations

Dr. Musto of Yale predicted in his 1973 book, *The American Disease*, that during the 1980s there would be a growing backlash against the use of illegal drugs and alcohol.[58] By the mid-1980s, Congress passed an anti-drug bill in which 1.7 billion dollars were authorized to augment law enforcement efforts against drugs, as well as treatment and education. The amount increased in subsequent years. Businesses respond to public values. Companies want to be perceived by their customers as upstanding in the community and reflecting the values of society. So as the larger society became more critical of drug use, business began to exhibit more conservative values as well.

Public relations is of particular concern in sports, since sports heroes are role models for young people. Widely publicized drug use by sports figures, such as the cocaine related death of basketball player, Len Bias, and the general public alarm about drug use by children who worship sports figures, inspired the professional sports organizations to take up drug testing to restore the credibility of the players and teams. The sports employee assistance programs reflect the intense concern of management about drugs.

For example, Richard Alderson, manager of the Oakland A's baseball team, said, "It's not just a question of occupational safety. We view drug testing as a way to make a statement that we are not on drugs, regardless of what the public thinks. We believe that testing acts as a deterrent, and in many instances I have traded drug testing clauses for higher salaries with my players."

Everyone Is Suspect

Workers, however, usually have concerns quite different from those of their employers or the general public. Joel Youngblood, an outfielder who played for the San Francisco Giants, had not been implicated in the drug scandals that rocked baseball. Indeed, there was no evidence — not even a hint of rumor — that he was anything but squeaky-clean in the drug department; yet because Youngblood balked at including a drug testing clause in his contract, he became baseball's unwanted man.

What irked Youngblood was the proviso that the Giants could test for drugs at anytime, day or night, as often as they liked. "It puts you in a position of having to prove your innocence," his agent said. "It's like having the police coming to your house at 3 a.m. just to look around. No reason."

During the winter Youngblood's agent had worked out the details of the next year's contract. But when he held off on the drug testing clause, however, the Giants withdrew their offer. No one else in the league would touch Youngblood, either. Suddenly, this nine-year veteran had become baseball's untouchable.

Gary T. Marx made the problem clear when he said in the *New York Times*, "In the novel *Gorky Park*, the police inspector asks the central character whom she suspects of having stolen her ice skates. She replies, 'Everyone.' The inspector responds, 'So do I.' In the same way, people in our society who advocate the indiscriminate use of drug tests and 'lie detectors' appear to suspect everyone.[88c]

"Mandating drug testing turns the basic idea that people are innocent until proven guilty on its head. By testing everyone, including those about whom there isn't a whiff of suspicion, the presumption is that we are all guilty," said David L. Kirp, Professor of Law and Public Policy at the University of California, Berkeley. [88]

The American Civil Liberties Union opposes indiscriminate urine testing because they believe it is unfair and unreasonable to force millions of American workers who are not even suspected of using drugs, and whose job performance is satisfactory, to submit to degrading and intrusive urine tests on a regular basis. The ACLU questions the fairness of treating the innocent and the guilty alike.[76]

> *At issue in the dispute over drug testing is nothing less than whether workers may be subjected to "police state" tactics in the workplace, whereby their bodies may be seized and ransacked through the compelled extraction and analysis of bodily fluids without the fundamental protection of a warrant based on probable cause and in spite of common-law rights all supposedly enjoy. And because urine testing detects not on-the-job impairment or drug use, but **prior** exposure to drugs which could have occurred days or weeks before the test while the worker was off duty, drug testing effectuates a form of employer control of workers' personal lives **outside** the context of the workplace.*
>
> *Random or mass urine testing reverses the presumption of innocence upon which much of our jurisprudence is built, and violates the strong prohibition of dragnet searches sweeping in the many who are innocent in order to find the few who are guilty which is the hallmark of a free and democratic society. . .*
>
> *If the lessons of history are to teach us anything, it is that we must be vigilant against the public hysteria of the moment and adhere to basic constitutional principles and democratic values which are the hallmarks of a free society. The drug problem though real, must be distinguished from the drug **testing** problem.*
>
> Edward Chen & John True[225]
> Civil Liberties Attorneys

Arguments For Testing

✦ *If you have done nothing wrong, you have nothing to hide.*

✦ *The tests are valid because they are based on neutral scientific measurement.*

✦ *It is for your own good, because drug use is a medical problem.*

✦ *It can offer proof of innocence.*

✦ *It is voluntary.*

✦ *It is legal.*

✦ *If you question the means, you do not care about the end.*

✦ *If you do not use drugs, you have nothing to hide. Why object to the testing?*

Chapter 10
Right To Privacy

Innocent people do have something to hide: their privacy. This "right to be left alone" is, in the words of the eminent Supreme Court Justice Louis Brandeis, "the most comprehensive of rights and the most valued by civilized men." Urine tests may be considered an invasion of privacy because the tests can disclose numerous other details about one's private life, such as whether or not an employee or applicant is pregnant or being treated for various medical conditions in addition to evidence of illegal drug use.

Even though indiscriminate testing may be the easiest way to identify drug users, some people think it is "un-American." There is a long tradition in the United States that general searches of innocent people are unfair. This tradition began in Colonial America, when King George's forces searched everyone indiscriminately in order to uncover those few who were committing offenses against the crown. These general searches were deeply resented by the early Americans. After the Revolution, and fresh from the experience of the unfairness of the indiscriminate searches, the Fourth Amendment was passed. It says that you cannot search everyone, innocent and guilty alike, to find the few who are guilty. You must have good reason to suspect a particular person before subjecting him or her to intrusive or degrading searches.[76]

The fundamental legal question is whether drug testing in the workplace is compatible with the protection of personal privacy embodied in the Fourth Amendment's prohibition of unreasonable searches and seizures. Indiscriminate drug testing threatens traditional Fourth Amendment values. Perhaps more than any other provision of the Bill of Rights, the Fourth Amendment expresses an essential quality of democracy — the defense of personal dignity against violation by the state. We ought not experiment with these rights. They are fragile. Once damaged they are not easily repaired. Once lost they are not easily recovered.

Adherence to tested Fourth Amendment principles is particularly important when, as now, there is widespread clamor for a simple solution to a serious social problem. The saddest episodes in American constitutional history have been those occasions, such as the internment of Americans of Japanese descent during World War II, when we have bent our principles to the zealotry of the moment. What is expedient is not necessarily fair, or constitutional. A war on drugs is a good idea, but not if its first casualty is the Bill of Rights.

Office of the Attorney General, Maryland[69]

Urine Testing: Search And Seizure?

A preliminary question is whether the collection and testing of a urine specimen is a "search" or "seizure" within the meaning of the Fourth Amendment. A *search* occurs when an expectation of privacy that society is prepared to consider reasonable is infringed. A *seizure* of property occurs when there is some meaningful interference with an individual's possessory interests in that property.

The Supreme Court ruled in 1989 in *National Employers Union* v. *United States Customs Service* that taking a urine specimen for drug testing purposes *is* a search or seizure under the Fourth Amendment. However, it is not necessarily a violation of that Amendment, because only unreasonable searches and seizures are prohibited; so an inquiry into the reasonableness is essential. The greater or more demeaning the intrusion, the more substantial must be the reason for conducting the search. The right to "be free from unreasonable governmental intrusion" applies whenever an individual may harbor a *reasonable expectation of privacy.* An expectation of privacy is legitimate in Fourth Amendment terms if the person has an actual or subjective expectation of privacy, and the expectation is one that society is prepared to recognize as reasonable. The Maryland Attorney General concluded, "in our view, state employees as a group have an actual, subjective expectation that their bodily functions will not be subject to government intrusion. Nothing about State employment gives employees reason to suppose that their urination is subject to supervisory inspection and probing. It states the obvious to say that state employees, like everybody else, expect to dispose of their wastes in private."

Reasonableness

It has been suggested that an employee's expectation of privacy at work can be rendered "unreasonable" by the simple expedient of the state's telling employees that they will be subject to searches. This argument has been challenged, however. A citizen who becomes a state employee cannot be compelled to give up his or her constitutional rights as the price of gaining that employment. "The government could not avoid the restrictions of the Fourth Amendment by notifying the public that all telephone lines will be tapped, or that all homes will be searched" concluded *U.S.* v. *Davis* in the 9th Circuit.

Some people have suggested that drug testing will be less intrusive if the actual giving of the sample is not observed, since most people do not expect to be observed while they are urinating. However, the absence of supervision means that an employee who does use drugs is able to substitute someone else's "clean" urine or otherwise tamper with the sample. To safeguard against this possibility, the federal testing program calls for supervision of an employee's urination if "the agency has reason to believe that a particular employee may alter or substitute the specimen to be provided" (Ex. order 12,564, Sec. 4d). For Fourth Amendment purposes, a less intrusive but also less effective program is as problematic as a more intrusive but more effective one.

> If a blanket search program has little or no effectiveness, it is in substance merely a kind of harassment, a show of power, or a 'fishing expedition,' and therefore, per se, unreasonable under the Fourth Amendment.
>
> U.S. v. Davis, (1973)[69]

Determining Reasonableness

Reasonableness depends on two things: the degree of intrusiveness of the search and seizure; and the public or private interests at stake. For a relatively innocuous search or a very compelling public interest, such as public safety in the case of an airplane pilot, the reasonableness of the search is greater.

Testing that does not involve observing of the sample is less intrusive, and therefore considered more reasonable. However, such testing is considerably less effective. The more effective type of testing, which involves actual close observation of the sample to prevent anybody from tampering with it, is more effective, but then it is also more intrusive and thus less reasonable, unless there is a very strong reason to actually suspect that person of using drugs.

Probable Cause

It is impossible to fully define either "probable cause" or "reasonable suspicion" in the abstract. As a comparative matter, reasonable suspicion is less stringent than probable cause. Even reasonable suspicion must be founded upon objective facts and rational inferences derived from practical experience, rather than unspecified suspicions, and must be directed toward a particular employee to be tested.[69]

Under a "for cause policy" a urine sample may be requested if a reasonable suspicion exists that an employee may be using drugs.[68] *Reasonable suspicion* exists when there are specific objective facts and reasonable inferences from work experience that suggest the employee is under the influence of drugs. These may include slurred speech, an on-the-job accident, frequent absences, tardiness, or early departure from work. Since reasonable suspicion is established by combining fact and judgement, it is not possible to predict or describe every situation that may arouse reasonable suspicion.

There have been some significant court cases around the issue of probable cause. For example, in *McDonnell* v. *Hunter*,[53] the 8th Circuit Court declared unconstitutional on Fourth Amendment grounds the routine searches of prison guards and their vehicles by the Iowa Department of Corrections. In this incident, the court directed the department to revise search procedures so that they would be based only on probable cause.

Reduced Expectation Of Privacy

The context of the situation is very important in establishing the reasonableness or unreasonableness of a search. In part, context has to do with what is needed to actually perform that job, and whether the employee could or could not threaten public safety.

Some categories of state employees can reasonably be expected to have somewhat diminished expectations of privacy, given the nature of their work. Someone who becomes a police or fire officer must know what the job entails and the special obligation of those who enforce the law to obey it themselves. Hence police officers may, in certain circumstances, enjoy less constitutional protection than the ordinary citizen. But even where police officers and fire fighters have diminished protection, they may be tested only if the reasonable suspicion standard is met. For example, in the *McDonnell* v. *Hunter* case just mentioned, in which prison guards' cars were being searched, testing was approved only on the basis of reasonable suspicions based on specific observable facts and reasonable inferences drawn from these facts in light of experience, that a given employee was abusing drugs.

In the case of *Capua* v. *Plainfield*,[69] an investigation began when anonymous tipsters warned officials in Plainfield, N.J., that some of the city's police and firemen were using illicit drugs. The city cracked down, staging a surprise urine test for all 244 members of the police and fire depart-

ments. Twenty employees, including two cops, tested positive for marijuana or cocaine and were given the option of resigning or being suspended.
Sixteen suspended firemen filed suit in Federal court, and U.S. District
Court Judge H. Lee Sarokin ruled that Plainfield's "mass round-up urinanalysis" violated the constitutional prohibition against unreasonable
search and seizure. "The threat posed by widespread use is real. The need
to combat it manifest," Judge Sarokin wrote in his decision, "But it is important not to permit fear and panic to overcome our fundamental principles
and protections."

However, in the Plainfield case, the court also held that testing of these
employees under the "individualized reasonable suspicion" standard would
meet Fourth Amendment standards. In other words, the mistake that the
city of Plainfield made was conducting a wholesale mass testing unannounced, without any reasonable suspicion of particular individuals.

In *Amalgamated Transit Employee* v. *Suscy*, [53] a Transit Authority employee came under suspicion by two supervisors who believed that he was
under the influence and therefore had him tested. In the ensuing lawsuit,
the court held that the blood and urine testing of this municipal bus driver
was permissible under the Fourth Amendment, citing the valid interest in
protecting the public. This decision reinforced the notion that an employer
should be able to test employees if public safety is an overriding concern.

In *National Employers Union* v. *United States Customs Service* and
Skinner v. *Railway Labor Executives Associations*, both plaintiffs argued that
"particularized suspicion" was essential to justify compulsory drug testing
of employees. But the Supreme Court disagreed and found that drug
testing can be constitutional even without particularized suspicion that an
individual employee is in fact a drug user.

Supreme Court Justice Anthony Kennedy, writing for the majority in
the 1989 landmark *Skinner* v. *Railway Labor Executives Associations* decision,
agreed that drug tests are "searches" according to the Fourth Amendment.
But he concluded that the search was reasonable when the "diminished"
privacy interests of railway workers were balanced against the "compelling" interest in deterring drug use on the rails. "The expectations of privacy
of covered employees are diminished by reason of their participation in an
industry that is regulated pervasively to insure safety," said Justice Kennedy. In the related decision of *National Treasury Employees Union* v. *Von
Raab*, he concluded that Customs employees who carry firearms and those
involved in drug interdiction have the same "diminished expectation of
privacy."

Compelling Interest

The reasonableness of the search, e.g., drug testing, is determined by
balancing the employee's privacy expectations against the government's
interest in conducting the search. In *National Employees Union* v. *United
States Customs Service*, the Supreme Court identified three governmental
interests:

1) "ensuring that front line interdiction personnel are physically fit, and have unimpeachable integrity and judgement;"

2) providing "effective measures to prevent the promotion of drug users to positions that require the incumbent to carry a firearm;" and

3) "protecting truly sensitive information from those who, under compulsion of circumstances or for other reasons, might compromise information."

The Court weighed the interference with privacy resulting from giving urine for testing against the government's compelling interests. The Court concluded that, while requiring urine samples could interfere with privacy, the governments need to conduct such searches of employees engaged directly in drug interdiction and of those who carried firearms took precedence.

In the related case, *Skinner* v. *Railway Labor Executives Associations,* the Court characterized the government's interest in promoting railroad safety through drug testing as "compelling" and, therefore, "not an undue infringement on the justifiable expectations of privacy of covered employees."

While somewhat ambiguous, the Supreme Court's decision in the Customs case strongly suggests that protection of "sensitive information" related to drug enforcement investigation and national security are also compelling government interests. There is speculation that it may be applied to the broader context of commercially sensitive information. If future cases result in such rulings, then the range of employees subjected to testing could be greatly expanded.

Voluntary Consent

In general, the courts have supported the idea that voluntary consent to a search satisfied the Fourth Amendment. The Department of Justice has taken the position that when a public employee is told that drug testing is a condition of employment and does not quit, this is in fact consent to the testing. The Office of the Attorney General of the State of Maryland, in an extensive study, rejected this notion of consent. They say, "a valid consent to a search must in fact be voluntarily given, and not be the result of duress or coercion, expressed or implied. It flies in the face of economic reality to suppose that an employee voluntarily consents to a drug test when the alternative is losing his or her job, or, for that matter, that an applicant voluntarily consents when the alternative is being denied the job. Agreement to a search motivated by fear that refusal will lead to loss of one's livelihood is not voluntary consent."[69]

Nor can voluntary consent fairly be inferred from a person's decision to accept a job with the knowledge that drug testing is a condition of that job. In both *McDonnell* v. *Hunter* and the *Security and Law Enforcement Employees* v. *Carey,*[53] the prison employees were told at the onset of their employment that they would be subject to certain searches. In McDonnell, the employees actually signed a consent form expressing their agreement, among other things, to submit to a urinanalysis or blood test when requested by the prison administrator. In Carey, they were given a rule book in which one rule said that any employee on duty would be subject to a search. Nevertheless, the court held that neither circumstance gave rise to voluntary consent. In both cases, the courts ruled that it was coercion and not consent. If the choice to decline the search carries with it significant adverse consequences, then the alternative, submitting to the search, does not reflect voluntary consent.

"Consent" in any meaningful sense cannot be said to exist merely because a person (a) knows that an official intrusion into his privacy is contemplated if he does a certain thing, and then (b) proceeds to do that thing. Were it otherwise, the police could use the implied-consent theory to subject everyone on the street after 11 p.m. to physical search, merely by making public announcements in the press, radio, and television that such searches would be undertaken.

Two Views

We're convinced that under the circumstances, this test will be proved to be constitutional. We're in a situation . . . where the country has a real serious problem on its hands. And I think, under the circumstances, a drug testing program is appropriate. Let me try to draw a parallel. A number of years ago, we used to be able to get on airplanes and fly from city to city without going through magnetometers and having our baggage searched at the gate. We developed a serious problem. We couldn't take an airplane flight without ending up in Cuba. We had to put in a fairly comprehensive program in our airports to stop this from happening, and the courts, when weighing the problem against the intrusion in one's personal life, decided this was constitutional.[11]

Stephen Trott
Justice Department

If the government were to announce that all telephones would be hereafter tapped, perhaps to counter an outbreak of political kidnappings, it would not justify, even after public knowledge of the wiretapping plan, the proposition that anyone using a telephone consented to being tapped. It would not matter that other means of communication exist . . . it is often a necessity of modern living to use a telephone. So also it is often a necessity to fly on a commercial airliner, and to force one to choose between that necessity and the exercise of a constitutional right is coercion in the constitutional sense.

U.S. v. *Albarado* (1974)

The question of whether or not testing is voluntary is very important, because a valid consent would excuse the need for a warrant or for probable cause prior to testing. In a private business setting, an employment policy posted publicly is generally taken to mean that all of the employees have consented to the policy. However, this may not be legally valid. A lawsuit (*Luck* v. *Southern Pacific*) in California was filed by a pregnant woman who worked for the company for six years as a computer programmer, refused to take an unannounced test administered to everyone in her department. Luck was fired because she did not consent to the test. She sued for wrongful termination. The jury was instructed that Southern Pacific had to show that it was "necessary" to test Luck "in order to achieve the public interest of safety in the operation and maintenance of the railroad. Southern Pacific failed to prove necessity and the jury awarded $485,000 in a unanimous verdict.

Southern Pacific appealed the ruling and in the Spring of 1990 the Court of Appeal decision upheld the jury award in favor of Barbara Luck. The California state appeal court ruled that employers must have a "compelling interest" when asking their workers to submit to random drug tests if the employees are not in safety sensitive positions. The ruling applies to all California employers, public and private. However, it does not speak to the issue of testing job applicants. The "compelling interest" requirement for a person already employed is more stringent than the existing requirement used for job applicants. Applicants may be tested if the employer's right to know outweights the applicant's right to privacy. Luck's attorney summaried by saying, "By this decision, employers (in California) must exercise extreme caution before they require any employee to submit to any test as a condition of employment."[242]

Chapter 11
Government Responds

President Reagan issued an Executive Order in 1986 calling for a "drug free workplace" and requiring each government agency head to establish a program to test for the use of illegal drugs by employees in sensitive positions. The word "sensitive" was vaguely defined and it was left to the agency heads to decide what it meant. President Bush continued the federal drug testing program and, despite staff protest, mandated testing of White House personnel.

Reagan insisted, in issuing the Executive Order, that it would not be used as a punitive measure to fire or otherwise hurt people. He promised that if people were discovered to be drug users, they would receive help.

But when the Office of Personnel Management released its written regulations they departed dramatically from Reagan's assurances to federal workers that drug users would not be fired. Nonetheless, the administration began moving ahead with its program of drug testing of federal employees, despite court decisions that widespread random testing was unconstitutional, and despite reservations among some of the top advisors to the White House.

The regulations contained a dismissal provision. In fact, employees could be fired for a single incidence of illegal drug use, and had to be dismissed for a second offense. The regulations did not require the agencies to prove in any way that the drug affected the employee's work. The definition of "sensitive" position was so broad that more than half of the federal workers were included. Under the regulations, disciplinary action was required to be taken against federal workers other than those who voluntarily turn themselves after a single confirmed positive drug test. Discipline could include a written reprimand, putting the employee on leave, suspending the employee, or firing, and anybody who refused to take the test could be fired "as failing to meet a condition of employment."

Unions' Challenge

Several federal employee's unions, including the National Federation of Federal Employees (NFFE), filed suit. The constitutionality of the program was challenged on the basis that the regulations ignore the concept of the connection between the on-the-job performance and discipline. NFFE attorney Pierce said, "the law is very clear that there here must be a connection, 'a nexus' between a disciplinary act and an employee's performance. A nexus must show that there is an actual relationship between off-duty behavior and actual performance." For example, under the Civil Service Reform act, if a federal employee is caught shoplifting, that person cannot be fired simply because of that arrest, because there is no nexus, no demonstrable relationship between that arrest and actual performance on the job.

The regulations required that each agency offer counseling and rehabilitation to help employees overcome drug addiction and that employees who failed the test, refused to take it, or failed to complete treatment or counseling successfully could be reprimanded in writing, suspended for 15 days or more, or placed on leave. They also provided that employees must be notified 60 days before the actual testing could begin.

Shortly after Reagan's Executive Order, the Custom Service instituted a widespread program of testing custom workers that met with an instantaneous lawsuit, *National Treasury Employees Union v. Von Raab*. The suit was filed in New Orleans and Judge Collins ruled that the drug testing program run by the Custom Service was unconstitutional. He said that examining custom officials' urine constituted a "warrantless search" made in a "total absence of probable cause or even reasonable suspicion." Judge Collins issued a permanent injunction against the agency program.

The United States Supreme Court, in a narrow 5 to 4 vote in 1989, upheld testing of customs personnel carrying firearms or employed in drug interdiction, but questioned testing of clerks, lawyers and accountants. Attorney General Dick Thornburgh welcomed the Supreme Court decision, and promised that testing would be tailored "to fit the rules."

The Drug Free Workplace Act Of 1988

The Drug Free Workplace Act of 1988 requires federal grantees and contractors having a contract for property or services of $25,000 or more to certify to the contracting agency that they will provide a drug free workplace. The act is the first extension of federal anti-drug legislation into the workplace of federal contractors and grantees. The act neither requires nor prohibits drug testing, however.

National Drug Control Strategy

In the fall of 1989 President Bush released The White House's drug control strategy on prime time television and followed it up with a text, *National Drug Control Strategy,* describing a comprehensive blueprint for controlling drug use and sales. Portions of the strategy pertaining to drug testing at work are reprinted in Appendix A. President Bush defends drug testing at work, inspite of charges that it is an invasion of privacy and test results are often inaccurate. President Bush says:

> *Despite broad public support for drug testing, the practice remains controversial. The chief criticisms are that testing is an invasion of privacy, that the results may not be confidential, and that they are not sufficiently accurate. Federal guidelines published in 1988 respond to these concerns, providing significant protection for tested employees. By clearly specifying steps to be followed from specimen collection to reporting of results, onfidentiality is maintained. If laboratories engaged in drug testing met standards equivalent to those prescribed form the Federal drug-testing program, the chances of an individual being wrongfully accused of using illegal drugs would be greatly reduced.*
>
> National Drug Control Strategy [237]

President Bush continues by setting forth a national mission statement that has direct significance for employers and employees alike.

> *The Federal government has a responsibility to do all that it can to promote comprehensive drug-free workplace policies in the private sector and in State and local government. Employers will be encouraged to:*
>
> *1) develop and communicate to all employees a clear drug policy setting out expectations of behavior, employee rights and responsibilities, and actions to be taken in response to an employee found to use illegal drugs;*
>
> *2) establish an Employee Assistance Program or other appropriate mechanism;*
>
> *3) train supervisors on how to identify employees who use drugs;*

4) educate employees about the established plan; and

5) provide careful means to identify employees who use drugs, including drug testing where appropriate.

The Federal government will also move quickly to implement and strengthen regulations for the Drug-Free Workplace Act of 1988, which requires Federal contractors and grantees to have drug-free workplace plans in effect.

National Drug Control Strategy[237]

Who Has A Right To Privacy?

The Fourth Amendment was enacted in response to King George's indiscriminate searches of colonist's homes. The goal is to prevent such excesses by government. It doesn't say anything about the behavior of private individuals, organizations, or employers.

Federal and state constitutions protect all citizens against unreasonable government searches and seizures of person and property.[53] In general, the federal protection applies only when the challenged action is taken by government officials. In fact, private employers often use the state action requirement as a defense against constitutional challenges to their drug testing policy. On the other hand, it is not a black-and-white issue. If a private employer uses the police or other government officials in the search, and the counter-claim is that the employer is acting as an "agent" of the state, then the constitutional standard is usually held.

Privacy rights of private employees may be protected by special federal or state laws or union contracts. In general, however, employees of private companies must look to their own state's laws to protect their right to privacy. For the most part, employees of private companies have little protection against the mandatory drug testing programs that have been adopted by Fortune 500 companies. The ACLU believes that it is unfair that government workers are protected in their rights to privacy, but their counterparts in private industry are not.

States Protect Privacy, Too

Ten states (Alaska, California, Flordia, Hawaii, Illinois, Louisiana, Montana, New York, South Carolina, and Washington) have express privacy provisions in their constitutions. Some of these state constitutions have a more developed right to privacy than the federal constitution. For example, the California constitution under Article 1, Section 1, specifically guarantees a person's right to privacy, and this provision has been interpreted to apply to both private and governmental activities.[68]

California's Right To Privacy

All people are by nature free and independent, and have certain inalienable rights. Among these are enjoying and defending life and liberty, acquiring, possessing, and protecting property, and pursuing and obtaining safety, happiness, and privacy.

Constitution of the State of California, Article 1, Section 1. [53]

A leading California case addressing the general privacy rights is *White* v. *David*.[53] The California Supreme court ruled that the California right to privacy prevents government and business from secretly gathering personal information, from overly broad collection and retention of unnecessary personal information, and from improper use or disclosure of properly gathered personal information. The court set forth a list of "mischiefs" that the right of privacy was intended to correct.

White Mischiefs

1. *Government snooping and the secret gathering of personal information.*

2. *The overly broad collection and retention of unnecessary personal information by government and business interests*

3. *The improper use of information properly obtained for a specific purpose, for example, use for another purpose, or the disclosure of it to a third party.*

4. *The lack of a reasonable check on the accuracy of existing records.*

The White "mischiefs" may not apply to employee drug testing, however. The White decision addressed secret or overly broad information gathering and improper disclosure.

In 1989, in the first ruling of its kind in California, a state appeals court upheld a private company's drug testing of its job applicants, regardless of the safety-sensitive nature of the position. [241] The 3-to-0 decision upheld a pre-employment drug and alcohol screening program at Matthew Bender & Co., a subsidiary of the Times Mirror Co. The court specified that its ruling applied only to testing of applicants and not to employees, whose rights against testing may be greater.

Information Management

In his national drug control strategy, President Bush asserts that success in the war on drugs depends on "comprehensive information management." However, he cautions that the necessity for greater information collection and control must be balanced with the protection of individual privacy and civil liberties. Nonetheless, some civil libertarians are worried that the President's information management is really people management in disguise.

> *Success in the war on drugs depends in no small part on having comprehensive information wherever it is needed to make sound policy and operational decisions. The information management challenge is particularly acute given the number and diversity of Federal, State and local agencies involved in the drug war. It is not only a question of having enough information; it is also a question of making the information that is available, and that will become available, accessible to those who are involved in the fight against drugs.*
>
> *Except for the small fraction of information in government hands that is sensitive and must be closely held, wider access to drug-related information is essential. Many agencies are involved; each must be aware of the drug problem's full range and complexity -- coherent and coordinated policymaking depends on it. Our national policy must be to maximize the sharing and use of relevant information among appropriate government organizations and to minimize impediments to its operational use. All such information sharing must of course be conducted with careful attention to the protection of individual privacy and civil liberties.*
>
> National Drug Control Strategy [237]

Compelling Interests

California privacy decisions after White have stated that the right to privacy is not absolute; it must be offset against other compelling interests. On the use of drugs, for example, at least one California court has held that an individual has no constitutional privacy right to use or possess cocaine at home (*People* v. *Davis*). In addition, California does not recognize a constitutional right to use or possess marijuana in one's own home (*NORML* v. *Gain*).

An infringement of a constitutional privacy right must be justified by a "compelling interest" under traditional California constitutional privacy analyses. Showing that the state's interest cannot be satisfied in a less intrusive manner is necessary in some instances. To meet the compelling interest test, the justification for the privacy intrusion must be very substantial. [228]

Drug testing cases in California present competing constitutional interests. The right to pursue and obtain safety, to preserve and protect property, and to pursue and obtain privacy are all protected by the constitution. Drug testing cases in California often pit the constitutional interests of employers, employees, co-workers and the public against one another.

How to resolve the clash of the constitution rights of safety and privacy is an unresolved California constitutional question. The use by police of drunk driver "checkpoints" that involve stopping and checking drivers at random, without any individual suspicion, was approved by the California Supreme Court (*Ingersoll* v. *Palmer*) and may help set the standard for the future of drug testing. The Court found that right to privacy was safeguarded by prior general public notice of location of the checkpoints and by stopping each motorist only very briefly if there is not suspicion of wrongdoing. However, as civil rights attorneys Edward Chen and John True point out, "no one has ever suggested that motorists be subject to random detentions and urine tests wherein they run the risk of losing their driver's license if such urine tests come up positive. . . . even sobriety checkpoints require probable cause based upon observation of behavior and appearance together with failed performance of a field sobriety test before the police can require the production of blood or urine."[225]

Privacy Off The Job

The concern that drug or alcohol testing may infringe on non-work activities merits consideration. The courts must counterbalance the interests of the employer, co-employees, and society against those of the employee being tested for drugs. Tests can identify drug use during an employee's off-duty hours. An employer's interest in an employee's personal matters is not compelling unless an employee's use of drugs affects the workplace. But employees with traces of drugs in their system during working hours may violate the employer's anti-drug rules. This is especially true if the rules require that employees be drug-free at all times. Even though employees may not be impaired when tested, it is argued that they can be expected to be impaired at some future time when test results reveal past use. Some employers feel that an employe's use of drugs while off-duty is itself a hazard that they have a responsibility to curb. On the face of it, use of drugs during off-duty hours is probably a weaker privacy interest than other personal matters not concerning the workplace.

> *May employers exercise control over off-the-job conduct simply because there is some correlation with job performance? If so, employers would have the right to control many aspects of worker personal life which could influence performance and productivity, including domestic disputes, personal financial woes, sleeping and eating habits, cigarette smoking and indeed any personal condition which affects an employee's overall physical and mental health. This argument has no logical limit,*

and it leads logically to frightening consequences. If drug tests are permitted, why not psychological tests and genetic screenings?

Edward Chen & John True
Civil Liberties Attorneys[225]

Privacy Is Evolving

Differences can exist between federal and state laws. For example, consider the Oregon election of November 1986, when at the peak of the national "War on Drugs," Oregonians could have legalized marijuana use in their state, even while in the rest of the nation employees in private and public business were being tested, put into treatment programs, and sometimes fired for the use of marijuana.[92] The Oregon ballot contained an initiative signed by 90,000 Oregonians to legalize marijuana. While the initiative was defeated by a 2 to 1 vote, it was on the ballot nonetheless.

In the Oregon initiative, "private" means "not public." In common-sense terms, private means that marijuana could not be used in a location where it would intrude upon the sensibilities of other people who might be offended. This notion of private is comparable to the definition used in the statutes prohibiting public indecency or public drunkenness. Had the initiative passed, it still would have been illegal to possess marijuana in parks, school grounds, or any place visible to the public.

During the Oregon initiative process, Governor Vic Atiyeh rejected a proposal by the President's Commission on Organized Crime to test all state workers for drug use. Atiyeh was quoted as saying he would not require drug testing as a condition of employment in the state of Oregon, because in his opinion it was "not necessary," and that drug use by state workers in Oregon was not a "major problem." As far as Governor Atiyeh was concerned, what employees did in their off-duty time was none of his business as long as it did not negatively affect their job performance. The Governor further cautioned private employers against using drug testing on employees, because in his opinion, such drug testing "involves an unfair presumption of guilt."

Another dramatic instance of the different interpretation of privacy in a state versus federal context is provided by the Alaska Supreme Court unanimous ruling on marijuana in *Ravin* v. *State* (1975). The court ruled that the Alaskan constitution protects an individual's privacy, and agreed with the NORML and ACLU attorneys that marijuana did not represent a significant enough risk to society to allow the state to invade an individual's privacy. In the years following the court's decision, several surveys indicate basic support for the reform. If anything, the surveys demonstrate support for legalizing the sales of small amounts of marijuana and perhaps total legalization.

The Supreme Court of Alaska discussed the Ravin decision, in *Harrison* v. *State* (1984). A state trooper had been arrested in a dry county with alcohol in his possession. The trooper claimed that the Ravin case provided a precedent for his possession of alcohol. He argued that if you are allowed to possess marijuana, you are surely allowed to possess alcohol. The Alaskan Supreme Court saw things differently, however. They examined the effects that alcohol was having in Alaskan society and compared that to marijuana. They found that there was no comparison, and that the state had more cause to regulate, even prohibit, alcohol than it did marijuana.

Vague State Guidelines

Many employers are afraid and want state guidelines for testing programs. But attempts to implement state laws regulating employer drug testing tend to set off heated debates that usually end up in a stalemate. For example, California State Senator John Seymour proposed three Senate Bills in 1986 and 1987 designed to create statewide rules for on-the-job drug tests. The response was emotional. During one hearing, Senator Nicholas Petris of Oakland dramatically pulled out an empty mayonnaise jar and dared the bill's supporters to take a urine test immediately. California Senator Bill Greene, Chairman of the Senate Industrial Relations Committee, repeatedly asked why the labor law needed to be changed and pointed out that California employers already have all the freedom they could possibly have by virtue of the fact that there are no laws prohibiting or regulating such testing. Seymour holds the California Senate Industrial Relations Committee responsible for the death of his early bills. Persisting, in 1989, he drafted Senate Bill 1120 calling for a drug-free workplace and regulation of state contractors and state grant recipients.[238]

Late in 1986, Governor Deukmejian issued Executive Order D-58-86 calling for a drug-free state workplace. The Personnel Board struggled with the task of balancing employer needs and applicant rights. The final regulations do not mandate drug screening of applicants for any classification in state service. Rather, they set forward a framework within which a department may request to institute an applicant screening program and they regulate such testing.[238] Simultaneously the California Department of Personnel Administration established rules under which employees serving in sensitive positions in state service will be subject to urine testing when there is reasonable suspicion.[238] The rules[239][240] were finally implemented in 1989 (see Appendix C).

By the late 1980s several states, including Montana, Iowa, Vermont, Minnesota, Connecticut and Rhode Island, had passed laws restricting the drug testing of employees by private employers. In contrast, Utah has enacted a pro-testing drug law and drug testing legislation is pending in many other states. That states can differ so widely in their legislation on drug testing is a matter of significance for multistate employers who must comply with local and state laws.

Cities Take A Stand

San Francisco and Berkeley have ordinances that protect workers in private industry from indiscriminate drug testing. The San Francisco law says that no employer doing business in San Francisco "may demand, require, or request employees to submit to, or to take or undergo any blood, urine, or encephalographic test of the body as a condition of continued employment," unless three conditions are met:

1. The employer has reason to believe that the employee's faculties are impaired on the job.

2. The employee's impairment presents a clear and present danger to his or her own safety or to the safety of others.

3. The employer must, at the employer's expense, have the samples tested by an independent laboratory, and give the employee an opportunity to rebut or explain the results.

Bill Maher, San Francisco Supervisor, the author of the ordinance, pointed out that the California legislature set minimal standards for protection, and that local governments could create greater rights. As an example, he offered municipal rent control laws that create greater tenant rights, local laws banning discrimination based on sexual preference, and various more extensive civil rights. He said in San Francisco there had been no outcry from business, and that no business left San Francisco as a result of the ordinance. He claimed that drug testing was "putting the Bill of Rights on hold." Maher claimed that these decisions should remain in local control, and to do otherwise was to return to the 1950s. "It used to be a red under the bed; now it's a narc in the bathroom. It was a bad idea in the '50s, and it's a bad idea now."

But feelings in San Francisco are far from unanimous. Quentin Kopp of the San Francisco Board of Supervisors debunked the law. "The San Francisco ordinance applies only to existing employees, and its prohibitions apply only to tests that are made as a condition of continued employment. The ordinance doesn't say anything whatsoever about applicants. The San Francisco ordinance fails altogether to accommodate legitimate employer interest other than safety, such as the need to preserve productivity, reduce staff, or maintain product quality. The ordinance prohibits the testing of other municipal employees, such as bus, subway, and cable-car operators, and it effectively prevents testing of private employees, such as truck drivers, forklift operators, and heavy construction workers, whose jobs could also endanger public safety on a daily basis. Finally, many employers sponsor employee assistance and/or rehabilitation program for drug- and alcohol-impaired employees, and these employers typically require on-going tests to ensure that the employee remains drug- or alcohol-free . . . In short, this hastily contrived ordinance presents too many serious problems for it to be considered a model for legislation in other locals."[79]

Many feared that the "Maher Bill" would proliferate throughout California but few cities enacted local drug testing controls.

Chapter 12
Self-Incrimination
And Due Process

ACLU lobbyist Dauphne Macklin cautioned that drug testing programs are frequently implemented in a way that could violate the Fifth Amendment. She pointed out that voluntary consent to drug testing forces employees into self-incrimination and denial of due process of law.

There is little in the legal literature about drug testing threats to the Fifth Amendment. Blood and breath tests have been held not to violate a person's Fifth Amendment protections against self-incrimination by the Supreme Court. If urine testing fits into the same category as blood and breath tests, then a self-incrimination defense is not likely to stand. The Supreme Court, in *Skinner* v. *Railway Labor Executive* rejected the defense that urine drug testing is a form of self-incrimination.

The Fifth Amendment

No persons shall be held to answer for a capital, or otherwise infamous crime, unless on a presentment or indictment of a Grand Jury, except in cases rising in the land or naval forces, or in the Militia, when in actual service in time of war or public danger; nor shall any person be subject for the same offence to be twice put in jeopardy of life or limb; nor shall be compelled in any criminal case to be a witness against himself, nor be deprived of life, liberty, or property, without due process of law, nor shall private property be taken for use, without just compensation.

Polygraphs

The self-incrimination issue is central in the debates abound polygraph testing. Lie detectors, known formally as polygraphs, are devices that purport to detect untruthful answers by measuring changes in blood pressure, pulse rate, and perspiration. Courts have never accepted the scientific claims for these machines, and they are barred as evidence. Private industry, however, has embraced them.

In the 1980s, as many as 2 million polygraphs were administered in the private sector each year.[98] Finally workers in the private sector brought suit, and the House of Representatives passed the Polygraph Protection Act, which prohibits private employers from giving lie detector tests to most current or prospective employees.[100] Many utility workers, pharmaceutical workers handling controlled substances, day-care workers, and employees of private security companies could still be polygraphed, however. In a California State Supreme Court ruling that outlaws the practice of forcing employees to take polygraph tests, Chief Justice Rose Bird wrote, "The device is designed so that an examinee cannot prevent a response to highly personal questions even by remaining silent. This method of interrogation thus strikes the very heart of the privacy guarantee."[83] Even so, there are exceptions to California's Employee Polygraph Protection Act, including employees involved in national security activities for the federal government, as well as security service firms and pharmaceutical manufacturers, distributors and dispensers, and employees of private firms who are reasonably suspected of involvement in a workplace incident such as theft or embezzlement that resulted in economic loss to the employer.

Whatever their scientific basis, lie detectors can serve as scarecrows. Many people think the machines work, and when facing a test, blurt out confessions. Abuses have occurred. In Florida, for example, managers at a Zayre's Department Store discovered a $500 theft. They tested everyone who had access to the store safe, including an assistant manger named David. He failed twice and was fired even though he proclaimed his innocence. The investigation continued until another man who had cleared the polygraph was caught. However, Zayre's would not rehire David without an admission of guilt. He sued for defamation, and the store later settled for $250,000. Zayre's no longer uses polygraphs.[98]

The Honesty Test

In response to the expense of polygraphs and the controversy surrounding them, many employers turned to personality tests or written honesty tests, some of which market for less than $10.00 a test. For obvious reasons, employers would like to be sure they are hiring honest persons, but it is virtually impossible to get to know people before they are hired. Honesty tests are specialized variations of personality tests. A large number of questions are usually included to increase reliability, but most questions simply represent different ways to probe for dishonest behavioral tendencies and attitudes. Interpretations are made by comparing an individual's profile with those of persons independently judged honest, possibly with polygraphs, and dishonest, possibly by courts of law. Some tests measure an individual's test score against the response pattern of normal persons as well as those clinically diagnosed as suffering from such psychiatric disorders as depression, hysteria, paranoia, and schizophrenia.

Typical Questions

Would you answer "yes" or "no" to the following:

✦ *When you are wrong, do you usually admit it?*

✦ *Do you ever worry about what other people will think of you?*

✦ *Did you ever cheat in school?*

✦ *Have you ever thought about cheating anyone out of any thing?*

✦ *Did you ever lie to a teacher or policeman?*

✦ *Have you ever stolen anything from an employer?*

Stanton Corp.[98]

Proponents claim that personality tests can predict which applicants are at risk of drug abuse, those who are unsuitable for employment in stressful positions, such as flight-control centers or nuclear plants, and even those who would function well in jobs that involve frequent rejections, such as sales, or physical threats, such as in psychiatric nursing. As Dr. Hommer B. C. Reed, a neuropsychologist at Tufts University New England Medical Center pointed out, often the tests are "disarmingly ingenuous."[98] He singled out as an example from one of the tests, "The amount I stole from my employer was (a) 0, (b) $5, (c) $25, (d) $100, (e) $500." This was accompanied by a space for explanation. No single answer, or group of answers, is considered significant without taking into account the total pattern of responses. Sometimes the test determines that you are lying by the "no" answer to a question like, "Did you ever cheat anyone?" or "Have you ever stolen anything?" The presumption is that everyone has cheated or stolen at least once.

Prompted by concerns that employers would use written tests to pry too much into an employee's background, as some lie detector tests have done, Massachusetts enacted a law that prohibits employers from giving honesty tests that amount to "paper and pencil" polygraphs. Considerable concern has been expressed about who is actually being screened out by these devices. Not only could they screen out capable and honest employees, but they might also screen out people more likely to join unions or to challenge practices on the job as being morally or ethically improper.

The issue has serious repercussions. For example, a grand jury awarded $450,000 to an employee of a fast-food chain who was fired because a polygraph examiner said that the employee's denial of having used cocaine was untruthful. Aside from the polygraph results, the only "evidence" suggesting otherwise was "rumors" of drug use outside of work that the supervisor had heard.

> *The next epidemic in America, which has already started, . . . is test abuse. Let me put it to you this way. Would you want your doctor making a decision to operate on you on the basis of a single blood or urine test? Now, most people in America, I hope, would be horrified by that thought. Yet, everyday in America we are operating on our workers. we are severing them from their jobs and their livelihood, and sometimes from their freedom, on the basis of a single chemical test.*
>
> Dr. Ron Seigel[84]

Due Process

Denying an employee due process may be in violation of the Fifth Amendment. The question is whether or not the drug testing process and results are arbitrary. This question is usually met by testimony regarding the accuracy of urine testing procedures and a factual demonstration that the procedure was followed.

The issue of abuse of drug testing has become very serious as a result of questionable practices by employers. A very dramatic case of alleged drug testing abuse involved Georgia Power.[91] Leslie Price and Susan Register were two workers employed in a nuclear power plant. Register, a mechanical expeditor, and Price, a quality-control inspector, were concerned about plant safety and reported apparent violations to the Nuclear Regulatory Commission. Subsequently, the two were told they had been "hot lined," and were ordered in for drug tests. Susan Register testified to being forced by a nurse to drop her pants to her ankles, bend over at the waist with her knees slightly bent, hold her right arm in the air, and with her left hand angle a specimen bottle between her legs. She described sobbing, wetting herself, and vomiting. She was fired for insubordination for refusing to take the test. Price gave her urine sample and was told that her sample was positive for marijuana. She was fired for misconduct. Had she been fired for drug use, the Nuclear Regulatory Commission might have ordered the company to recheck, at great cost, all the work she had inspected as a quality-controller. This is a dramatic example of how drug testing might be used to punish whistle-blowers.

Employers are not the only sources of potential abuse. A spiteful employee, for example, could report having heard rumors that another employee was suing drugs, causing that person to be tested. This could be considered harassment. Since these tests have a high rate of errors, that person could come up with a positive test, even though drugs were not used. Many are concerned that drug testing could be used in subtle ways to dissuade union organizing, or that particularly outspoken employees could be subjected to testing and have the future of their employment put in jeopardy.

Workers at Pacific Refining Company in Hercules, California, filed a class-action suit after the company ordered its employees to take urine tests.[89] Hercules required all employees to come in, partly disrobe, and expose themselves so that a witness could verify the urine specimen. Three people refused to take the test and were fired, even though the company said that employees who tested positive would not be fired. The company said it had to fire those who refused because they needed 100 percent participation. The ACLU and Attorney John True of the Employment Law Center worked with the employees on the case and a restraining order was issued to halt the testing. It was one of the first tests of drug testing and right-to-privacy laws in California.

The plaintiffs asserted that there was no reason to believe that there was a drug problem at the refinery. The decision to do the testing was made at the home office in Houston, because of a belief that drug use is "pretty pervasive" in society. True pointed out that the test in no way showed anything about impairment on the job, but it could indicate pregnancy or ingestion of legal medications, which would be an invasion of privacy.

The right of employers to test employees for drugs is evolving. Testing of strongly suspected drug users, crews involved in accidents, and person-nel in sensitive positions has been upheld by the Supreme Court. However, a minority of employees use drugs, have sensitive positions, or are involved in serious accident.

Justice Scalia was with the 7 to 2 Supreme Court majority upholding post-accident testing in *Skinner* v. *Railway Labor Executives Association*. He dissented from the narrow 5 to 4 majority upholding testing of some, but not all, customs employees. Justice Scalia noted that only five of 3,600 customs employees tested positive for drugs. Of the 30,000 federal employees tested in 1988 under the random spot checking program only 203 tested positive, a rate of 0.7 percent.[206]

The Supreme Court seems to be shifting on the Fifth Amendment away from the negative requirement of "particularized" suspicion for reasonable searches. Critics question this erosion of privacy, primarily of the innocent. Does this prepare the way for dragnet office searches, blanket AIDS testing, or regular searches of travelers, they wonder. Contrasting the documented record of alcohol and drug abuse among railroad workers with the data on customs workers, Justice Scalia wrote that there is no "real evidence of a real problem that will be solved" by drug testing. He added, "Symbolism, even symbolism for so worthy a cause as the abolition of unlawful drugs, cannot validate and otherwise unreasonable search."[205]

Given the narrow 5 to 4 vote and limited scope of the Supreme Court decision in *National Treasury Employees Union* v.*Von Raab*, it is likely that there will be limits to drug testing. Responding to the Court's decision, Dr. Michael Walsh of NIDA, National Institute for Drug Abuse, said, "The issue in our program has always been who. The most difficult decision is where to draw the line. Nuclear people are obviously in, and clerical people are obviously out, but there are a lot of people in the middle."

In 1989, there were over 40 lawsuits challenging drug testing before federal courts. It will be years before the line is clearly drawn as to who can be tested for drugs and under what circumstances.

My major problem in defense of railroad workers accused of Rule G violations is that the provision for due process is extremely attenuated, limited, or nonexistent. Perhaps in agreements or the Railroad Labor Act, there is language generally addressing that issue, but in practice, the railroad management almost unilaterally, without exception, keeps defendant employees from having any semblance of due process defense. We're presented, perhaps only at a hearing and not before, with a laboratory report that most people in the collective bargaining adjudication procedure have no familiarity with.

They're not giving it to them before the hearing, so it can be scrutinized by independent consultants who know what they're looking for. . . . it's hard for a local griever to know what to look for in order to defense a case or even see the most fundamental problem with a report.

. . . we are given no raw data from the laboratories, . . . On every successfully challenged case . . . it has been through quirk, a luck-out, somebody divulging something that clearly would never have been divulged.

. . . my emphasis is access to raw materials for independent consultant analysis, which oftentimes can divulge the source of the wrongful allegation against the employee. Lack of access to that information is totally the antithesis of due process. . . Retesting of the original sample from the original bottle, that's the primary first step. . . The problem is getting the sample.

Current railroad employees have no obligation from their perspective to give you access to it. And then, if they do, they say it will be retested at our lab, not your lab. . . .Ninety-nine percent of the cases will never get to the sample to do that testing.. . .

Kenneth Rogers [238]
Trainman, United Transportation Union
Hearing on Status of Drug Testing in the Workplace

Good drug testing progras build in due process to protect employees from abuse and minimize employer liability. These include demonstrating a drug abuse problem exists in the company or within the industry, careful attention to how employees are selected for testing to prevent harassment or discrimination, strict adherence to forensic standards, preservation of the sample, permission for employees to use the lab of their choice for retesting, and advanced disclosure of the testing procedure to employees. California's testing program for applicants and employees (see Appendix C) incorporates due process safeguards. Programs that are carefully crafted to include due process are less susceptible to legal challenge.

Guidelines For Employers

Chapter 13
Deciding On A Drug
Testing Program

Alcohol and drug use has been around for a long time, and has caused problems at work. However, employers have traditionally tended to dismiss the problems of alcohol and drug addiction. In fact, many employers are unaware of the extent of their own company's problems. Some estimates say that 50 percent of the executives from leading insurance, banking, and financial, and transportation companies believed that alcohol and drug use was "not really a problem for their organization."[3]

Supervisors are usually reluctant to accuse someone of abusing drugs. Likewise, many employers would like to look the other way, thinking that it is the smartest way to avoid legal action. Of course, just the opposite is true. There is a common belief that problem employees, those who do abuse substances, will be screened out during pre-employment interviews. However, that often does not happen, even now that pre-employment drug testing is in vogue.

The tendency is to deny the whole issue. To even start having a drug testing program is to imply that there may be drug users in the company, which is a serious social stigma that companies do not want to bear.

On the other hand, employers who ignore alcohol or drug use in their companies can face problems, such as "vicarious liability," which means that the master is liable for the servant's actions. For example, if a blue-collar worker has an accident on the job because of substance dependency, that employee can actually turn around and sue the employer! Additionally, if an employee has an accident on the way home after work, the employer can be sued for negligence for keeping a drug- or alcohol-dependent person on the job without rehabilitation. On the other hand, an employer should be extremely careful never to terminate an employee for anything other than job performance. If an employer fires a worker for drug addiction or alcoholism, and communicates that reason to someone else, the employer can be sued for defamation of character.

There are cases holding employers directly responsible for failure to screen applicants carefully or for retaining incompetent or dangerous employees. Since the behavior of drug or alcohol abusers can present serious problems for co-workers and others, an employer must be alert to any sign that an applicant or current employee may cause such danger. Failure to act reasonably when information was or *could have been* available can expose an employer to substantial liability. Even when there is no evidence of negligent screening or supervision, an employer may be held vicariously liable for the negligent or violent acts of an employee.[53]

Drug Testing Pros And Cons

"Many companies jump into drug testing blindly, and realize after the fact — after they've collected samples and taken adverse action against employees — that they haven't really thought about the many parameters involved in developing a drug policy," comments Dr. J. Michael Walsh, Chief of the Clinical Behavior Pharmacology Branch of the National Institute on Drug Abuse (NIDA).[118] "Drug testing is a deceptively simple solution. People think, 'All we have to do is start drug testing, and we'll get rid of this problem.' Probably the main point made at the NIDA conference was that drug testing can be a useful tool within . . . an overall program of treatment, prevention, and education. It is not a necessary tool, but it could be a useful tool in identifying people with drug problems."

It is difficult to identify drug-using employees solely by their behavior.[68] More importantly, drug use is difficult to prove without the support of objective drug test results. Positive identification of drug use is the main reason for implementing a urine testing program. A testing program can also identify drug use early, potentially reducing harm to the employee, the employer, and co-workers. A pre-employment screening program can identify drug users before they enter the company's work force. Drug testing not only makes it difficult for an employee to deny drug use, but test results provide strong evidence if employee disciplinary action is necessary. Urine testing may allow employers to pinpoint the causes of other sorts of problems, such as absenteeism and decreased output. Random testing has been shown to have significant deterrent effect on drug use.

Determining The Extent Of Drug Use By Employees

Direct Evidence

♦ *Substantial observed or known drug use by employees*

♦ *Security department or undercover investigation reports indicating substantial drug use or drug transactions*

♦ *Drug paraphernalia found on premises*

♦ *Complaints of drug use by co-workers*

♦ *Employees arrested off-duty for drug use*

♦ *Medical claims implicating drug use*

♦ *Results of fitness for duty examinations*

♦ *Drug use at other company sites*

Indirect Evidence

♦ *Accidents on the job*

♦ *Accidents off the job*

♦ *High absenteeism*

♦ *Employee difficulties in concentration*

♦ *Decreased employee productivity*

♦ *Employees with poor interpersonal relationships*

♦ *Increased medical/benefits claims*

♦ *Increased wage garnishments/personal bankruptcies*

William F. Adams, Controlling Drugs and Alcohol in the Workplace: A Summary of Drug Testing Law and Legislation and Guide to Corporate Policy Development, Orrick, Herrington & Sutcliffe, San Francisco, October, 1988.[229]

Direct Impact On Business

Drug testing takes time, costs money and can impact adversely on employee morale. Employers who institute drug testing programs with little planning can find themselves accused of violating employees' right to privacy.

Consequently, establishing a clear relationship between drug use and damage to the company is essential. When employers cannot demonstrate that its business is directly affected, the testing program is unlikely to survive scrutiny.

In deciding whether or not to institute a drug testing program, employers must establish a line between drug use and business concerns. The employer should gather direct and indirect evidence of drug use in the workplace from all reasonable sources. Next, the employer should identify the areas of the business that are at risk. finally, the employer should be prepared to demonstrate the ineffectiveness of less objectionable methods.

Employee Morale

When considering a drug testing program, employers must weigh the effect of a drug testing program on employee morale. For example, Tom Peters, author of *In Search Of Excellence*, says that if "future competitiveness depends on treating people as an important part of the institution, the least respectful thing I can imagine doing to a human being is telling him to piss in a bottle once a month."[102]

Louis L. Maltby is vice president of Drexelbrooks Engineering Company, a small instrumentation company in Horsham, Pennsylvania, which has decided not to have any drug testing. He argued, "We just don't think you need to test to keep the workplace drug-free. After all, drugs are just a symptom of something else. What you really want is a committed, dedicated workforce, people who like their jobs and care enough not to come to work stoned. What we do is select and nurture employees who are going to do a good job. We think that if we do that, the drug problem takes care of itself. We're incredibly careful about the people we hire. You're saying you can have a drug testing program and have the kind of employee relations I'm talking about. I say you can't. The two are inimical. Ours is based upon a relationship that doesn't come from a paycheck. When you say to an employee, 'You're doing a great job, but just the same I want you to pee in this jar and I'm sending someone to watch you,' you're undermining that trust."[82]

Cost

Cost justification is an important factor in any business decision. The bottom line is whether drug tests are worth the money they cost, and any employer considering a drug testing program must weigh the costs of the program against the benefits. For example, if there are serious potential liabilities because of public safety, as there is with transportation or manufacturing of chemicals and explosives, an accident caused by one stoned employee could cost the company and the surrounding community an extremely high price. In those cases, a drug program is almost always worth its cost. On the other hand, if the goal of the program is to deter drug and alcohol use, there may well be other, less expensive ways in which to accomplish that end without instituting an expensive company-wide testing program.

What Tests Actually Show

The chief concern in drug testing is not the accuracy of the test, but the degree of the job-relatedness of the test results. Therefore, it is important to have a good understanding of what a positive urinalysis result does and does not show. *A positive urinalysis shows that a person has used a certain substance at some time in the past* (which might be hours, or it might be weeks), *but it does not show whether the person was intoxicated or under the influence of the drug at the time the urine was given.* This is a critical point, as some companies have learned after the fact.

For example, in one arbitration case in a mining company, a one-time mass test led to the firing of a few employees. However, the court ordered that the employees be reinstated because they were fired under a company policy that prohibited employees from being under the influence of a drug or alcohol. The tests showed only that they had used a drug or alcohol, but not that they were under the influence. The arbitrator recognized that the positive urine tests only showed recent drug use. Had there been a written policy prohibiting the use of controlled substances altogether, the firing probably would have been upheld.[68]

Urine tests cannot detect causes of worker impairment *other* than drugs, such as fatigue, domestic problems, financial woes, grief, low worker morale, or organic disease.

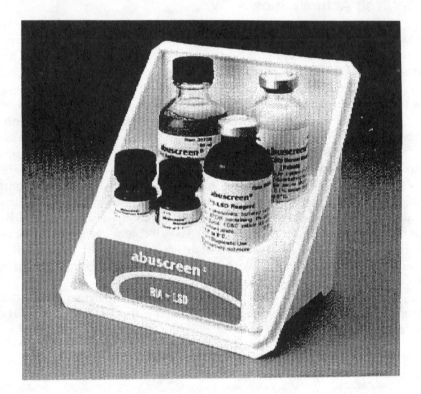

Abuscreen ® Radioimmunoassey from Roche Diagnostic Systems is a low cost drug screen. Shown here is the RIA for LSD which offers a positive cutoff set at 0.5 ng/ml. (From product literature of Roche Diagnostic Systems, Division of Hoffman-La Roche, Inc.)

Chapter 14
Establishing A Drug
Testing Policy

In order to decide what levels of drug testing are proper for the work environment, a company should first define the severity of the problem in its own house. One approach is to conduct a sample screening of the work force population from the top down or a representative sample of the employee base by a "blind" screening (with no way to identify individuals who test positive). A 10 percent problem should be addressed differently than a 50 to 70 percent abuse problem. Once the extent of the problem is defined, one or all of the procedures can be implemented by a company if properly managed.[106] It is very important to think through the reasons for having a drug program, weigh the issues, and decide on an approach.

Approaches To Drug Testing

There are five basic approaches to drug testing: the military approach, a medical approach, a security approach, the business approach, and the legal approach.

The Military Approach

Unlike companies in the private sector, the military does not conduct pre-enlistment drug testing. The military believes that it can take its recruits and shape them up into good soldiers. The centerpiece of the military testing program is that it is stringent. Entire units can be screened for drugs without notice, and individuals can be randomly selected for tests as well. Any commander who thinks there is a probable cause can have subordinates tested. For an officer who fails a drug test, dismissal is all but automatic. However, whether or not the military model can be applied to the larger public is questionable. The military, after all, is an authoritarian organization, and the kind of stringent measures that it employs would undoubtedly cause an uproar in a corporation or college.

The Security Approach

The security approach is based on the notion that drug users pose a risk to company security and to co-workers' safety, and on the belief that drug users must be quickly and permanently removed from the company's work environment. The approach calls for immediate dismissal or punitive actions. Here, firms actively look for drug use by urine-screening the employees, and by random searches of work areas by private security officers, often using trained dog patrols and undercover agents. This approach is expensive, usually lacks support from labor unions, and contributes to strained relationships between employers and employees.

The Medical Approach

The medical approach involves treating troubled workers primarily through employee assistance programs (EAPs), which provide treatment services or refer individuals to professional rehabilitation sources. Here a company demonstrates concern for its employees' health and well-being, and at the same time saves money by rehabilitating workers rather than firing or replacing them.

EAP programs usually work by employee self-referral. Some people believe that this is why they are less effective than they might be, because even a successful EAP might be missing half the employees who need help because of substance-abuse. In the security approach, substance-abuse is viewed as a crime; in some other approach it might be considered an immoral activity. In the medical approach it is viewed as a disease that is treatable, with high recovery rates.

The Business Approach

The business approach takes a broader view of substance-abuse in the workplace, and combines considerations of company policy, security, and treatment in setting up a substance-abuse program. Here the concern is with the performance of the individual and the cost of drug abuse. If employees are under the influence of drugs or alcohol, they are costing the company money because they are not working efficiently, because of absenteeism, and because of safety and security problems. The view in the business approach is one of the bottom line and the healthiness of the entire organization.

The Legal Approach

Here, the underlying concern has to do with protecting the organization from potential liability for accidents caused by employees who have been abusing substances on the job. Employee rights must be honored; yet, at the same time, the company must be sheltered from liability. The legal approach, like the business approach, involves planning and developing a comprehensive company program.

Establishing A Company Policy

The first step, if the organization does decide that it is going to have a drug testing program, is to formulate a company policy.[112]

Points In A Company Drug Testing Policy:

+ *The need for a substance-abuse policy*

+ *The company's position on use and possession of substances on company premises*

+ *Responsibilities of both the company and the employees to insure public trust, public safety, and fitness for duty*

+ *What sanctions will be taken if the policy is violated*

+ *Which job categories will be subject to testing*

+ *Circumstances under which employees will be tested*

+ *Consequences of refusal to undergo testing*

+ *Consequences of a positive result*

+ *The company's position on rehabilitation opportunities*

+ *Responsibility of employees to seek treatment*

+ *Provisions for confidentiality*

A company policy is a clearly articulated statement that spells out the company's attitude toward drug use on and off the job as it affects employee productivity. The policy is publicized throughout the company, and is included in the employee handbook, the supervisors' handbook, and the supervisory training program. How drug users will be dealt with is clearly spelled out, and usually rehabilitation through an EAP is offered.[105]

A company drug testing policy statement is a vehicle for communicating the company's expectations regarding drug use to its employees. It describes what urine tests will be performed, under what circumstances samples will be requested, and how test results will be used. Such notice is vitally important. An employee's expectation of privacy can be reduced if they know that all employees are subject to urine testing in certain circumstances. If employees can show that they were not fully informed about such a policy, disciplinary action may be overturned.[68]

The policy and procedures should clearly advise employees of the circumstances under which they will be tested, the consequences of refusing to submit a urine sample, and the consequences of a positive test result. Again, if the employees can show that they did not know about the policy and procedures, or if the employer cannot demonstrate that employees have been advised, disciplinary action may be overturned.

The question of who can be searched, and when, is important for a new substance-abuse policy. A union contract may affect the policy and must be considered. The contract may prevent the company from implementing a new drug abuse policy unilaterally. It may be necessary to negotiate the policy with the union. Any changes, even in the enforcement of the existing policy, should be reviewed alongside an existing labor agreement, and agreed upon by union representatives. Dramatic changes abruptly and unilaterally carried out can generate problems that will delay implementation of any effective drug control policy.

The September 1989 issue of *Employment Law Update*, a newsletter published by Rutkowski and Associates, contains an alcohol and drug abuse policy that can serve as a model for developing a company policy (see Appendix B). Of course, it is important that each provision be carefully tailored to the unique needs of the company and not just boiler plated.

Searches

A company should develop and publish explicit guidelines on searches of employees' lockers, vehicles, packages, and personal property, and on when investigatory interviews with security personnel and other employees will be permitted. It also must be decided whether undercover investigators furnished by law enforcement agencies will be utilized and what the arrest procedures will be.[117]

Generally, searches are less likely to draw legal attack when they are conducted only in situations where there is reasonable suspicion that drugs are present, rather than on a random basis.

Chapter 15
Picking Tests And
Selecting Labs

The tests used must be tailored to the employer's purpose in testing. The methodology and the detection limits as well as the selection of a laboratory to preform the tests are crucial.

Screening Tests

A screening test is intended to determine whether or not a drug-like component is present in the sample. Screening is often used with large groups of people where there is no known relationship between their performance or activities and the test taking. If the purpose of the drug testing is for screening, then the test needs to be inexpensive (because it is used for a large group of people), easy to administer (possibly by people who have minimal training), and relatively quick in yielding results, possibly on the spot. For example, some types of tests might even use litmus paper, although it would not necessarily be recommended for the employers themselves to actually do the testing.

Confirmatory Tests

In contrast, the confirmatory test is used to ensure that what is revealed by the screening test is actually an abused drug instead of, for example, an over-the-counter medication, an unusual food, or an error of some sort. Confirmatory tests are also used when there is some behavioral indication, such as slurred speech, staggering, nystagmus eye movement, or even an accident. The cost of the confirmatory test is higher so fewer are given. The time it takes to yield the results is also less important, but the specificity of the test is extremely important, and the sensitivity may be very important as well.

Cost Of The Tests

Laboratories can provide drug screening for five or six commonly abused drugs for approximately $10.00 per individual tested. A confirmatory test, on the other hand, typically costs between $25.00 and $50.00 for confirming a single positive drug test, and the cost can be substantially higher (over $100) if the confirmatory test involves a multiple blood test.

Sensitivity

Another issue that must be determined before implementing a program is the sensitivity of the test. Sensitivity refers to how readily the test can detect the presence of a drug. The most common type of screening test is a test for the presence of the drugs in urine, although screening methods can be applied to blood and saliva as well. Police officers who stop motorists who appear to be under the influence may use saliva or breath tests, but employers typically use urine tests. A "positive" or "negative" result is relative, not absolute. That is, if it is above or below the cut-off value, it is labeled "positive" or "negative." It is therefore extremely important to find out in advance what the laboratory's cut-off point for positive samples will be. The cut-off points should be reviewed to ensure that the laboratory can detect the drugs of interest within an appropriate length of time after use by an employee or job applicant. The cut-off point can be rather high, making the test less sensitive, or low, making it more sensitive. The sensitivity of the test should depend on the company's purpose for testing. For a broad screening, it might be a good idea to have a somewhat insensitive test, to detect only people who are under the influence at the time of testing, or who have used a drug very recently, or who seem to have used a large amount of a drug. In a safety situation, it might be smart to have a much more sensitive test, which would flag a wider range of people.

One typical screening test used is thin-layer chromatography (TLC), which may not detect drugs at low concentrations, but can detect the presence of many drugs simultaneously. It is therefore an inexpensive way to screen for many drugs at one time.

A confirmatory method should not only be as sensitive for the drug's presence as the screening method, but also permit specification of the drug that was detected. The confirmatory test should always be one that uses a different process than the screening test. Never use the same type of test twice for both screening and confirmation. The confirmatory test is usually based on a different chemical principle than the nonspecific screening method. These tests include the gas chromatography(GC) and the gas chromatograph/mass-spectrometer (GC-MS). These methods require extensive instrumentation and experienced operators. They provide the best means available to identify a specific drug present, but are expensive.

Choosing Test Sensitivity Level

If the company decides to launch into a drug testing program, one of the first questions is, "What kind of errors can you tolerate?" We have already seen in our exploration of the issues and the data that errors in drug testing programs are inevitable. There is no such thing as a perfect drug testing program. There will inevitably be innocent people who are accused of being drug users. And there will be guilty people, drug users, who will be measured as nonusers. So, do you want a program that will catch only the extreme drug users and let many casual drug users by? Or do you want a program that will indicate all drug users, of even the slightest amount, but will also give a positive result on many people who are merely eating poppy-seed bagels and taking Nyquil® cough medicine?

If you are faced with public-safety issues, as with airline pilots and train engineers, it would perhaps be better to get a positive result on a person who is not abusing substances. On the other hand, if you are just using the program to deter drug use, and you do not have public-safety issues, it might be better, in light of the serious consequences to the individual, to let some people escape who are occasional or recreational users, or even regular abusers, on the grounds that sooner or later they will be detected.

Choosing Detection Limits

Most tests for drug abuse have low detection limits. A laboratory will usually be unable to detect, or will not report the presence of, drugs taken more than a few days prior to the tests. To avoid detection, a drug user generally needs to abstain from most drugs, including marijuana, for a week or even less. Chronic daily users, on the other hand, may need to abstain for up to three or four weeks to avoid detection, depending on the individual's previous level of use and the sensitivity of the tests.

The *cut-off value* refers to the concentration of the drug that will be reported by a laboratory as a positive indication that a drug or its metabolites are present in the sample. Some cannabinoid tests may be too sensitive for employee testing, since they can react positively to a sample from a person who has been passively exposed to marijuana smoke, particularly when the results are reported at cut-off levels such as 50 nanograms per mililiter.

However, a higher cut-off value, for example, the use of a 200 nanogram per milliliter cut-off value in an EMIT® test, gives reasonable sensitivity and is less likely to result in the reporting of a false positive. The use of a high cut-off value increases the job-relatedness of a test. However, the test can not measure the degree of employee impairment. The smoking of a single joint by a nonuser is not analogous in effect to that of a single joint for a chronic user, much as one stiff drink to a nondrinker is more impairing than it would be to a moderate drinker. Yet the same drink may set an alcoholic off on a binge. Still, the use of a higher detection limit is a way of creating an error bias.

The common tests for alcohol use have very short detection limits, and the correlation between the results of laboratory urine tests and actual blood-alcohol concentration is well understood. Thus, blood tests detect recent use of alcohol, as well as actual impairment.

Drug testing laboratories are very much aware of the consequences of reporting false positive test results. In practice, they may use higher cut-off points for positive results rather than use the full sensitivity that their methodology is capable of providing. This technique leads to less sensitive screening for drugs, so that only a few samples with high drug concentrations will need to be confirmed. Another way to reduce the chance of a false positive test result is to use a less sensitive method to confirm the initial screening results. Since the initial positive screening result cannot be confirmed, the overall result is reported back to the client as a negative result. In either case, the net effect will be an underestimation of the actual drug use, and many false negative test results.[105]

Choosing Your Errors

Errors in drug testing are inevitable. The actual question is: what type of error can you accept? There are two types of errors: a drug user can test negative, or a non-drug-user can test positive. If the consequences of the test are used as a basis for disciplinary action, employment, promotion decisions, or criminal investigations, then a false negative is the safest error. It is better to let a few of the "guilty" go undetected than to wrongly accuse the innocent. Drug abusers who escape detection in one testing are likely to be detected in a subsequent testing.

On the other hand, a false positive might be the better error in a research or treatment setting. If testing is intended to evaluate work fitness, such as that of a pilot commanding a passenger plane, then it would be safer to stop a functioning pilot from making a flight than to fail to detect an intoxicated one.

Selection Of A Drug Testing Laboratory

Doing the initial drug screening within the company can reduce the cost of testing and still provide good quality laboratory data. By sending only those samples that test positive at the company's initial screening, a company can significantly reduce the cost of its drug testing program — provided drug use is not widespread. In this situation the training and skill of the person performing the analysis are crucial to the success of the program. There are many drawbacks, however. People who have minimal training in understanding what the tests mean can make mistakes, causing positive results for people who have not been abusing drugs. What effect might these positive results have on those persons' reputations? The in-house program can also suffer from many problems of access to the tests and samples. For these reasons, most companies conducting large-scale testing programs prefer to have a laboratory perform the drug screening even thought it costs more. Confirmatory testing is almost always done in an off-site lab.

Considerations In Choosing A Testing Laboratory:

✦ *The laboratory should be licensed, inspected, audited, and in good standing with state authorities. The laboratory should use the National Institute on Drug Abuse Guidelines as the standard for "good laboratory practices."*

✦ *The laboratory should confirm all positive results by a fundamentally different method of testing. Under no circumstances should a sample be screened once and then reported without a confirmation test being performed.*

✦ *The laboratory should adhere to forensic procedural standards, including strict chain of command to guard its samples from the possibility of tampering. Samples should be locked away when not going through the testing process. Visitors should not be permitted in the testing area.*

✦ *The laboratory should have a substantive quality control program that dictates standard operating procedures to ensure the integrity and repeatability of results.*

✦ *The laboratory should be willing to defend its procedures with expert testimony, at a fee, if questions arise.*

✦ *The laboratory should save all possible samples for a reasonable time, at least 30 days, which would permit retesting if a question arises.*

✦ *The laboratory should participate in an outside proficiency test program to monitor the quality of its performance. Ideally, the program should consist of blind analysis of samples having known levels of various drugs.*

Test Procedures

No testing method is guaranteed to be error-free, but there are methods of selection and guidelines a company can follow to insure the highest degree of accuracy in drug testing. A company should demand certain procedures, and monitor the lab to make sure these conditions are being met, so that its employees are protected from false positives, and so it is protecting itself from false negatives.

Remember that any quick testing method risks high levels of error. If a company is promised high quality results with returned reports in two to four hours, it should be aware that it is risking a high number of errors. Quality work takes at least 24 if not 48 hours from receipt of specimen. No method or equipment exists that can shorten the time it takes to test, confirm, and produce results that can be counted on in a sensitive area.

Incidences of poor testing generally come from casual selection of laboratory vendors. Make sure that the laboratory managers are well versed in substance-abuse testing. Ask for references and call them.

Questions To Ask Prospective Testing Labs

✦ *Who has accredited the laboratory?*

✦ *How does it maintain quality control?*

✦ *Does the laboratory insist upon a release form from employees?*

✦ *Does it provide help with policy statements?*

✦ *Has it done work for treatment facilities?*

✦ *Does the lab insist on confirmation testing of all positives, or is it willing to provide reports from a single-method general screening?*

✦ *Does it follow forensic standards and how is the chain of custody maintained?*

✦ *Is the lab willing to defend its data in court?*

✦ *Does the lab participate in an external quality assurance program?*

Be aware that drug testing labs may not have to be approved or certified by any state or federal agency to conduct business. Even if a lab has been approved or certified by some organization, such credentials generally imply only that the overall lab operation meets minimal requirements for personnel space and safety. It usually does not imply that the lab employs sound analytic methods or can perform tests reliably.

Labs can and do make errors. A good lab will attempt to minimize these errors by having a quality assurance program, which should include internal measures to prevent breakdowns in procedures, and participation in an external quality-assurance program, such as those conducted by the College of American Pathologists, the American Association of Bioanalysts, and the California Association of Forensic Toxicololgists. These programs submit urine samples to laboratories at fixed times during the year and evaluate the accuracy of the results. Ask if the lab subscribes to any of these programs, and ask to review any evaluation made of the lab.

Another approach is to ask the lab to test a set of drug-free and drug-containing urine specimens before awarding a contract for services. Labs will often provide free analyses under these conditions to obtain the contract.

Cost Of The Lab

Price in selection of a lab should be the last consideration. You usually get what you pay for. The cost to a company of one badly botched lab test can be far greater than any savings in the lab testing fees.

Evaluating The Lab

Once you have selected your lab, continually evaluate its performance. You can do this by requesting data from external quality-assessment programs, and by conducting your own blind assessment of the lab periodically. An easy way to do this is to occasionally split a specimen and submit it under two different names or sample identifiers. Lab results should be identical for the two specimens. If the blind method is used, it is probably better to attempt to get a specimen that has drug metabolites in it. These can be gotten sometimes from external quality-assessment program, through consultants, or by recycling positive drug specimens identified by the lab itself.

Breath testers for alcohol should be periodically calibrated and tested for accuracy. Here a man uses an Alco-Equilibrator ™ (the white cannister) to check calibration of a hand held Sober-Meter ™ electronic breath alcohol sobriety tester. Both products are from Luckey Laboratories, Inc. The tester measures blood alcohol content (BAC) from .00 to .10 gms %. (From product literature of Luckey Laboratories, Inc.)

Chapter 16
Protecting Employee Rights

Consideration of employees' constitutional rights is imperative when setting up a company drug testing program. The program must be designed in such a way that it does not violate, and in fact protects, employee rights. This strategy will minimize exposure to lawsuits, and maximize the company's ability to have its program upheld in court if a lawsuit does occur.

The mechanisms employers use for *selecting which employees to test* is an extremely important consideration. The legality of the testing program is often determined by the way in which individual employers are selected for testing. Random testing programs are most likely to encounter legal resistance. Testing of job applicants or employees in connection with periodic physicals has drawn little attention in the courts. Testing under conditions of reasonable suspicion, when employers were clearly informed of the policy beforehand, has withstood legal challenge.

Employer attorney William Adams recommends that random testing be used only in high risk, safety-sensitive jobs, especially those in which it is difficult to supervisor day-to-day work. He cautions employers to be prepared to demonstrate the ineffectiveness of less objectionable methods.

How To Limit Company Exposure
To Legal Challenge[101]

✦ *Develop a specific drug abuse detection program. This program should be developed in consultation with all parts of the company that might be affected, such as union representatives, occupational safety and health personnel, security staff, and legal advisors.*

✦ *Modify private employment contracts and collective bargaining agreements to reflect the company's policy.*

✦ *Document the relationship between job performance and drug use.*

✦ *Use random testing only in high risk, safety-sensitive jobs, particularly where it is difficult to supervise day-to-day work performance.*

✦ *Demonstrate the actual or likely ineffectiveness of less objectionable methods of drug detection.*

✦ *Inform all job applicants of the policy. Employees should be given advance notice of any disciplinary action that might be taken as a result of confirmed drug use on the job. If drug tests are to be administered, employees and job applicants should consent to these tests. If penalties are to be imposed for failure to take tests, these penalties should be described in advance.*

✦ *Establish a grace period after the policy is announced and before it is implemented.*

✦ *Notify employees of positive drug detection results, and give them an opportunity to contest disciplinary action based on the results. Consider referring employees to medical help or employee assistance programs before taking punitive action.*

Privacy

Insuring the privacy of employees is important. In general, employees have a "reasonable expectation" of privacy. For example, people using the toilet or urinal usually have an expectation of privacy. Observation of these activities can be considered to be violating that reasonable expectation. If an employee can demonstrate that this expectation of privacy was violated, the company can face legal action. However, the employee's expectation of privacy can be reduced if the employer clearly informs all employees about the drug testing program, when and how it will occur, and so forth. This notification reduces but does not eliminate expectation of privacy. Disclosures should be written up in the employee's handbook. Any documents given to applicants should also have some disclosure statements.

For example, drug testing programs that gather samples without disclosing that they will be tested for drug contents probably constitute an invasion of privacy. Also, drug testing that unnecessarily focuses on off-duty conduct may be open to a privacy challenge, more so than testing that detects only drug use that would affect work performance.

Off-Duty Behavior And Privacy Rights

Most people have a reasonable expectation that what they do in their off-duty time, away from the job, is their business and not the business of the employer. Generally, the courts would support that opinion. There are exceptions, however. For example, when the employer can show a relationship between off-duty behavior and the job, disciplinary actions may be taken. Even for illegal behavior, such as the use of illicit drugs, it is the employer's burden to establish the link between that misconduct and the employee's job performance. For example, what link can be shown between occasional weekend use of marijuana and the job of a stock boy, clerk, or even a professional? It could be argued that casual use in this situation is no more damaging or job-related than casual use of alcohol. It is important for the employer to keep in mind that the burden is on the employer to prove this link. There are several standards generally used to evaluate off-duty misconduct and whether or not it constitutes grounds for discipline. Most involve demonstrating a threat to public safety or to organizational productivity.

Injury To The Company

A jail term leading to the loss of production or depriving the company of the employee's unique skills could harm the business. Claimed harm cannot just be speculative, however. The employer has to prove that the employee's drug use would constitute real and actual harm. For example, the company's reputation might be damaged by an employee going to jail. However, unless that harm is so obvious as to be virtually self-evident, showing the existence of a harm, such as loss of sales, can be difficult. Showing the need for high public confidence in the employer is one approach. For example, a court upheld the firing of an air traffic controller who was found in possession of cocaine at a concert, because drug use and possession would detract from the public's confidence in the agency.[68] The courts will take into consideration the degree of notoriety of the incident and the type of conduct related to the employee's position in assessing damage to the company.

Inability Or Unsuitability To Perform

Absence without authorization, including a jail term, can provide the basis for discipline. Absence or physical inability to perform often go hand in hand with damage to the company. Breach of trust or dishonesty can render an employee unsuitable for a job. When this standard is used, arbitrators usually review the employee's previous record to lessen a severe action or justify termination. A positive urinalysis showing only recent drug use generally does not prove that an employee is unable to perform his or her job responsibilities.

Safety Of The Public And Co-Workers

For employees whose jobs are directly related to safety, such as pilots, vehicle drivers, crane operators, and railway workers, the relationship between safety, job performance, and drug use seems clear. Generally, even on the safety concerns, the courts look at the extent of the employee's drug use when considering the legality of a discharge. For example, in one case, firing of an employee was upheld because evidence showed extensive drug use; however, a second case was dismissed because the employee had a good record, and it could not be shown that he had endangered other employees.

Negative Attitude

Employees may be discharged if co-workers refuse to work with them as a result of off-duty conduct. Cooperation and team work are vitally important to productivity and morale in most companies. Drug abusers often exhibit negativity toward the company and co-workers. This can lead to conflict and dissent.

Adverse Effect On The Employer-Employee Relationship

The most difficult case standard involves serious confrontation between employee and employer that creates a situation where they are unable to work together. Such ill-feeling may be evident if an employee is identified as a drug user but refuses to participate in a drug treatment program.

Reasonable Suspicion

It is sensible for an employer to respect the employee's notion of privacy where possible and appropriate, even if the law might permit the employer to engage in all sorts of observational methods. Testing only when there is reasonable suspicion greatly reduces the degree of legal risk. Labor attorney William Adams reports that an employer's testing policy is likely to be upheld when there is a strong indication that a particular employee has recently used or is under the influence of drugs or alcohol. Generally, employers should probably avoid intrusive monitoring of employees, such as the use of cameras, unless there is real justification for these methods.[101]

Factors Affecting Reasonableness Of Drug Tests

Here is a checklist of factors that may affect the reasonableness of a drug testing program:

 ✦ *Accurate test methodology*

 ✦ *Reliable chain of custody*

 ✦ *Need for tests due to safety, security or integrity of company business goals*

 ✦ *Documentation of past drug use in company*

 ✦ *Inappropriateness of ineffectiveness of other, less intrusive means of achieving the company's goals*

 ✦ *Efforts to minimize intrusiveness of specimen collection*

 ✦ *Procedures for protection of confidential records and test data*

 ✦ *Availability of rehabilitation option or periodic monitoring before discipline results*

 ✦ *Existence of clear notice of the program and its requirements that may result in discipline or termination*

 ✦ *Existence of other safeguards against error, such as permitting employees to explain positive results that might be in error and retesting the same sample in questioned cases*

 ✦ *For random testing there should be additional justification on the basis of substantial safety or security factors; difficulty in monitoring employee performance for signs of drug use*

From William Adams, The Dos, Don'ts and Whys of Drug Testing, *Labor and Employment Law Update*, Orrick, Herrington & Sutcliffe, April, 1988.[228]

 In general, the rules for violation of privacy have to do with "reasonable suspicion" and "probable cause."[69] It is impossible to fully define either term in the abstract. As a comparative matter, reasonable suspicion is less stringent than probable cause, although reasonable suspicion must be founded on objective facts and rational inferences derived from practical experience, rather than inchoate "unspecified suspicion," and must be directed toward the particular employee to be tested.

Reasonable Suspicion Standards

In cases where reasonable suspicion standards can be satisfied, mandatory testing of a public-safety employee does conform with the Fourth Amendment's protection of privacy.[68] Reasonable suspicion may be based on indications that an employee is under the influence of drugs. Indications may include slurred speech, accidents, frequent absences, tardiness, and early departures from work. Since reasonable suspicion is established by combining facts with judgment, it is not possible to predict or describe every situation that may create a reasonable suspicion.

Even when reasonable suspicion or probable cause exist, it is not smart for the employer to try to force a sample from the employee. For example, UPS was sued in 1986 because a company nurse demanded that an employee who had been a drug user, and had been through a drug treatment program, provide immediate samples of his blood and urine for testing when he returned from vacation. When the employee objected, the nurse disregarded his protest and "plunged a needle into his arm and extracted blood." Such forced methods are unwise and should be avoided. An employer should always do everything possible to get the sample with the consent of the employee to avoid such legal actions.

Gathering Confidential Information

Additionally, the gathering of information should be for a particular purpose with a particular employee. In California, for example, the state constitution specifically protects privacy from what is called overbroad and unnecessary information gathering. Employers should not gather whatever information they can get, or they could be in violation of the employee's right to privacy. In California, to be lawful, the employer must establish that there is a compelling need for the test, and that there are no less intrusive ways of meeting that need.

Employers investigating drug or alcohol abuse by workers may wish to obtain an employee's medical records to see if there is a history of drug or alcohol abuse. However, doing so can be dangerous, since most states set a premium on the right to privacy of medical records. Access to and release of medical information is highly regulated. Information containing medical, psychiatric, or psychological material is classified as "confidential information." It simply cannot be obtained without the prior written voluntary consent of the individual to whom the records pertain. Therefore, an employer should not depend on these records; if they do become available, the employer must be scrupulous in maintaining their confidentiality.

Employers who do get positive drug test data from an employee must maintain the privacy of that data. They cannot give data to other employees or employers. Claims for defamation of character may arise if an employer investigates an employee and shares the findings or suspicions with third parties, including other employees who have no need to know, particularly if the findings are wrong or unreliable.[53] There may also be grounds for defamation lawsuits if the employer explains to third parties the reason for any adverse actions, such as termination, that it takes against an employee, especially if the third party is a prospective employer. The wisest policy is to issue no information without a signed release from the affected employee.

Due Process

When implementing a company drug testing program, the company must be proactive in making sure that employees are given due process. Due process means that legal procedures are followed that guarantee a person's rights, and that decision making is not arbitrary. The most important way in which a company can ensure that employees are granted due process is to disseminate a written company policy on drug testing that specifies the rules about drug use on and off the job, what kinds of testing procedures will be use and when they will be used, how they will be used, and what sanctions will be taken if controlled substances are found. It is also important to be sure that the drug testing, the actual taking of the sample, and the analysis and use of its outcome are not in any way arbitrary.

Nondiscriminatory

Title VII of the Civil Rights Act prohibits discrimination based on race, creed or religion. This statute says an anti-drug policy may not single out minorities, women, or other protected groups. Therefore, an employer may be required to demonstrate that the rule is job related and not discriminatory. One way to demonstrate that the program is not discriminatory is to give the test to all applicants or to all persons in a particular job category.

For Cause

Another way that the employer may ensure due process is to make sure the drug testing is done for cause. "For cause" means that testing may occur when reasonable suspicion exists that the employee is using drugs, that is, when there are specific objective facts and reasonable inferences in light of work experience that suggest the employee is using drugs. Staff members trained in recognizing signs of drug or alcohol abuse are able to make this kind of decision more reliably than untrained staff members, and their judgement will be more likely to withstand the scrutiny of a court arbitrator. Grounds for reasonable suspicion include slurred speech, on-the-job accidents, frequent absences, early departure from work, and tardiness.

Forensic Standards

Use of forensic standards in the gathering of the samples and in conducting the analysis of the sample is an effective way to ensure due process. Unless you follow proper procedures and forensic standards, an employee can argue in court that the results are tainted by procedural errors and are therefore unreliable.

Consent

Due process can be demonstrated when an employee actually consents to the test. Of course, the consent must be free consent, not forced. There is some debate over this issue, because people naturally wonder whether consent is genuinely free if the possibility of being fired is implicit in the situation.

Inform Employees

Informing employees, either in their employee handbook or by placing notices on employee bulletin boards, about the drug testing program, how it will work, and what the sanctions will be taken for positive results is another way to guarantee that the employee has been granted due process. Employers should be aware that people who have abused alcohol or drugs, who have been involved in formal rehabilitation, and who have been certified as having been "cured," are protected by Title V of the Federal Rehabilitation Act of 1983, which protects handicapped people from discrimination by federal employers. The drug or alcohol abuser who has been in a program is usually considered to be handicapped. A federal employer cannot legally refuse to hire such individuals. However, once hired, these people can be tested, and can be reprimanded or fired if the employer can establish a clear connection between unsatisfactory on-the-job performance and some kind of drug use as indicated by the testing.

Search And Seizure

If the employer is going to conduct a search, the search procedure should be announced well in advance as company policy, and described in detail in writing to all employees. Whenever possible, the employer should seek written consent from employees to search before proceeding with an intrusive search. Searches should always be conducted so that employee dignity is preserved. Without a properly announced search policy, it may not be possible for an employer to search a purse or lunch box stored in a locker. In fact, searches are very touchy, and usually employers should avoid searching altogether.

Employers should be very careful in taking possession of any incriminating evidence that belongs to the employee. The smartest thing to do is to call in the police, and have the police take possession of the evidence; if the employer takes any evidence before any police involvement, criminal prosecution might be affected by mishandling of the evidence.

Chapter 17
Implementing A Drug
Testing Program

Getting support from all parties involved in the company's drug testing program is critical to its acceptance and success. Support of unions is particularly important. Unions can be of great benefit, or they can resist a drug testing program bitterly if they feel that the testing may be used to harm or fire employees.

Unions Are Concerned

A study of union opinion revealed that unionists feel that drug use in the workplace is a serious problem and is likely to increase.[109] Of the executives responding to an inquiry about union cooperation, 31.5 percent say that unions associated with their company are cooperative with management. The majority of union literature is concerned with labor's involvement with drug programs, which labor leaders support because they want to seek alternatives to termination of unionists detected as users. In order to get union support, management needs an alternative to automatic termination of detected users. Joint programs, with active participation of both labor and management, have been found to be more effective than programs run solely by management or the union. In this cooperative action, management program resources and union reassurances of protection to the user can be successfully combined.

According to union people, the most effective approach to the drug problem is preventative education in the workplace, school, and community. While there is a trend toward less primitive reactions to detected drug users, the respondents in this study perceived that terminating users is still the most typical management policy for dealing with drug users. Managers usually view drug use as a problem arising outside of and "imported" into the regular workforce. Unionists believe that drug use is normally begun prior to joining the workforce through peer associations made in school and in the military.

Even though they believe drug use begins in the social arena, unionists feel that the problem is best confronted within the workplace. Specifically they feel that management and union efforts would be most effective if directed toward preventative education rather than toward in-house counseling or referral to outside agencies. Unionists perceive that drug use in the workforce is relatively high, and is likely to increase in the future. They see management as tending to take a primitive approach to this problem, although growing awareness of the need for more humane management policies is apparent.

Get Union Support

Both the union and the employer are concerned about the benefit of employees. Remember to emphasize that the program is aimed at preventing drug abuse when introducing a drug testing program to unions. Control of alcohol and other drug use in the workplace makes it safer for all employees, by preventing abusers and substances from getting into the workplace, or by removing abusers from the work station.

Any changes, even in the enforcement of existing policies, should be reviewed alongside an existing labor agreement and agreed upon by union representatives. A union contract will probably affect a company drug policy. It may prevent a company from implementing a new policy of drug testing unilaterally, for example. It may be necessary to negotiate the policy with the union.

There has been a marked change in attitudes regarding drugs among union members. According to Gunter Neurenburg of the Crowley Maritime Corporation, a large transportation and oil exploration company with 4,000 employees, "Something has changed. The employer is all of a sudden the good guy. Seafarer [the union] came to us and demanded we begin drug testing." Mr. Neurenberg recommended that employers get the master trade agreement of the Teamsters or other unions regarding drug testing to see how they deal with union policies and agreements about drug testing programs.

According to George Cobbs, the Northern California Alcohol Representative for the International Longshoremen's and Warehousemen's Union, generally the unions will support pre-employment screening for detection of drug use in job candidates, but typically do not support random testing of those on the job. It is very important that companies look at their union contract, if random testing is under consideration, because most union contracts will not allow random testing without bargaining for it. Unions typically feel that the random testing is an avoidance of the problem and violates the rights of employees. However, where a job involves public safety issues, an employer working with the union can often bargain for random testing because of the union's concern for the safety of lives and property.

On the other hand, unions will often support testing for probable cause, provided that it is across-the-board testing of all employees, including management and executives. One source of discontent is that, in many companies, only the blue-collar workers are subjected to testing, whereas the management rarely gets tested. Unions feel that this is a subtle form of discrimination and control.

Unions fear that drug testing can be used to weaken unions or interfere with strikes. Typically, they will support drug testing when it's used for rehabilitation purposes — that is, if the employer does not use test results for punitive actions.

In a typical union labor agreement, the discharge of an employee is reviewed by an arbitrator.[68] The arbitrator's job is essentially three-fold. First, the arbitrator must decide whether the situation alleged by the employer is true. For example, was the urinalysis for the employee positive for the drug in question? Was the test accurate enough to prove the use of the drug? Was the chain of custody of the sample clear, and was the test performed properly? Second, the arbitrator must decide whether the employer violated the labor agreement. Third, the arbitrator must decide whether the sanction imposed was fair and equitable, or too harsh. An arbitrator who feels that the sanction was too harsh is empowered to reverse the sanction in favor of a lesser penalty. Labor agreement compensation is generally limited to orders of reinstatement and back pay. The employer's liability exposure is somewhat limited compared to the employment-at-will situation, where damages may be awarded for such things as mental anguish.

Supervisor Training

Other than the employee's family, supervisors are usually the first to recognize the symptoms of drug use. Supervisory training is essential to avoid witch-hunting situations. If time permits, it is best that a team of supervisors reach the decision to test an employee. The team members should document their reasons and observations as soon as possible, while the cause is fresh in their minds and details can be recalled.[106]

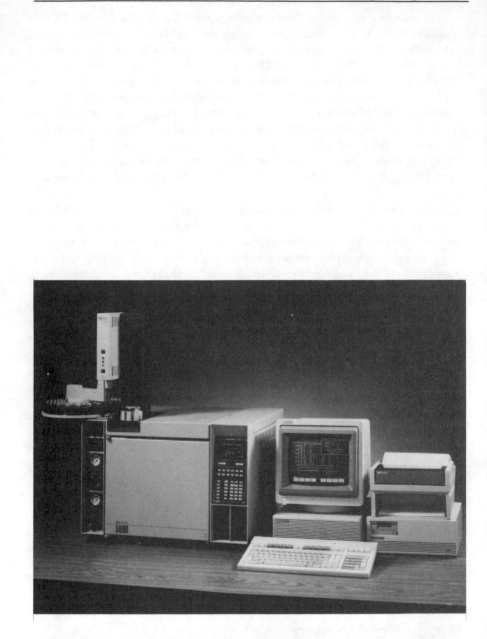

The HP5890A gas chromatograph with HP7678 autosampler manufactured by Hewlett Packard, Inc. Gas chromatography/mass spectrometry (GC/MS), the most accurate and expensive method of drug testing, is used to confirm positive results of drug screening and when forensic standards are required. Most drug testing labs that conduct GC/MS analysis use Hewlett Packard instruments. (Photo by Pete Nuding provided by Hewlett Packard, Inc.)

Chapter 18
Responding To
Positive Results

When positive results come back from initial testing, it is a mistake to assume that there are actually positives for drug use. Instead, view initial positives as a need to confirm results with a more sophisticated, more reliable test based upon a different testing methodology.

Confirmatory Tests

The second test is called a confirmatory test. A confirmatory method ideally should be more sensitive than the screening test and permit identification of specific drugs. Many screening tests are not specific, but in confirmation a test which indicates which kind of substance was used is required. This is particularly important because the use of over-the-counter drugs may have caused the first positive result. A valid confirmatory test requires the use of a testing method based upon a chemical principle different from that used in the less specific screening method.

Two confirmatory methods are gas chromatography (GC) and gas chromatography/mass spectrometer (GC/MS). These methods require special instrumentation and a highly skilled operator; therefore, they are more expensive, and require specialized labs. However, they provide the best means available to identify the specific drugs present.

The terms "positive" and "negative" are used in a relative rather than an absolute sense in drug testing. Since different drug testing methods have different sensitivities for drugs, it is not surprising that one laboratory, using one method, may call a sample positive for a drug, but another laboratory testing the same sample, but using another method, might call the sample negative.

An employee who feels that the urinalysis test results are unconfirmed, or that the tests were improperly performed, could bring a negligence action against the employer in state court.[101] The bases of such an action would be that the person conducting the test and the employer who ordered the test have a legal duty to see that the manufacturer's directions are properly followed, and that the screening test is confirmed in a proper manner. Failure to fulfill this duty, and subsequent harm caused to the employee by loss of work or by other disciplinary action, could be the basis for a lawsuit. Despite the additional cost of confirming a screening test, it is advisable for the employer to confirm all positives on screening tests, by means of reliable and appropriate confirmatory tests.

Discipline And Termination

The appropriate response to positive test results depends on a variety of factors, including the nature of the job, the employee's past employment record, whether drug use can be shown to have taken place on the job, and the severity of the employee's drug abuse problem.

If the drug test confirms other evidence that the employee was under the influence while on the job, there is a stronger case for termination or other serious discipline than if the employee was only using the drug off the job.

What the employee does off the job is usually of no consequence or concern to the company. There are exceptions to this rule, however. If the employer can show a relationship between off-duty behavior and the job, then disciplinary action may be taken. Even with illegal off-duty behavior, such as the use of illicit drugs, it is the employer's burden to establish a link between that misconduct and job performance, and this can be difficult to prove. There are several standards generally used to evaluate off-duty misconduct and whether it constitutes grounds for discipline.

The Particular Problem Of Marijuana

Marijuana presents several unique problems in the workplace, reflecting its unique place in our society.[111] It is illegal, but in many jurisdictions its use or possession is no more serious than a minor traffic ticket. It is the most used illegal drug in our country, particularly among younger people. In general, its use is not considered as serious as the use of cocaine, LSD, or so-called "hard drugs" such as heroin and methadrine.

This ambivalence toward marijuana is manifested in arbitration decisions. Some arbitrators will sustain discharges for simple marijuana use on company premises, and others will not. The case for discharge improves where several incidents of usage occur, however, or when a large quantity is found in the employee's possession, since sale of the drug on company premises then becomes the major issue.

Another complication is that marijuana traces appear in urine for days after use. This problem is substantially aggravated in jurisdictions that have decriminalized marijuana, and in which the community has relaxed attitudes towards its use. An employee who uses marijuana at home without criminal implication can be penalized on the job for having done so.

The problem is further exacerbated by passive inhalation. A non-user who has a spouse, roommate, or friend who smokes marijuana can get positive test results. Clearly, an employer has no right to discipline employees for the behavior of their friends, or to dictate where they may go for recreation and entertainment, if it is otherwise lawful. To discipline or discharge an employee for "dirty" urine under these circumstances could be to invite a lawsuit based on the torts of intrusion or defamation. Therefore, when drug screens for marijuana are used, it is imperative to look for more than a trace, which could be a result of passive inhalation.

Test Sensitivity

Cannabis metabolites tend to be stored in the fat cells for long periods of time. The positive result could be indicating usage several days or even weeks in the past, and may not be correlated with impairment of job performance.

Most other abused drugs have much shorter detection periods than marijuana, so laboratory detection periods commonly used are brief enough to be considered strongly job-related. If the first results are confirmed by a second test, chances are that the drug was actively affecting the person. However, that's not the case with marijuana.[53] In general, to deal with this issue, employers should make sure that the confirmatory test is less sensitive to the presence of the cannabis metabolite, in order to maximize the possibility of detecting actual presence during a period when it would still be influencing the person. Many cannabinoid assay tests may be too sensitive for employee testing, because they can react positively to a sample from a person who has been passively exposed to marijuana smoke.

The use of a 100 nanograms/milliliter cut-off value in an EMIT® test provides reasonable sensitivity, but is unlikely to lead to a false positive result. A negative finding in such a test sample is strong evidence that THC is not present in the system of the tested individual in excess of the detection limit. At the 100 nanograms/milliliter cut-off, most marijuana use at low to moderate levels will be undetectable beyond 24 to 72 hours, although chronic use may be detected for a longer period. Use of this higher cut-off value thus increases the job related value of the test.

False Positives

Another problematic aspect of testing for marijuana is the false positive that may be caused by melanin.[210] Melanin is the pigment that imparts color to the skin. Dr. James Woodford[186], a chemist in Atlanta, Georgia, did tests showing that several of the tests that the military had given confused results for cannabis with those for melanin. Serious concerns were raised that the tests may be discriminatory against people of negro descent, who have a high degree of melanin in the liver and skin. However, it has since been discovered that there are various conditions of the liver and kidney that increase considerably the amount of melanin breakdown products that are present in the urine. As many as 20 to 25 percent of the population may have some of these melanin related conditions, regardless of race.

If the sample is tested immediately, the cross-reactivity of the melanin seems to be rather minor. However, the longer the period that has elapsed since the sample was given, the greater the likelihood that the melanin will test positive for THC when the individual has not consumed any cannabis at all.

In light of all the problems in testing cannabis, it may be advisable for an employer not to test for cannabis when screening employees, but to reserve cannabis tests for situations, such as accidents and treatment programs, where the testing is more closely monitored and confirmed.

Passive Inhalation

Passive inhalation is another cause of false positives. In 1983, Ferslew, Manno, and Manno demonstrated that people who were present while marijuana was smoked by others tested positive, even though they did not smoke any themselves.[44] Researchers were exposed to 13 male subjects individually smoking marijuana cigarettes calibrated to deliver 0, 37.5, or 75 micrograms of delta-9 THC per kilogram of body weight. The researchers' urine was collected 2.5 hours after each smoking period, and just after waking the following morning (the first void). The urines were tested by the EMIT®-d.a.u. cannabinoid urine assay, and measurable concentrations of cannabinoids were detected in the urine.

Evaluation Standards

✦ *Does it cause injury to the employer's company? Has company's reputation has been harmed, or has a jail term or time off from the job led to a loss of production or deprived the company of the employee's unique skills?*

✦ *Does it lead to inability or unsuitability to perform work?*

✦ *Does it threaten the safety of the public or co-workers?*

✦ *Does it lead to negative employee attitude, such as other co-workers refusing to work with the person?*

✦ *Does it lead to adverse effects on the employee-employer relationship, such as confrontations and hostilities that make it difficult for them to work together?*

Follow Established Procedures

An employer who discharges or disciplines an employee for suspected or proven drug use or abuse should act reasonably in light of the stated personnel policy and the employee's work record in order to avoid liability.[53] The employer must follow the company's termination procedures when dealing with an employee suspected of illegal drug use in the workplace, as it would for terminating an employee for any other reason. Restrictive laws affect employers the least when discipline relates to absenteeism, unacceptable performance, or safety violations. Employers are accorded particularly wide latitude if health or safety is at risk. Since drug and alcohol use is commonly linked to increase of hazards on the job, employers will have more freedom to discipline employees if the affected job involves safety risk to co-workers or the public, such as jobs related to public utilities, or transport, or involving machinery.

Be Fair And Reasonable

An employer should handle any termination for drug- or alcohol-related offenses in the same reasonable manner as other terminations.[53] In general, the personnel manager or equivalent should review the facts for objectivity, and to ensure that proper procedures have been followed and consistently applied. In particular, employers should beware of a double standard in which executives or other key personnel are not subjected to anti-drug and alcohol policies, but other employees are subject to discipline.

A checklist of procedures can be reviewed with a legal counsel. An employer should be consistent in procedures and practices. Mistakes and inconsistencies can be minimized by using the checklist. If legal counsel is involved in the investigation, it is possible to protect the confidentiality of the process and documentation by use of the attorney-client privilege.

An employer should always provide an employee under investigation with a full opportunity to be heard on the subject. It is advisable to interview the affected employee to determine the nature and substance of any potential claim by the employee if there is any misunderstanding. This interview should be documented with a file memorandum made immediately afterward. Strong disciplinary actions, including termination, may be required and can be accomplished with minimal legal risk, so long as the action is based on fair and reasonable policies that have been communicated and followed in good faith.

Progressive Discipline

A policy that emphasizes purely disciplinary sanctions as a response to a positive urinalysis may cause both the courts and the arbitrators to favor the employee. The concept of progressive discipline is well-established and a better alternative. A purely disciplinary approach to drug use can damage employee morale, increase the company's training cost for new employees, and increase the adversarial relationship between management and labor. Disciplinary decisions will be reviewed in a variety of forms, depending on the nature of employment (either public or private) and the presence or absence of a union agreement.

"Employment-at-will" theoretically allows an employer to fire an employee whether or not there is a valid reason. In the private sector, an "employment-at-will" situation may exist if there is no union agreement or other specific contractual agreement between management and employees regarding disciplinary procedures. However, many courts now give a discharged employee grounds for suit against an employer if a discharge is in bad faith, abusive, wrongful, or against public policy. Sometimes the employer's personnel manual or policy statement has been seen as constituting an implicit employment contract, or as superceding a signed contract which provided for discipline-at-will. Therefore, even in an employment-at-will situation, an employer should ensure that the company policy and procedure accurately state the consequences of urine testing. These policies and procedures should be followed carefully.

Arbitrator Review

When there is a labor agreement, typically any discharge will be reviewed by an arbitrator. The arbitrator will look at several issues. First, the arbitrator will decide whether the situation alleged by the employer is true. One factor to consider is what kind of drug the result indicated. It makes a difference whether it was for marijuana or cocaine, for example. Was the test accurate enough to prove the use of the drug? Was the chain of custody of the sample clear? Was the test performed properly?

Second, the arbitrator will decide whether the employee violated a company rule or the terms of the labor agreement. In the absence of clear rules, the arbitrator may overturn the discharge on the basis that the employee lacked fair notice of the consequences of his actions.

Third, the arbitrator will decide whether the sanctions imposed are fair and equitable, or too harsh. An arbitrator who feels the sanctions are too harsh is empowered to reverse the sanction in favor of a lesser penalty. Here is where questions concerning off-the-job conduct, the employee's past records, severity of the conduct and other mitigating and condemning information will be considered. The arbitrator may ask if progressive disciplinary actions were applied, and, if not, why not. Labor agreement compensation is generally limited to orders of reinstatement and back pay, whereas in the employment-at-will situation, damages may be awarded for such things as mental anguish.

Handling Refusal To Be Tested

An employer policy may call for termination of employees who refuse to undergo drug testing. In general, company policy should link the severity of the discipline for refusing to take the test to the nature of the job or the needs of the particular workplace. Employers should not require involuntary administration of a drug test.[53] Employees who refuse to take the test may be permitted to resign instead, or be subjected to some predetermined discipline instead of taking the test. Employers might offer the option of undergoing rehabilitation instead of discipline, for example. Another approach might be to bar employees who refuse to take the test from particular job categories, for example, vehicle or equipment operations, until they have taken and passed the test.

Termination

Terminations of union members who refuse to submit to a test are carefully examined by arbitrators to be sure that the employee understood why he or she was required to submit to testing, and whether he or she knew the consequences of a refusal. If there is any doubt about whether the employee knew about policies requiring submission of urine samples, or about negative consequences for refusal arbitrations tend to be resolved in the employee's favor, especially when the employee's job is at stake.

The best way to avoid legal issues associated with refusal to submit to tests is twofold. First, the company needs to publicize to employees the details about when urine samples may be requested and what happens if a request is refused.

Second, when a specimen is requested, it is a good idea to remind employees of the requirements of the policy. If a union is involved, employees should be allowed to consult with union representatives to eliminate any possibility that an employee can claim ignorance or misunderstanding of the policy.

When it is clear that the employee knew that refusal to submit a urine sample was grounds for discipline, the legal question becomes whether the company sanction was appropriate or whether it was too harsh.

Rehabilitation

The final draft of the National Institute on Drug Abuse (NIDA) report on drug testing says, "Employers should consider providing an opportunity for employees who test positive for drug abuse to enter a drug treatment program and be eligible for reinstatement in an appropriate position on successful completion of that program. It may also be appropriate, in certain situations of casual or infrequent abuse, to allow an employee to demonstrate by one or more future negative tests that the drug abuse has been stopped. An employer is justified in terminating the employment of employees whose tests yield results indicating substance abuse after appropriate opportunities for treatment for such abuse have been provided."[118] These recommendations are particularly relevant in a situation where an employer is dealing with a recreational user who smokes marijuana on weekends and who tests positive. Such persons may not need rehabilitation, and the problem may be addressed in other ways than termination or drug treatment.

Use Of Legally Prescribed Drugs On The Job?

Firing or disciplining the employee who uses legally prescribed drugs would be ill-advised, because the employee has done nothing wrong except, perhaps, in not informing the company about the need for a prescribed drug. Discipline would be possible in theory, but *only* if the company policy had specifically referred to legally prescribed drugs and had required disclosure of such use. Even so, the company should not impose any measures beyond progressive discipline. On the other hand, the underlying issue with legally prescribed drugs, just as with illicit ones, is their effect on job performance. If the prescribed drugs are found objectively to be interfering with job performance, then there is a question about whether that person should remain in that job or be moved laterally, or whether some other action should be taken.

Abuse Of Prescription Drugs

Prescription-drug abusers are typically middle-class, or upper-middle-class, law-abiding citizens who obtain drugs from physicians rather than dealers. These abusers are not thought of as criminals or individuals who are dangerous to their communities, and they probably don't think of themselves as drug abusers either. But legal drugs can be dangerous. The National Institute For Drug Abuse has established that abuse of prescription drugs causes 60 percent of hospital emergency-room admissions for drug overdose, and 70 percent of all drug-related deaths.

An employee on prescription drugs presents unique problems in the workplace. The employee may need the drugs for therapeutic reasons. Nevertheless, the employee has no right to report to work in an impaired state, especially if that impairment poses safety risks. In upholding the disciplinary suspension of an employee for being under the influence of prescription drugs and alcohol, arbitrator James C. Reynolds stated:

> *The union questions the fairness of a rule that results in an employee being disciplined for taking medication as prescribed by his physician.*
>
> *The rule clearly makes no exception for that situation. To provide such an exception would not be appropriate, in my opinion. The purpose of the rule is to safeguard the employee and fellow workers from injury which might occur as a consequence of the employee being under the influence.*
>
> *Whether that influence resulted from the employee taking medication as prescribed, or using drugs without benefit of prescription, is not relevant to the fact that the employee was under the influence and therefore a risk in the workplace.*
>
> *An employee who is taking prescribed medication which would diminish his capacity to work safely should take sick leave rather than report to work under the influence.*
>
> James C. Reynolds, Arbitrator[111]

It is advisable to require every employee on prescription drugs to report the use and duration of such prescriptions to the medical or personnel departments, so that decisions can be made about what tasks the employee can perform safely. Moreover, supervisors should *never* confiscate prescription drugs from an employee who has a prescription.

When the employee has no prescription, otherwise legal drugs become contraband and may be treated as illegal drugs. Company drug abuse policies should specifically define illegal drugs as including legal drugs obtained without a prescription.

Chapter 19
Employee Assistance Programs

Employee assistance programs (EAPs) have enjoyed spectacular growth and acceptance in recent years. The reason for growth in such programs, at a time when many employee benefits are being scaled back, is that EAPs are financially beneficial to the employer. If employees are treated and rehabilitated, the cost in dollars as well as human life is usually far less than that of tolerating poor performance, absenteeism, industrial accidents, worker's compensation cases, turnover, retraining, increased medical costs, and other expenses attributed to the impaired employee.

Employee assistance programs offer confidential assistance to workers troubled by either personal problems or substance abuse. They have proven to be cost-effective investments for the companies that implement them.

History Of EAPs

The first EAPs were established by businesses in the 1940s to combat the alcoholism that was affecting performance of white collar workers.[112] These early EAPs were staffed primarily by recovering alcoholics, or other lay people, who could refer troubled employees to community treatment programs, or Alcoholics Anonymous. More than 5,000 U.S. companies now have EAPs. Most of these programs have been established since the early 1970s in response to the rise in employee substance abuse and its impact on job performance and absenteeism. Many EAPs provide counseling services for family problems, marital and sexual difficulties, legal and financial troubles, and social or emotional dysfunction. These programs are referred to as broad brush in scope, because they attempt to deal with a wide variety of problems that can affect worker performance and productivity.

Certain EAPs claim to have strong success rates, and to be cost-effective for companies to maintain. For example, approximately 70 percent of the employees who enter General Motors Corporation's treatment and aftercare program recover sufficiently to resume work satisfactorily. In addition, lost work time for these GM employees has been reduced by 40 percent, sickness and accident benefit payouts by 60 percent, and job accidents and disciplinary actions by 50 percent. GM estimates that for every dollar spent on its EAP and outside treatment, two dollars are returned in regained work productivity, during the three-year period of this study.[112]

IBM's EAP Is A Model Program

IBM tests all job applicants for drugs. If the result is positive, the individual is rejected for employment and must wait six months before he can re-apply. If an employee exhibits a decline in work performance, unexplained prolonged absences, or other erratic behavior, his supervisor may report such observation to the company's medical department. Following a consultation with a company physican, a medical evaluation may be required, including, at the physican's option, a drug test. Employees in "Safety-Sensitive" positions cannot continue to perform their jobs without a drug test, and refusal to take one could result in termination. when there is a positive result, and no medically-acceptable explanation can be found, the company assists the employee in seeking treatment. In order to return to work, the employee must become and remain drug-free, participate in an appropriate rehabilitation or treatment program, and consent to be monitored by the company physician, including periodic, unscheduled urine testing.

National Drug Control Strategy[237]

Creation of an EAP which allows the employee with a drug problem to participate in a treatment program is beneficial to the company because it can retain qualified and productive employees. A drug/alcohol policy that tempers discipline for substance abuse with opportunities for rehabilitation tends to increase arbitrator's support for urine testing programs. In a case involving a bus driver, for example, an arbitrator upheld a company's screening policy, and noted with favor that a first positive urinalysis result would not lead to termination, but to identification of the problem and the need for treatment. However, a rehabilitation first policy, once adopted, must be followed through, lest employees fight disciplinary action by claiming they were denied an opportunity for treatment, or were discriminated against for refusing a treatment offer. In one case, the firing of an alcoholic employee who admitted to alcoholism, but sought treatment only when asked to leave, was overturned as being a violation of the company's policy.

Guidelines For Establishing An EAP

The goals of an employee assistance program are to identify troubled employees, to motivate them to seek and accept help, and to select the most appropriate treatment and cost-effective care.[110] Companies of any size can start an EAP at a minimal investment.

Assign An Employee Assistance Program Coordinator

This can be a full-time or part-time position, depending on the size of the company. Generally, a full-time coordinator is needed only for companies with more than 2,500 employees. The coordinator could be someone who is already working for the company. The coordinator must understand the problems associated with drug or alcohol abuse and emotional or mental problems, and act in an evaluation and referral capacity. The coordinator estimates the nature and the scope of an employee's problem, and may provide limited counseling. The coordinator, especially if selected from current staff, must be someone in whom all employees, from the bottom to the outside sales management, can confide.

Formulate A Policy

Management must define its view of the program and the types of problems it will deal with, and assure confidentiality for all employees. Once an employee assistance program and policy is set up and put into place, employers should follow it. Any deviation, particularly a significant one, may result in liability for breach of contractual obligation. If an EAP of some type is offered, participation by affected employees should not be made mandatory. This policy should be readily available, posted on employee bulletin boards, and printed in the employee manual.[110]

Decide On Implementation Procedures

Managers should never make a diagnosis themselves. They should know their employees, and can identify changes in behavior as they relate to job performance. When they suspect an employee has a problem that is interfering with work, the manager typically meets with the person and

then refers him or her to the EAP coordinator, who evaluates the problem
and decides how to handle it.

Decide On Appropriate Treatment Programs

If an employer has tolerated marginal or unacceptable behavior for
some time without action, it often becomes difficult to deal with, and is more
likely to worsen rather than improve. If the employee's contract or performance does not warrant termination, the employer should thoroughly document the situation, and institute measures for treatment and/or corrective
discipline.

The EAP coordinator should survey local resources to find out what
type and quality of services are available. These may include outpatient
clinics, counseling groups, private practice, medical professionals, and
credit counseling. The coordinator should also examine the company's
medical insurance plan to see what types of treatments are covered by
insurance. The company may want to change its coverage to include these
types of services.

Train Managers And Supervisors

Training generally includes an overview of the kinds of problems
employees suffer from and their causes, the kinds of behavioral signs to look
for and techniques for approaching and referring problem employees.
Employers should also train supervisors to intervene when work performance first becomes noticeably affected, even if the cause is not positively
known to be drug- or alcohol-related. Absence from the workplace,
decreasing work performance, wide mood swings from depression to
short-fused anger, injuries at work, disappearance during work hours, or
severe family problems are often symptoms of substance abuse. Employees
with physical symptoms or behavioral patterns suggesting drug use should
be referred to the employee assistance program. Managers and supervisors
should never attempt to conduct drug counseling themselves.

Promote The Program

Employees and their families must be aware of the program. The
preventative aspects can be stressed. Encourage employees who need help
to get it before it affects their work.

Evaluate The Program

Means for deciding if goals are being met and if the program is cost-
effective should be developed. Work performance should be judged
separately from EAP participation, although such participation can be
considered a positive sign of an employee's willingness to work through
personal problems.

Multidisciplinary Team Approach

Ideally, an EAP involves the family of the troubled employee, both in preventative education and in treatment. A model EAP recognizes that identification, intervention, and treatment require a multidisciplinary team approach, because drug use is a physical, emotional, and cultural disease. A team approach is important in deciding on the type of treatment called for and in helping the troubled employee develop nonchemical coping skills needed for the recovery.

Alcoholism and other drug addictions are relapsing diseases. A model EAP should both anticipate and be prepared to deal with this phenomenon. Supervisors and others involved should understand that a relapse is not invariably treatment failure, but may be another step in the recovery journey. However, the program should not allow an attitude of relapse permissiveness. Relapse requires further structure and self-discipline, as the key to recovery continues to be personal accountability. A model EAP has carefully structured aftercare, based on the belief that alcohol and other drug addiction are treatable diseases with high recovery rates. Most EAPs rely on self-referral.

Arbitrators appear to favor EAPs. In the absense of an EAP, arbitrators tend to order reinstatement in cases where the employee has sought post-discharge treatment, and has testified to an awareness and control over the drug problem. Similarly, arbitrators are less sympathetic to employees who suffer relapses after treatment. It is to the advantage of the astute employer to define the EAP treatment as a "last chance" and to have the employee sign a "last chance agreement." An effective EAP is never a revolving door.

Chapter 20
Drug Abuse Prevention
Without Testing

A sound drug use prevention program for a plant or office has six basic elements, each of which is potentially linked to the other.

Recognition

It is essential not to ignore alcohol or other drug abuse in the workplace. Failure to address the problem is likely to cost an employer thousands of dollars. When left unaddressed, these problems usually do not solve themselves. Rather, they progressively worsen, until they cause absenteeism, tardiness, industrial or home accidents, poor job performance, friction between workers or with supervisors, loss of business, excessive claims for sickness and accident benefits, or a combination of these problems.

Conduct A Survey

It is often helpful to make a detailed survey of the workplace to discover the types of drug related problems that exist. Review of employee records is a good place to start. Absence of reported employee problems could be a danger signal. Failure to document work related problems on employee records increases the difficulties of discovering and correcting these problems. Attorney William Adams suggests a number of direct and indirect indicators of drug use in the workplace on page 85, Chapter 13.

Tour The Workplace And Talk With Employees

Look for employees who appear particularly unhealthy. Look for visible signs of loss of sleep, lack of alertness, bloodshot eyes, inattention to work, failure to meet reasonable schedules, flushed faces, or use of breath fresheners. Be sensitive to the smell of marijuana or alcoholic beverages. If a person is suspected, but there is no proof, do not jump to conclusions. Serious, adverse legal consequences could follow. When there is a record of impairment, safety violations, and broken work rules, the employer might first confront the employee and offer help such as time off, counseling or a drug rehabilitation program. Additionally, the employer can observe the employee's behavior and talk to co-workers.

Prevention

Prevention of drug problems starts with pre-employment screening. This includes various kinds of blood and urinalysis testing, as well as the review of health history, medical records, physical exams, criminal records, reports from previous employers, and family data. Treat alcohol abuse as drug abuse. Alcohol, like any other drug, should be banned from company meetings, including sales meetings.

Policy

Have a sound company policy and work rules. The corporate policy should strictly prohibit the possession of intoxicants or illegal drugs on company premises. The company should have rules that impose stiffer penalties on employees who sell intoxicants or illegal drugs than on those who are merely using them. There should be a specific rule against coming to work under the influence of any drug, including alcohol, and the company should have separate rules regarding work safety and the operation of machines and vehicles.

Special precautions are advisable for isolated work stations and night shifts. For example, employees working on drilling platforms in the ocean should be systematically inspected for readiness to work prior to going onto the worksite, and there should be routine inspection of the worksite itself, sometimes even with use of drug sniffing dogs. Finally, actions should be taken to reduce the entry of drugs into the workplace. This may include policies for outside vendors, delivery trucks, shipping department, and even security guards.

Containment

Companies can contain drug problems by cracking down on drug dealers, investigating the cause of employee accidents, monitoring sickness and accident benefit claims, and uniformly enforcing company policies and work rules. A good containment strategy will not wait for the later stages of drug problems to develop. Positive health promotion, including the opportunity for physical exercise appropriate to overall health, is beneficial. A drug awareness program and efforts to motivate employees toward positive, drug-free goals is useful.

Drug users seldom hide contraband in their lockers or at their work stations, because they do not want to risk being caught in possession of the drug. They hide the drugs somewhere in or on the premises, so that they will have access to them. A good containment strategy minimizes opportunities for unobserved employee drug us and eliminates hiding places, by restricting access and increasing the prospect of the discovery of hiding places.

Assistance

The key to the early identification of problems in the workplace is for supervisors to listen to employees and to understand their requests for help. People who are experiencing a problem, including addiction problems, will drop hints of their concerns and problems. A good listener will offer to assist the employee with personal problems to get appropriate help. Maintaining confidentiality is essential. Make it clear that the employer is not going to use personal information against the employee.

Supervisors should never try to diagnose the employee's problem, or discuss the use of inappropriate chemical substances. A problem of misguidance should be avoided. Covering up the problem with well-intentioned, sympathetic tactics is not helpful. Assistance may require constructive confrontation, because most drug users, including alcoholics, minimize their drug use, delude themselves about the seriousness of their problems, and deny much about their addictions. Employees with physical symptoms or behavioral patterns consistent with drug use should be routinely referred to a physician, psychologist, or an employee assistance program.

Focus on documented instances, witnessed behavior, and impaired work performance. The supervisor, personnel director, and manager — sometimes with the help of the spouse and other peers — can confront the employee, and give him or her a choice between assistance or job action leading to termination. However, any counseling should be left to trained professionals, and it is a good idea if the company refers employees to either a program it has investigated or its own employee assistance program (EAP).

Drug use rarely occurs in isolation. It is usually a response to home pressures and personal problems. Often, drug use on the job can be prevented by EAP programs that offer counseling for non-drug problems such as legal, marital and financial difficulties.

Education

Drug education is both a form of prevention and a means for involving employees in early intervention. Set aside 15 to 20 minutes for a face-to-face presentation to employees. A presentation given by a recovered abuser or an individual with a drug treatment experience is very helpful. Such a person can share relevant personal experiences, and point out that everyone is prone to personal problems that adversely affect work performance. Confidential assistance should be offered in a nonthreatening manner. Encouraging employees to ask questions, and share their personal experiences is important.

Employee assistance programs are enhanced by the use of wall posters, materials, newsletters, employee benefit fairs, informational payroll stuffers, and direct mailings to the home. At least one direct mailing to the home is important, because it can insure that the family has access to information. It can provide information about confidential, low-cost or no-cost intervention, and outpatient care. Intensive training of key employees is also a good idea.

How To Identify Drug Dealers

Cocaine and heroin users frequently become drug dealers to sustain their habit. Marijuana users often sell a joint to a friend. Drug dealers must come into contact with other persons to ply their trade. Hence they seek out exposure to co-workers. Employees who leave their work stations or who seek jobs that bring them into contact with many people are a higher-risk group for drug dealing than other employees. Cocaine, crack, and heroin users are more likely to be selling drugs than other types of drug users. The most common places for drug sales are high-traffic areas, such as cafeterias, restrooms, and toolrooms, which are used by numerous employees. Transactions may be made by mail-delivery personnel, forklift drivers, or others who routinely travel throughout the plant.[114]

Dealers and users can be identified by a variety of techniques, such as confidential employee informant "hot line," undercover investigators, video surveillance (excluding bathroom stalls), and supervisor surveillance of bathrooms, offices, and private areas.

Guidelines for Employees

Chapter 21
Preparing To Be Tested

More than five million workers were tested for drugs in 1987. The American Management Association reported that 20 percent of the companies it surveyed were carrying out some sort of drug testing. Employees of Fortune 500 Companies, the federal government, a state government, or anyone holding a sensitive position, such as a schoolteacher, or people attempting to adopt a child, may face a drug test. [129]

Obviously the primary objective of people in this position is to pass the test. Even those who use no drugs or chemical substances at all can still be confronted with a positive result on the test. It could be that there is melanin, the skin pigmentation, in the urine, for example. Or perhaps the person to be tested took an over-the-counter substance for a cold. Obviously, the major concern of people who do use drugs is going to be how to get through the test without being detected and what to do in the event of a positive result.

Preparing For The Test

Probably the worst thing people who have used chemical substances in the recent past can do is to do nothing and then try to cope with a positive result from a defensive position. Education is an important first step. Anyone facing a drug test should find out about drug testing in general and the company's program and policies in specific beforehand.

Homework is needed to prepare to pass the test. The first step is to find out as much as possible about what tests are going to be given. Depending on which test is used, a different strategy for passing the test is needed. The test most commonly given is a relatively crude screening test, such as the EMIT® or RIA. A crude test is one that detects a substance in the urine in terms of yes/no, e.g., yes, there is a metabolite in the urine, or no, there is not. However, such tests do not identify the substance. This can be particularly problematic to people who have taken over-the-counter drugs, because they could come up with a positive result without having taken any illicit substances.

In some circumstances, such as an accident investigation or a criminal preceeding, more sensitive tests are used. These can detect traces and determine what compounds are in the urine. The gas chromatography/ mass spectrometer (GC/MS) test is the most common. Companies don't usually use these more expensive, more sensitive tests for random testing and general screening.

Where To Get Information

Information can be gotten simply by asking questions. Supervisors and other employees who have already been tested are good sources. Finding out from co-workers the step-by-step procedures they went through is helpful in preparing to be tested. Company announcements are another information source. Personnel officers can explain the procedures and provide additional information. Union stewards are another source employees can consult. Unions usually have guidelines for handling the testing process, and inform their members about what pitfalls to avoid.

Another source of information is the drug test manufacturers themselves. Some of them have 800 phone numbers. Syva Company in Palo Alto, California has both national (800-227-8994) and California (800-982-6006) toll-free numbers. Roche Diagnostic Systems, located in New Jersey, also has a toll-free number (800-526-1247) and a toll line (201-751-6100). These companies will send packets of information and respond to inquiries.

Avoiding Suspicion

A subtle manner prevents needless suspicion. Being "cool" is the best approach. It is only reasonable that when an employee asks a lot of questions, that an employer may wonder why. Astute employees prepare for comments like, "Well, why are you asking all these questions? Do you have something to be worried about?" Preparing in advance to respond to such inquiries helps reduce defensiveness. The best approach is sprinkling questions with statements indicating that the job is important and that the purpose is merely to be informed. For example, an employee might say, "I've read that there are a lot of errors on these tests, and my job is important to me. I want to make sure I understand what's going on so there won't be any screw-ups."

Important Questions

✦ *Who will conduct testing? Is it in-house or conducted by a lab or other vendor?*

✦ *What are the procedures for collecting the samples? Will I be watched? Is a special room used? If so, what is it like?*

✦ *How are the samples stored? How long? Who has access to the samples?*

✦ *What kind of training and certifications do the lab technicians have?*

✦ *How does the lab confirm positive results? Which tests are used to confirm?*

✦ *Does the lab send the sample out to a different lab, or does it do the confirmation?*

✦ *What happens to results? Who gets notified? How long are results kept?*

These kinds of questions become significant if an employee has the misfortune of getting a positive result. Having information in advance can help employees prepare for and avoid false positives. Generally, if the testing is done in-house, it is easier to get information than if it is conducted by an independent lab. In-house testing is usually the simple EMIT® or RIA screens and tends to be more casual, whereas tests overseen by a lab or consulting group tend to be more closely monitored and standardized.

Basic Steps Of Testing

Employees who know the testing procedures in advance can better prepare for the experience because they know what to expect.

Being Observed

Although many testing labs and testers believe that actual observation is the best approach, in actuality urination itself is seldom carefully observed. It is still regarded as excessively intrusive and humiliating to both the collector and the employee to have the urine flow from the meatus into the bottle be watched. Standard practice now includes the presence of an "over-the-shoulder" or outside-the-stall monitor, and a coloring agent used in the toilet, so that the toilet water can't be scooped up.

The Dry Room

Sometimes the collection room is a "dry room." This is a small room where urine test subjects can give their sample with little or no opportunity to get pure water to dilute the sample. First, employees are directed to a changing room, where they remove their clothes and dress in a hospital gown. This is to prevent people from bringing in a balloon full of clean urine hidden in their clothes. Employees are directed to the dry room, usually a bathroom with water taps sealed off, and only enough water in the toilet to handle the spillover from the sample.

Angela Rinaldo followed me into the bathroom and closed the door. Mirrors covered the lengths of one wall, ceiling to floor. On the counter, next to the sink, sat a little white bottle with my name on it.

Rinaldo frisked my arms to make sure I had nothing up my sleeves. She told me to scrub my hands, my lower arms, and beneath my watch. She slipped on a green surgical glove and handed me a white styrofoam cup, the kind you drink coffee in at the office.

I was told to hold the cup with one hand, keeping my other hand visible, resting on my knee. I had to urinate while Rinaldo watched.

"This is just as embarrassing for us as it is for you," she told me. "We're both in this together."

Rinaldo is Vice-President for Operations for Allvest, Inc., a rehabilitative service for adult offenders. Allvest also conducts urine analysis tests for court ordered clients, government agencies, and the public.

Rinaldo wrote something down on a form. Then she told me to pour the urine sample into the little white bottle with my name on it, and seal it with special tape. 'Warning:' it said, 'Sealed evidence. Do not tamper.' Once the bottle was sealed, she scribbled something on the form.

Then she locked the little white bottle up in a refrigerator. Again she wrote on the form.

Rinaldo was meticulous. On the form she documented everything, from the second the sample was taken to the moment it was placed behind lock and key. The whole process took less than five minutes.

That was it. The results would be ready in 24 hours.[52]

Federal Government Guidelines

Guidelines were issued in the spring of 1987 for collecting and testing federal workers. They are as follows:

✦ *The employee must go to a special collection site to give a urine sample in a toilet stall or behind a partition to permit officials to control the conditions of collection in order to prevent cheating or contamination.*

✦ *The worker must take off outer garments and leave them outside the stall, along with purses or briefcases, to prevent the carrying of substitute samples, water, or chemicals into the stall.*

✦ *The worker must wash and dry hands before entering the stall; this is to prevent the carrying of chemicals under the fingernails, of the carrying of moistener or soap into the stalls to put into a sample bottle.*

✦ *After washing hands, the worker must remain in the presence of a collector before entering the stall; this is to prevent access to a water fountain, faucets, soap dispenser, or cleaning agents that could dilute or contaminate the sample.*

✦ *Blue dye must be placed in the toilet bowl before use to prevent a worker from dipping water from the toilet bowl to dilute the sample.*

✦ *The worker giving the sample in the stall is not to be observed directly, but the collector may watch for "any unusual behavior" that could indicate attempts to dilute or contaminate the sample.*

✦ *The worker is to provide slightly more than two ounces of urine to assure an adequate amount for proper testing. The worker may be given drinking water by the collector to aid in achieving the minimum amount.*

✦ *The collector will take the temperature of the sample within four minutes after it is given; this is to prevent dilution of the samples with water or substitution of a "clean" sample. If the temperature is not 90.5 to 99.8 degrees Fahrenheit, a new sample is to be taken, with the collector directly watching the worker giving the sample.*

✦ *The collector must observe the sample until it is sealed and labeled to assure there is no substitution or misplacement, and the worker must sign a certificate that he or she has personally secreted the sample.*

Technician at AN Laboratories, Inc. in Houston, Texas prepares blood samples for drug testing. (Photo by Jim Knowles, copyright © 1986 Picture Group, Inc.)

Chapter 22
Passing The Test

Abstain

The best preparation is abstinence. Cautious employees should simply take no chemicals whatsoever into their systems and should definitely not use any drugs — legal or illegal. Abstinence must include all over-the-counter medications because they can come up as positives. Even though a person doesn't use any illicit drugs or prescription drugs, a false positive is still possible. In most cases, a false positive casts suspicion on the unfortunate employee and results in further testing. This is particularly alarming when a employee's livelihood and reputation are at stake.

Table 22.1
Over-The-Counter Medications To Avoid[186]

Alka-Seltzer Plus®	Nyquil®
Allerest®	Primatene®
Bronkaid®	Sinutab®
Contac®	Sudafed®
Donnagel®	Triaminic®

Detection Periods

The length of time spent in abstinence is important, because each drug has its own life-cycle. Table 21.2 shows the time periods after which drugs commonly tested for become undetectable as found by Anaclinn-Roche Biomedical Labratories. These times seem very short. Abby Hoffman, in his book, *Steal This Urine Test*, reports longer times. PharmChem's detection periods are in Appendix D.

Table 21.2
Times For Drugs To Become Undetectable

Name	Anaclinn-Roche	Hoffman
Amphetamines/stimulants	3-4 days	20-25 days
Antidepressants	3-6 days	—
Alcohol	—	1-2 days
Cocaine	26 hours	2-4 days
Demerol	24 hours	—
Heroin & Morphine	48-72 hours	10-14 days
LSD	—	20-40 days
Marijuana/THC	5-7 days	14-30 days
Methadone	72 hours	—
Methaqualone	—	14-21 days
Phencyclidine (PCP)	5-15 days	10-14 days
Phenobarbital	30 days	10-14 days
Propoxyphene (Darvon)	72 hours	—
Tranquilizers (Valium, Librium)	16-24 days	—

Source: Anaclinn-Roche Biomedical Laboratories data are cited in Miners, Nykodym and Traband[186] and *Steal This Urine Test* by Abby Hoffman [120]

The retention time can vary dramatically from person to person, depending on the person's weight, fat level, and metabolism, and the amount of drugs that they have used. According to Dr. John Morgan, Medical Professor and Director of the Pharmacology Program at the City University of New York, a heavy marijuana smoker who was incarcerated continued to secrete the acid metabolite for more than two months. [129]

The length of the detection period depends on the sensitivity of the test used. The EMIT® has two cutoff sensitivities, high and low. The low cutoff level detects a concentration one fifth of the high level. Knowing more about the sensitivity of the test to be used may help to determine how long to abstain. The rule of thumb is, when in doubt, go without!

Flushing The System

With this strategy, the person facing a test puts as much liquid through the system as possible, in order to get as much of the drug out as possible. Removal of 100 percent of the metabolites in the system by flushing is rarely, if ever, possible. However, flushing can dramatically reduce the concentration of metabolites in the urine.

Street-lore cites many ingestants that people have tried, but these methods have questionable (if any) results. Golden Seal, cranberry juice, vinegar, and aspirin are sometimes mentioned. U-R-KLEAN, a tea claimed to clean urine, is distributed by Houston Enterprises in Tempe, Arizona.[211] These substances have highly questionable results in altering the body chemistry and employees wanting to clean their urine would be wise to test their effectiveness beforehand.

Employees who know they are going to be tested might drink large quantities of water and other nonalcoholic liquids the night before and during the morning before the test. This dilutes their samples and thereby reduces the possibility of a positive result on a broad screening test.

The first urine in the morning after waking from sleep is called the first void and has the highest concentration of metabolites. People being tested would be wise to avoid giving a sample from their first urine of the day. Also, Hoffman even suggests not sleeping the night before testing or, alternatively, getting up earlier than usual in order to take into account the biological cleansing of metabolities into the urine.

Another method of diluting is the use of a diuretic known as Lasix, manufactured by Hoechst-Roussel Company.[123] Its generic name is furosemide. Other diuretics may also function to dilute the urine, because diuretics cause the kidneys to step up the secretion of water. A *High Times Magazine* article suggested taking 80 milligrams of Lasix, and urinating two or three times before giving the sample. Simultaneously, the employee could increase water intake. Furosemide is a prescription drug, but not a controlled one. Family physicians can sometimes be persuaded to give a prescription. Employees who can't get furosemide might try drinking a lot of coffee, because caffeine is a mild diuretic and should cause similar effects.

When a lot of liquid is consumed, urine will be very light with almost no color. Taking lots of Vitamin C for several days before the test can help correct this problem, since Vitamin C imparts a deep yellow color to urine.

Substitute

Employees fearing they may test positive sometimes substitute clean urine for their own. They may have gotten it from a friend whom they know is absolutely clean. It may have come from a vendor of urine.

In the late 1980s, Jeff Nightbyrd, operator of Byrd Laboratories began in business by collecting and selling "clean pee" for about $50 a bag. (Byrd Labs' address is 225 Congress, Box 340, Austin, Tx. 78701, 512-480-0085.) He

Drug Testing At Work

claimed to sell it for "experimental purposes only," and guaranteed that it was 100 percent pure urine. The urine was collected from a local Bible study group, tested, and then packed in plastic bags that included a tube through which it could be poured.

As of this writing, there is no known state law that prohibits the sale of urine. Further, the use and sale of urine do not come under the food and drug laws, which seem to have no jurisdiction over it. It is not clear whether or not people who bring urine and pass it off as their own are violating any laws.

Nightbyrd's first product was urine in its original liquid state, which sold for $49.95 a bag. But there were numerous problems with selling and transporting liquid urine, especially through the mail. Unrefrigerated urine has a short shelf-life of under 18 hours.

An attempt at freeze-drying urine didn't work either. Subsequently, Nightbyrd laboratories offered a powdered urine, having the color and consistency of corn starch, which reconstituted with hot, distilled water. This powder sold for $19.95 for two samples. Nightbird also solicits distributors and sells a pamphlet for $5 titled *Conquering The Urine Tests: A Complete Guide To Success In Urine Testing* which is distributed by Homestead Book Company in Seattle, Washington.

Of course, it isn't necessary to send away for mail-order urine. Some people use a sample from a friend or relative. However, this has been a mistake for employees who failed to confirm the contributor's drug-use history. For example, there was the case of a professional man who smoked marijuana occasionally on the weekends and who was facing a drug test. Quite concerned, he asked one of his children for a urine sample, and felt confident going into the drug test. You can imagine his surprise and humiliation when his test came up positive for cocaine!

How Samples Have Been Substituted

When the sample is given in a situation that is not observed and is relatively lax, such as a family doctor's office, a substitution is a simple procedure. The person just goes into the bathroom and puts the substitute sample into the container. However, most testing is conducted in a testing facility at the place of employment, in a testing lab, or, in the worst case, in a court-monitored situation. In these situations, people who are substituting must be extraordinarily cautious.

Condoms And Bladder Bags

One woman filled a condom with a substitute urine and placed it inside her body. When it came time to deliver the sample, she used her fingernail to break the condom, and the urine flowed into the container as if it were her own.

Other people have used a catheter bag hidden under a shirt, with a tube running down a sleeve to deliver the bogus sample. This is much more dangerous. A body pat-down, or undressing to put on a gown, will reveal the intent to deceive. This would then become presumptive evidence and trigger tighter testing procedures.

What Kinds Of Bags Have Been Used

Pharmacy or hospital supply centers sell Bard Dispoz-a-Bag® Drainage Bag, or the kinds of bags used by ambulant patients. Typically, the bags are inexpensive, at around $4 to $5 and come in different sizes. Some sympathetic pharmacists and clerks in pharmacy supply stores will give advice.

Abby Hoffman describes usings a large leg bag that allows for extra volume and the shape makes it easier to hide around the middle of the body. He says that after the bag is filled with clean urine, the air should be squeezed our completely and the bag sealed, and that a short piece of rubber tubing and valves be added for easy filling.

Hoffman says people can buy incontinence pants at a pharmacy or hospital supply store to help hold the bag in place. The bag is usually flattened on the skin around the abdomen. Once taped in place with surgical tape, the tube from the bag is brought down to the crotch. The on/off tap is placed within easy reach, but hidden from sight. When the person gives the sample, the fluid flows down. People usually practice the actual delivery of the sample with water in the bag.

Employees hoping to substitute a sample usually use a bag rather than attempting to carry the sample in a jar, since it is less likely that employees will be frisked or strip-searched. When employees are closely observed, the risk is higher, but motivated people have learned to hide the tube and use it without being seen.

Another approach that Hoffman describes is the use of a reservoir-tipped, nonlubricating condom. He suggests filling one and then putting a second one over it, to prevent bursting, and taping it as close to the crotch as possible. When it is time to give the sample, he advises his readers to use a presharpened fingernail to puncture the tip.

Time is a problem, because the urine doesn't keep longer than 18 hours. Consequently, the donor's urine must be collected the same day as the test.

People carrying a concealed container with a substitute urine in an observed situation have successfully avoided direct observation by claiming they just can't "go" when being watched. This is a common phenomenon which is referred to in the medical community as "blushing kidneys."

Dangers Of Substitution

Obviously substitution is a high-risk strategy and not recommended. The best approach is abstinence. However, some employees are desperate enough to try substitution. They may attempt to substitute cat, dog, or other nonhuman urine, or to manufacturing a facsimile of urine by using water and artifical coloring. These ploys are watched for and easily detected.

Temperature

Some programs call for testing the temperature of the urine. According to the federal government guidelines, if the temperature is not within 90.5 to 99.8 degrees Fahrenheit, a new sample is to be taken, with the collector directly watching the person giving the sample. If the government guidelines are being followed, the temperature will be tested within four minutes after giving the sample.

To avoid detection, sample that has been refrigerated in order to keep it fresh has to be warmed up before the test. Even if the temperature is not measured, detection is still possible. If the sample seems unusually cold it will probably be tested for temperature. One of the most effective methods used is holding a bag or condom close to the body, where it is kept warm at just the right temperature.

Adulterating The Sample

Another approach that is commonly attempted, and under certain circumstances has proved effective, is adulterating the sample, usually by adding something to it or diluting it.

Probably the most common adulterant used is salt. Not very much salt is needed. The EMIT® test is most easily nullified by this approach. Undetectable amounts of lye, common table salt, or household ammonia will neutralize the enzyme activity, insuring a "no drug content" read out on the sample. However, an absolutely negative result may in itself be suspicious, according to an article in *Journal of Clinical Chemistry*.[56]

The thin-layer chromatographic (TLC) results are not affected by salt. If it is an immunoassay screening test, the salt may neutralize the sample. However, trying salt on a confirmatory, highly sensitive test is unlikely to succeed. The manufacturers of the drug tests warn employers of the use of salt, and many consultants advise that the acid-to-base ratio or the pH factor of each urine sample be tested. If the employee has heavily salted the sample, or added some acid to it, it will probably show up as outside the normal pH range of urine. Employees suspected of tampering with their samples will be subjected to more questions and may have provoked greater suspicion than if they just got a simple positive.

Further, when salt is put into a sample, it is vitally important that no crystals of the salt remain undissolved in the bottom of the container. Employees who carry salt in pockets to the test are risking exposure. There are reported cases where employees who were asked to open their pockets or purses were carrying salt, and were terminated as a result.

Some people have smuggled salt and other substances into the testing bathroom on their hands or under their fingernails. If the test is being conducted under the federal guidelines, employees will be required to wash their hands and scrub their nails in the presence of a monitor. If the federal guidelines are not being followed, then a person might be able to hide salt under the nails. However, making sure the salt is completely dissolved is still a problem.

Other Commonly Used Adulterants

Nightbyrd describes other adulterants, such as two tablespoons of bleach or a capful of ammonia. However, the smell of ammonia is problematic. Alternatively, hydrogen peroxide, which is odorless, causes a chemical reaction and can alter the urine to the point where there will be a negative result.

According to an article from *Clinical Chemistry*, two drops of a liquid soap dropped into a urine sample is enough to make the EMIT® test record negative.[32] Another interesting adulterant is blood. If while giving a sample, the person pricks a finger and drop in three or four drops of blood, the sample will then test negative for cannabis, according to Dr. John P. Morgan, Medical Professor and Director of Pharmacology at City University of New York.[129] The use of blood as an adulterant is some serious drawback, however. Testing blood reveals *current* intoxication; so if the person has smoked marijuana within 6 to 8 hours the test will probably be positive. Whereas, if the marijuana use is not recent, but several days in the past, blood might be an effective adulterant — provided the person is not currently under the influence of any other drug.

Using bleaches that have blue dots in them is not effective: the blue dots make it obvious that the sample has been adulterated.

Table 22.3
Table Of Adulterants[129]

Adulterant	Amount*
Salt	1/2 teaspoon per 10 ml urine
Vinegar	5 drops per 7-10 ml urine
Bleach	1 drop per 5-10 ml urine
Liquid soap	1 drop per 5 mil urine
Liquid detergent	1 drop per 5-10 ml urine
Blood	1 drop per 5-10 ml urine

*Amounts of adulterants used to convert EMIT® positive urines to negative, based on results found by Dr. John Morgan. A typical urine sample is approximately 60 milliliters or 2 ounces. Dr. Morgan did not attempt to test samples of this size and it isn't known whether his findings will hold for full samples.

Diluting The Sample

The basic strategy in diluting the sample is to add water to the sample, so that its potency is reduced. This is much more effective than trying to dilute the sample by drinking a lot of water. Obviously, the amount of water put into the sample can be controlled, provided there is an opportunity to do so.

Finding Water

The diluting strategy is so enticing and so commonly attempted that usually the toilets where samples are given are filled with a blue dye. When the toilet water has not been dyed, the specimen cup can simply be dipped in and filled about half full with toilet water. The strategy is only effective in defeating the test when there is also some urine in the sample because the test can determine that the sample is only water. Water on the outside of the cup is a clue that this strategy is being attempted.

When the toilet contains the blue dye, some people open the back of the toilet to gain access to the clean water in the resevoir. In the back of the reservoir there is usually a plastic spout or tube, which carries the fresh water in from the pipe. Pushing the float down causes the mechanism to turn on the water. This can be quite tricky, however, because opening and closing the lid of the reservoir can make a sound.

Dilution Dangers

There are a couple of dangers in dilution. If the temperature is not high enough or not within the acceptable range, it will be detected. In *Steal This Urine Test*, Abby Hoffman describes rubbing the outside of the specimen cup with the hands to warm it up. However, this trick may not warm it up sufficiently. In regular bathrooms, water from the hot spout can be used, but this may create too high a temperature. Usually, if it feels tepid to the finger, it's near body temperature.

The second concern is the coloring of the sample. Obviously, a lot of water in the sample will make lose its yellow color and give the deception away. Hoffman suggests taking substantial quantities of Vitamin C before the tests — probably the day before and the morning of the test — so that the portion of the sample provided is very deep yellow in color. When it is diluted, the sample will show the typical pale yellow coloring.

Attempting to dilute the sample with saliva doesn't work. It is unlikely that the employee can produce sufficient amounts of saliva to make a difference. But more important, if a substance, whether illicit, prescription or over-the-counter, has been used it will be revealed by drug metabolites in the saliva. The likelihood of getting a positive result may be increased rather than decreased.

It was a small town, and the only clinic testing facilities was staffed by all women. Since all the testees were men, we decided to just have a gar-bage can lined with a plastic garbage bag to handle the urine spillover, so they could do it in private. There wouldn't be any water available for dilution. Well, one fellow who worked there, a marijuana user, was pretty worried; so he waited at the very end of the line, and was the last of about forty men to go in. He saw that the garbage bag was well over half full of

*urine; so he didn't furnish any of his own urine at all, just scooped up a cup
full of the collected spillover in there.*

*Well, of course," chuckles the consultant, "that sample came up
positive for everything: amphetamines, methaqualone, cocaine, opiates,
THC, everything. And when he was asked how that happened, he threw
up his hands and said, 'Hey, I was only smoking* **marijuana**!*[29]*

The Dry Room

Testing programs try to battle the problem of diluting the sample,
besides using the bluing color, with what is called the "dry room." The dry
room is usually a bathroom where the water taps have been sealed off, and
there is only enough water in the toilet to handle the spillover from the cup.
Usually, the resevoir tank is also secured, so there's no access to clean water
from that source.

Using Saline Solution

An approach that has been attempted with some success is the use of
an IV or intravenous saline bag. A 250cc intravenous solution bag can be
taped under the arm. Such a bag can be purchased in most drug stores and
medical supply houses, usually without a prescription. Only normal saline
solution can be safely used because it is undetectable as a contaminant.

Typically the bag is taped under the arm, where it stays warm, and the
tube is taped down the front of the body to the urinary opening. At the time
of the test, a small amount of urine is put into the testing cup, before the cup
is filled by squeezing the saline fluid out of the bag. Usually the observer
is on the other side of a partition, or stands behind the person giving the
sample, and so cannot observe the tube easily.

Chapter 23
Handling The Paperwork

Giving the sample is only part of what is required of the person being tested. Each person tested has to fill out a variety of papers and forms. How these are filled out can become important at a later date, particularly if there is risk of a positive sample. Because of the high error rate, anyone tested risks a positive result. It is advisable that everyone being tested pay close attention to the paperwork.

Consent Form

On the consent form, the person being tested gives permission to have his or her urine tested for drugs. It must be signed either by the person giving the sample or a custodian. Of course, anyone can refuse to take the test, and make a formal objection. However, doing so invites considerable suspicion and puts the person in a defensive position, even though refusal may be well within one's rights. So the consent form places the person being tested in something of a double bind, or damned-if-you-do, damned-if-you-don't proposition. According to an interview with Barbara Perkins, the public relations counselor with 3M Corporation, 3M's urine testing policy is that employees who refuse to be tested can be suspended without pay, and a written report must be issued on the incident.[200] Employees contemplating refusing to give a sample should consult with an attorney before the fact rather than afterward.

The consent form typically has the name of the company and the employer (in cases when these are different), the date, the name of the employee being tested, job title, and employee ID number. Typically, the employee signs a statement that the information given is correct regarding any medications that have been consumed, and that the information is complete and correct to the best of his or her knowledge. It typically says that the employee understands that the urine sample is going to be analyzed to determine the presence of drugs, alcohol, and other substances, and it will usually state that the signer is aware that the results will be given to the employer. The employee can legimately request that the test result be kept confidential from any and all other parties except for the one indicated on the form. It is also understandable that the employee would not want the results to become known at some future date, regardless of the nature of the result.

Disclosure

Along with the consent form, the employee being tested is usually asked to fill out a form disclosing what medications or drugs were taken in the past week. Usually the name of the medication, the reason for having taken it, how much was taken, when it was prescribed, and who prescribed it are requested on the form. Finally, the employee is asked to sign it.

Nightbyrd suggests that people cross out "7 days" and write in "30 days," because many of the common substances actually stay in the body much longer than seven days. He also suggested that employees be prepared to be questioned by the test giver for making this or any other changes on the form. They may be accused of being worried about the test. If this is the case, Nightbyrd suggests that employees have a prepared answer, such as stating that their job with the company is very important, and because they are aware that the error rate for false positives is well over 25%, they are being cautious in writing down anything that they have taken in the last 30 days. Nightbyrd also suggests that people being tested write their own disclaimer in their own language at the bottom of the form, such as, "This list is my best recollection. There may have been other legal medications or substances that I consumed which I don't remember at this time." Such a disclaimer could be helpful to employees who test positive and have to pursue a legal remedy.

Disclose Cross-Reactants

The medical disclaimer form provides an opportunity to list some of the over-the-counter or prescribed remedies that have been legally prescribed and that could test positive. This is a potential loop hole for people who are afraid they will test positive.

Employees may write down over-the-counter or prescription drugs whose cross-reactivity would cause a false positive for the controlled substance that may have been ingested. If a positive is revealed, the employee can point to the disclosure where the over-the-counter or pre-scription substance was indicated. Of course, the employer is likely to request a confirming test which will be more specific about which metabolite was in the urine. Nonetheless, having disclosed the cross-reactant before the first test will provide the employee's attorney with some leverage in the situation, should it escalate into the legal arena.

Table 23.1
Cross-Reactivity Table

Positive for	Cross-Reactivity	Examples
Marijuana	Ibuprofen	Advil, Nuprin
Amphetamines	Phenypropanolamine	Diatec, Dexatrim
		Cotylenol, Triaminic
	Ephedrine	Primatene, Bronkotabs
		Nyquil
Opiates	Dextromethorphan	Vicks Formula 44-M
	Amitripyline	Elavil
	Meperidine	Demarol
	Imprimine	Tofranil
	Perylamine	Mydol, Permensin,
		Primatene-M
Barbiturate	Phenobarbital	Primatene
Methadone	Diphenhydramine	Benadryl

Source: Abbie Hoffman, *Steal This Urine Test* (120)
Brand name medicines are ® registered

Having A Legal Prescription

An alternative strategy is obtaining a legal prescription from a sym-pathetic doctor for the substance the person may have taken or a substance that has a positive cross-reactivity for the one taken, and then that prescrip-tion is discloed on the form. For example, Hoffman suggests that a doctor may prescribe a codine-based cough syrup for an employee with a bad cold. If an opiate has been used, the cough syrup can be ingested before the test, and also disclosed on the form, stating that it was used recently. The doctor can substantiate that the employee has a legal prescription.

Some employees have been able to find sympathetic doctors by asking pharmacists for referrals. Obviously, during such questioning the person looking for a "script doctor" must be very subtle in the inquiry. The person might have asked, "I've just moved here and I wonder if you could help me find a good doctor? My old doctor prescribed me thus-and-such each month for thus-and-such problems. Would you know of a good doctor around here who works with people with problems like mine?"

On the other hand, it may not be a good idea to disclose any kind of sensitive medication, even when there is a legal prescription and a valid reason for taking it. For example, an employee may be taking a mood elevator or other psychiatric drug. The employer may wonder if he or she has psychological problems. Many companies have policies which do not allow any kind of job-impairing drug use, whether prescribed or not. In short, it is probably a good idea for anyone taking any legally prescribed behavior-altering drug, including sleeping pills and drugs for epilepsy, to meet with a doctor, and in some cases with an attorney, before taking the test and before filling out the medication self-disclosure form.

It would probably be foolish to disclose having smoked marijuana even if it was only occasional use in a community where marijuana has been decriminalized. There is considerable social stigma attached to the use of this substance.

Sending Results To A Personal Physician

An employee might ask that the results of the test be sent to a personal physican. This request could be written on the consent form, and becomes part of the conditions for giving the test. It is also permissable to request that information about the testing methods be sent to one's doctor. If the person being tested comes up with a positive result, the doctor may be able to provide information that will explain a false positive result, such as using a particular prescribed medication.

The Split Sample

It is not just people who have used drugs, prescribed or otherwise, who have reason to be concerned. People who are absolutely drug-free can still come up with false positives. Everyone being tested needs to take steps in advance to protect against this possibility. One way to do this is to insist on a split sample. One-half of the sample is sent to the company's testing lab, and the other half is refrigerated or frozen. If the lab results indicate a positive for a drug, and the employee states the drug was not used, the sample can be split again and one-half sent to the company's lab for retesting, and the other half to a knowledgeable lawyer to arrange for an independent testing at a different lab. This provides legal evidence for those who are unfairly accused. This strategy is advised in situations where testing is a result of an "incident," such as an accident or accused drug use.

Chapter 24
Defending Against A
Positive Result

If the testing was for a pre-employment drug screen and the test comes up positive, the chances are that the aspiring employee will never know about it. It is rare that an employer gives reasons for not hiring a candidate. The person usually receives a form letter saying that the company is sorry, but someone else was selected.

However, if a job candidate is told that the test was positive, then it is appropriate to request a second test. Of course, the request may be denied. A number of companies will not administer a retest, but will tell candidates who tested positive to wait six months and then reapply.

When the person receiving the positive result is already on staff and was administered the test because of an accident on the job or part of a random testing program, the first step is to request a confirmatory test. It is important to be sure that the confirmatory test is a more sensitive test based upon a different testing methodology and not simply another screening test. See Chapters 6 and 7 on testing which explains the differences between testing methods.

Get Information

The employee is wise to find out about the testing. It would have been better to have known about the testing methodology in advance and to have been prepared. The employee with a positive result should find out if there was a split sample where part of the urine sample was saved. If there was, the employee should ask if it was frozen. If it was not frozen, the sample will probably have deteriorated by the time of the initial results. If so, requesting a new test is the next step. The company is obligated to give employees who test positive an opportunity to be retested.

Admitting nothing is vitally important. The safest thing for employees in this unfortunate predicament is to deny everything and insist that the positive test result was simply impossible. Information gathering is paramount. The employee should find out everything he or she can about the test used, the procedures, whether forensic standards were followed, which lab was used, what test was used, what is the lab's track record, how long a period elapsed between giving the sample and the analysis of the sample, and what precautions were taken to prevent false positives. The answers to these questions will form the basis of the employee's defense.

Constitution Protections

Government employees have rights under the Fourth and Fifth Amendments. The Fourth Amendment protects against illegal search and seizure, and insures privacy. This means that there must be "probable cause" to test. If a positive result comes up in random testing, a defense may be that there was no cause to give the test in the first place. The Fifth Amendment states that a person cannot be forced to testify against him or herself. Employees in the private sector do not have these Constitutional protections, and their situation may be more precarious. See Chapters 10 and 12 on legal issues for more information on who is protected under the Constitution.

Union members who test positive can seek help from the union. Unions have proven effective and successful in carrying through legal proceedings to defend their members against unfair treatment in drug testing situations.

Challenging The Results

Results can be challenged on the basis of cross-reactivity. The employee can claim that another substance, such as an over-the-counter medication or a legally obtained prescription, was taken. The company will probably insist upon a confirmatory test administered under stringent conditions. Use of prohibited substances will be determined by the results of the second test. Employees who are faced with taking a confirmatory test are wise to cease using any illegal or over-the-counter substances immediately and hope they can get it cleared form their systems before the confirmatory test.

Other challenges include challenging the steps in the procedure, the chain of custody, whether or not there was probable cause to give the test in the first place, the monitoring procedures, and so forth. The assistance of an attorney or union are needed for these challenges.

Confidentiality

Employees should insist upon confidentiality, so that results are not given out to anyone while the employee is attempting to have the matter resolved and, hopefully, expunged from the record. The employee can submit a written notice requesting confidentiality, or request a letter from the union or an attorney. It is smart to send it by certified mail or by some other documented delivery method.

Revealing test results to third parties is a definite infringement of employees' rights in most states. All medical records are protected under legal standards of privacy in most states. In most states employers are required to take the necessary steps to insure confidentiality of employees' records. However, employees with positive results should never assume confidentiality — they should assert this right.

Maintaining A Paper Trail

Employees involved in legal entanglements are wise to keep copies of everything. Memorandum of important conversations with the employer or other company officials should be written and filed. Verbal exchanges and other incidents should be documented in a log or diary with notes on time, place, and names. Employees should ask ask that all requests and determinations be given to them in writing. Under the whistle-blowing laws, it is illegal for an employee to be fired for challenging the test results. Of course, it can still happen. Maintaining a "paper trail" is one of the best ways to reconstruct events

The Vocational Rehabilitation Act

If an employee has the positive result on the company record, there is one last strategy — the employee can claim to have a drug problem.

People already on the payroll are protected from employer discrimination on the basis of disease or handicap. Because substance abuse is defined as a disease by the American Medical Association and the courts, employees need only claim addiction to sidestep punishment.

Once an employee claims to be an addict, then direct disciplinary action is prohibited. Instead, the employee is referred to approved treatment, such as counseling or intensive drug rehabilitation therapy. The company would be enjoined from firing or disciplining the employee with a positive result, and would be required to offer the person the opportunity of rehabilitation. If the employee fails to work conscientiously toward recovery and to cooperate with therapy, then he or she could be disciplined or have employment terminated.

Suing

An employee with a confirmed positive test who does not claim the handicap of addiction may well face termination. When threatened with termination the assistance of the union or an attorney is essential. Trying to stop the termination is easier than attempting to become reinstated.

Experienced attorneys are often reluctant to take cases which involve Fourth and Fifth Amendment challenges, especially when drugs are involved. This can make it difficult to find an attorney to help because people who cite these protections tend to be perceived as an addict or drug abuse sympathizer. Government employees might begin the search for an attorney with the American Civil Liberties Union which claims preservation of Constitutional rights as its mission. The ACLU will probably not be too helpful to private sector employees but may be able to give referrals.

A lawsuit against an employer is usually based on the grounds of wrongful discharge, infliction of mental stress and, perhaps, slander and defamation, if the employer violated the confidentiality of the person's records. Establishing grounds for these challenges are very difficult. Those working in the private sector can't use the constitutional issues because the Constitution only protects people against actions of the State not those of private organizations.

Wrongful discharge cases are ordinarily hard to win. However, according to attorney Patrick Bishop, publisher of *Criminal Law Monthly*, the attorney should be able to convince the judge to have the employer disclose all the documents pertaining to the test results. Usually, the attorney will look for some violation of the forensic standards used in getting the sample, or in the types of tests used, or for some other flaw in the testing procedures. Attorneys Edward Chen of the Northern California American Civil Liberties Union and John True of the San Francisco Employment Law Center have outlined several innovative defenses using common-law theory and other torts in an article entitled, "Recent Developments in Employee Drug Testing."[225]

Whether or not the person should sue for reinstatement or for damages is another consideration. It is usually easier to retain an attorney when monetary damages are demanded rather than only reinstatement and back pay.

Some employees have been successful in legal challenges after years in the process. A San Francisco jury awarded $485,042 to a woman fired from her computer programming job with Southern Pacific Railroad because she refused to submit to urinalysis (*Luck* v. *Southern Pacific Transportation Company*). The New York Supreme Court ruled that mandatory testing of public school teachers is unconstitutional (*Patchogue-Medford Congress of Teachers* v. *The Board of Education*). In San Francisco, a federal court found that train operators could not be tested simply because they had been in an accident. The court ruled that the employer must have a "particularized suspicion" that the employee was under the influence of drugs or alcohol while on the job (*Railroad Executives Association* v. *Burnley*).

In the summer of 1988 a Santa Clara county judge halted mandatory testing of Stanford University athletes in a case in which two Stanford athletes sued the National Collegiate Athletic Association (NCAA) over mandatory testing. Judge Rushing found that the drug testing program invaded the athletes' constitutional rights to privacy, and his ruling prohibited the testing in all of Stanford's 24 sports.

The Stress Of Suing

The repercussions of a lawsuit can go beyond the current employment situation. The stigma attaches itself not only to the employee, but to the spouse and children as well. For example, friends and neighbors may suspect that the person was taking drugs when they hear about the lawsuit.

The process of a lawsuit is expensive and stressful. In court, the employer's attorney will usually try to make the person appear to be a drug addict. Private investigators ("private eyes") are often hired to dig up the employee's personal history. The employee may be confronted with transgressions from college days, for example, where he or she may have experimented with drugs or had friends who were drug users.

Preparing in advance is the best recourse. Employees should do what they reasonably can do to prevent getting a positive result in the first place. The best protection is not using drugs at all, including alcohol, over-the-counter, and prescription drugs in preparation for the test. Employees and athletes who have serious health problems should never stop taking their medication because of a pending drug test, however. In the case of prescription drugs, it is best to consult a physican.

Unemployment Benefits

Collecting unemployment benefits after being fired for refusing to take a drug test or after getting a positive result can be questionable and regulations vary from state to state. The California Unemployment Compensation Appeals Board has ruled that employees in hazardous jobs who are fired for refusing to submit to drug tests based on a reasonable suspicion of drug use are not entitled to benefits. However, in Oregon, an appellate court ruled that an employee who was fired after testing positive for drug use is entitled to unemployment benefits, since the test results alone do not show that the employee was fired for work-related conduct. Employees who contemplate refusing to be tested or who worry they may get a positive result would be wise to make inquiries before testing to the unemployment compensation departments in their respective states.

Appendix A

National Drug Control Strategy

Following is a reprint of sections of the *National Drug Control Strategy* as it pertains to the workplace.

Federal Implementation

Translates the general policy statement (see Chapter 11) into specific steps that the Federal Government will undertake.

Implementation Steps in the Workplace

✧ Ensure a drug-free Federal workforce through implementaiton of Executive Order 12564.

Each Federal agency will expedite the implementation of a drug-free workplan. Those agencies with certified plans will fully implement them, consistent with recent court decisions, by January 5, 1990. This implementation is to include Employee Assistance Programs or other appropriate mechanism, training for supervisors, rehabilitation for drug users, and drug testing. Agencies without currently certified plans will complete certification by January 5, 1990, and fully implement the plans by April 5, 1990.

In carrying out their responsiblities under Section 3 of Executive Order 12564, agency heads should review their testing designated positions periodically as significant new decisions on drug testing are issued by the courts.

❖ Promote drug-free workplace policies in the private sector and the State and local government that include clear penalties for use and drug testing where appropriate.

The Administration will issue final regulations for the Drug-Free Workplace Act that will require Federal contractors and grantees to:

a) adopt formal policies banning illegal drug activities in their workplaces;

b) individually notify employees working on covered Federal contracts or grants that they must abide by this policy;

c) establish an ongoing drug-free awareness program emphasizing education about drug use and providing information about counseling and rehabilitation; and

d) report convictions of employees resulting from drug offenses occurring in the workplace and appropriately penalize such employees.

ONDCP (Office of National Drug Control Policy) will convene an interagency working group to draft model legislation for drug-free workplaces in State and local governments and for their contractors and grantees. This model will reflect the key components of the Drug-Free Workplace Act of 1988 and the President's Executive Order for a Drug-Free Federal Workplace.

Further, Federal agencies which conduct workplace inspections including those in the Department of Labor and Transportation, will investigate whether the use of illegal drugs was involved in accidents in the workplace.

Recommended State Legislation

States and localities are already doing many good things in the fight against drugs. They provide the lion's share of resources and many of the best ideas.

The Anti-Drug Abuse Act of 1988 contained numerous Federal provisions that might profitably be adapted to State and local purposes. Several such provisions — and other recommended State legislation pertaining to the workplace — are briefly discussed below.

Drug-Free Workplace statutes

All State and municipal employers, including agencies, contractors, and grantees, should be required to take personnel action against employees found to be using drugs, or to be under the influence of drugs at work. Such action could include suspension, termination, or enrollment in a drug treatment program.

States are encouraged to examine the model Uniform Controlled Substance Act (UCSA) closely and to determine what changes to their existing laws might be apporpriate.

States should review their labor laws to ensure that private employers are not legally precluded from implementing drug-testing programs (including pre-employment screening).

State boards and agencies responsible for professional licensing should adopt policies whereby individuals would immediately lose their licenses if convicted for sale or distribution of illegal drugs. These policies should also call for the loss of licenses by individuals who use drugs, with reinstatement only after treatment and monitoring.

States should enact a range of penalties for persons caught using or possessing even small amounts of drugs, among them suspension of drivers' licenses for 1 - 5 years.

Reprinted from *National Drug Control Strategy*, The White House, September, 1989, For sale by the Superintendent of Documents, Government Printing Office, Washington DC. 20402 (call for pricing) and from Ronin Publishing, P.O. Box 1035, Berkeley, Ca 94701, $19.95 + $4.00 shipping & handling (California residents add 7.25% sales tax).

Appendix B

Sample Alcohol And Drug Abuse Policy

I. Statement Of Purpose

XYZ Company is committed to maintaining the safety and health of its workers, and will not tolerate any drug or alcohol use which endangers the health and well-being of its employees or threatens its business. To this end, company employees and supervisors will be educated on:

1. The Company's Drug and Alcohol Abuse Policy;
2. The danger of abusing drugs and alcohol in the workplace;
3. The medical treatment available for persons who seek treatment and counseling; and
4. The action that the company will take when employees violate the Alcohol and Drug Abuse Policy.

It is this company's belief that the use of illegal drugs and the abuse of other controlled substances, on or off the job, is not consistent with the law of the land. When employees use illegal drugs or abuse other controlled substances or alcohol, on or off duty, they threaten the company's business by tending to be less reliable, less productive, more accident prone, and less likely to report to work regularly in a mental and physical condition fit for work. This results in increased costs to the company, and jeopardizes the reputation of the company and the quality of its products, as well as the well-being of involved employees, their families and their co-workers.

Employees have the basic right to work in an environment that is free of drugs and alcohol, and to be able to rely on the fact that co-workers are not impaired by substance abuse. In the interest of maintaining a safe and healthy workplace that is free of alcohol and drug abuse, this company is committed to strictly enforce its drug and alcohol policy and to comply with the requirements of the Drug-Free Workplace Act of 1988 and the special Drug-Free Work Force Rules of the United States Department of Defense.

II. Procedures To Be Initiated By The Supervisor For Impaired Employees

Because this company recognizes the tragic effects that substance abuse can have on the productive work life of the employee, his co-workers and his personal life, it is committed to early identification and referral for professional medical treatment of substance abusers. However, its commitment to personal assistance does not waive any disciplinary procedures invoked by the behavior of an employee, particularly when the employee does not first come forward voluntarily to management with his/her substance abuse problem.

Supervisors will be trained to:

1. Detect and document any job performance or work behaviors that indicate personal problems;

2. Identify on-the-job use or impairment of drugs or alcohol;

3. Initiate the process of mandatory referral for impaired employees for medical assessment;

4. Require testing for employees who are suspected of drug or alcohol impairment on the job;

5. Utilize confrontation techniques to establish a violation of company policy;

6. Understand the drug testing procedures and technology;

7. Know when random testing is appropriate,

8. Be responsible for detecting substance abuse problems in their work area;

9. Encourage voluntary referrals to the company's Employee Assistance Program;

10. Know the procedure for conducting workplace inspections, and will be informed about the employee's right to privacy.

III. Authorized Use Of Prescribed Medicine

When employees are taking a medically prescribed drug that can alter behavior, physical ability or mental function, they must report the use of this drug to the personnel department, which will determine whether temporary job reassignment/medical leave is warranted until the treatment is finished. Employees must keep all prescribed medications in the original container, which identifies the drug, dosage, date of prescription and prescribing physican.

IV. Arrest Or Conviction Under Criminal Drug Statute

Employees must notify, in writing, the director of personnel within five days of any arrest or conviction of a criminal drug statute. This requirement is is set forth to comply with the federal contractor Drug-Free Workplace Act.

V. Policy Violations

XYZ Company specifically prohibits the following and will routinely discipline an employee up to and including discharge for any of the following:

1. Use, possession, manufacture, distribution, dispensation or sale of:
   a) Illegal drugs or drug paraphernalia;
   b) Unauthorized controlled substances; or
   c) Alcohol on company premises or company business, in company supplied vehicles, or during working hours.

2. Storing in a locker, desk, automobile or other repository on company permises any illegal drug, drug paraphernalia, any controlled substance whose use is unauthorized, or any alcohol.

3. Being under the influence of an unauthorized controlled substance, illegal drug or alcohol on company premises or company business, in company supplied vehicles, or during working hours. The term "being under the influence" of alcohol is defined as blood alcohol level of 0.04. The definition of "being under the influence" of unauthorized controlled substances or illegal drugs is testing positive at a specified mg/dl level.

4. Use of alcohol off company property that adversely affects the employee's work performance, his or others' safety at work, or the company's reputation in the community.

5. Possession, use, manufacture, distribution, dispensation or sale of illegal drugs off company property that adversely affects the employee's work performance, his/her own or others' safety at work or the company's reputation in the community.

6. Switching or altering any urine sample submitted for drug or alcohol testing.

7. Refusing to consent to testing or to submit a breath, saliva, urine or blood sample for testing when requested by management.

8. Refusing to submit to an inspection that is requested by management.

9. Conviction under any criminal drug statute.

10. Arrest under any criminal drug statute under circumstances which adversely affect the company's reputation in the community.

11. Failure to notify the company of any arrest or conviction under any criminal drug statute within five days of the arrest or conviction.

12. Failure to report to the personnel department the use of a prescribed medication which may alter behavior, physical ability or mental functions of the employee.

13. Failure to keep prescribed medications in its original container with a label that states the name of the drug, the frequency of dosage, the date prescribed and the name of the prescribing physician.

14. Refusing to sign a statement to comply with the company's drug and alcohol abuse policy.

15. Refusing to complete a medical questionnaire and consent form prior to testing.

16. Refusal to complete the toxicology chain of custody form after submission of a urine or blood specimen.

VI. Other Testing

If XYZ Company suspects that an employee's on-the-job performance may have been adversely affected in any way by drugs or alcohol, or that an employee has otherwise violated this policy, it may require the employee to submit to a breath, saliva, urine and/or blood sample for alcohol of drug testing. The employee will be in violation of this policy, if he/she tests positive for alcohol or drugs during this testing.

Whenever this company requires a standard physical examination, that examination will include a breath, saliva, urine and/or blood test for alcohol and drugs. A positive test for alcohol or drugs during this testing will be a violation of this policy.

Employees who transport company products and materials on interstate highways will be subjects to the random testing requirements established by the Federal Department of Transportation. (Note: We do not recommend random testing for employees other than that required by state and federal regulations.) An employee who tests positive for alcohol or drugs will be in violation of this policy.

Whenever an employee is involved in an accident involving fatality, serious bodily injury, or substantial property damage, the company may require the employee to submit a breath, saliva, urine and/or blood specimen for alcohol or drug testing. The employee will be in violation of this policy if tests for drugs or alcohol are positive.

Prior to testing of applicants and employees, the company will allow the person to list all prescriptions and non-prescription drugs taken within thirty days, and to provide an explanation for the use of these drugs.

Before testing, all applicants and employees must sign an approved form consenting to the testing and the release of test results to the company's personnel department.

If an employee tests positive for alcohol or drugs, he/she will be given the opportunity to explain the test results before any action is taken.

VII. Inspections

Whenever the company suspects that an employee's work performance or on-the-job behavior may have been affected in any way by alcohol or drugs, or if the company suspects that the employee has sold, purchased, used or possessed alcohol, drugs or drug paraphernalia on company property, the company may inspect the employee, the employee's locker, desk or other company property under the control of the employee, as well as the employee's personal effects or automobile on the company property.

The company will post the following "Right To Inspect" notice at or near each entrance to company property:

Right To Inspect

XYZ Company reserves the right to inspect the property and person of any individual or vehicle on company property. This right includes, but is not limited to, the inspection of the employee's vehicle, parcels, packages, purses, lunch boxes, briefcases, lockers, workstations and desks.

VIII. Condition Of Employment

Compliance with XYZ's Company substance abuse policy is a condition of employment. The failure or refusal of an employee to cooperate fully, sign any required document or submit to any inspection or test will be grounds for termination.

IX. Reservation Of Rights

XYZ Company reserves the right to interpret, change, rescind or depart from this policy in whole or in part without notice. Nothing in this policy alters an employee's status. The company hopes each employment relationship will be happy, productive and enduring. Nevertheless, employees remain free to resign their employment at any time for any reason or no reason without notice. Similarly, XYZ Company retains the right to terminate any employee at any time, for any or no reason, without notice.

X. Applicant Testing

Applicants will be required to complete the Applicant's Certification and Agreement form as a part of the routine application process. (A sample is available from *Employment Law Update*, Box 15250, Evansville, In. 47716, 812-476-4520) They will then be tested for drugs and alcohol as a part of the application process.

Note: An employer does not have any legal obligation to tell the applicant the reason for rejection of employment. If an applicant is rejected for failing a drug test, it may be advisable not to give this reason for not hiring the applicant. The employer can simply state to the applicant that not being hired was the result of failing the total interview process covering hiring requirements. This should also aid in avoiding lawsuits for defamation, based on a claim that the employer labeled the applicant as a "drug user."

XI. Employee Drug Testing

1. The employee will be asked to list all drugs consumed during the past thirty days, and will have the opportunity to explain the use of each one.

2. The employee will complete a consent or alcohol and testing form. The refusal to do so will be considered a violation of company policy, and the employee will be terminated.

3. Test results will be returned to the personnel director for review with the employee, and a copy of the test results will be placed in the employee's personnel file. All positive results will be given a second verification test.

4. If an employee tests positive after the second verification test, he/she will be disciplined up to and including discharge for violation of company policy. The termination of an employee or use of an employee assistance program will be the decision of management, depending on the circumstances in the judgement of management. All disciplinary action will be controlled by management.

Authors note: We are grateful to Rutkowski and Associates, publishers of *Employment Law Update*, for granting permission to reprint the **Alcohol and Drug Abuse Policy**. The terms in the policy were developed by Rutkowski and Associates and do not reflect the opinions or advice of the authors or publisher. The authors, the publisher and Rutkowski and Associates do not intend to render legal advice in providing this example company policy. It is presented here as an example only. Each company's situation, work force and needs are different and the company policy should be carefully tailored to fit the company's unique situation and state laws, especially as they pertain to privacy rights. The reader should employ legal counsel to determine the applicability of the material reprinted from *Employment Law Update* to their particular circumstances.

Procedure To Be Followed For Employee Who Is Under The Influence

Procedure to be followed in situations (particularly employers that have unions) where there is an employee who appears to be under the influence of alcohol, drugs or controlled substances or both. In an effort to establish if a violation of Company rules and regulations occurred, all inquiries should be made according to the following procedure.

1. Determine if an employee "appears" to be under the influence of an alcohol beverage, drugs, including controlled substances and prescriptions, or both.

2. If available, get another supervisor or management representative to personally escort the employee to the supervior's office.

3. Bring in a union representative (or any other representative the employee chooses) to be present during the investigation (*in this situation*).

4. Ask the questions indicated in "Questions for Suspected Alcoholic or Substance Users."

5. During the investigation, with the employee and union representative still present, complete the "Observation Checklist."

6. If the employee has previously agreed, have the employee take the "Basic On-Site Coordination Examination."

7. Complete the "Opinion Based on Observations Checklist."

8. If you conclude that the employee does not appear to be under the influence of alcohol or drugs, including controlled substances and prescription drugs, and he is able to perform his work duties, then have the employee return to his work station.

9. If you conclude that the employee *is* under the influence of alcohol, drugs or both, then suspend the employee pending final determination, in the presence of his union representative, and advise him of the Company rules(s) that he violated.

10. Make the necessary arrangements to have the employee taken home. Do not permit him to go home or drive by himself. If the employee refuses any assistance, such as by his union representative, then make sure the union representative and your company representative *can* verify that the *employee refused such assistance.* However, if an employee cannot control his actions, then under *no* circumstances should he be allowed to leave without assistance. You must call the local police chief or sheriff to warn them of the grievant's condition and refusal of assistance before the employee is allowed to leave the plant. Tell the law enforcement officials the employee's name and make of car.

Note: The reason for calling the local law enforcement authorities and providing assistance before the employee leaves the plant, is based on the Texas case of *Otis Engineering Corp.* v. *Clark,* 668 S.W. 2d 307 (Tex. 1983). In this case, an employee who was clearly under the influence while at the plant was ordered to punch out by his immediate supervisor. While attempting to drive home, the drunk employee killed two individuals in a traffic accident. The Texas Supreme Court found that the decedents' family could bring a wrongful death action against the employer holding:

> *"When, because of an employee's incapacity, an employer exercises control over the employee, the employer has a duty to take such action as a reasonably prudent employer under the same or similar circumstances would take to prevent the employee from causing an unreasonable risk of harm to others. Such a duty may be analogized to cases in which a defendant can exercise some measure of control over a dangerous person when there is a recognizable great danger of harm to third persons. Thus, you do all that you can to prevent an obviously intoxicated employee from driving home alone."*

11. Whenever possible, have a *management representative present throughout* the *entire proceedings* with appropriate *notes* being *taken* for future reference and supporting documentation.

Note: Review the procedure and questions with all your supervisors and other appropriate personnel.

Questions For
Suspected Substance Abusers

1. Are you feeling ill?_____ If yes, what are your symptoms?_____.

2. Are you under doctor's care? _____ If yes, what are you being treated for? _____ What is your doctor's name and address? _____ When did you last visit your doctor?_____.

3. Are you taking any medication?_____ What medication?_____ Who prescribed it? _____ When did you take your last dosage? _____ Do you have your prescription in your possession? _____ Do you have any additional medication in your possession? _____.

4. Do you have any pre-existing medical problems? _____ Diabetes? _____ Are you taking insulin? _____ Do you have low blood sugar? _____ Epileptic? _____.

5. Do you have a cold? ____ If yes, are you taking any cold pills? _____ Cough medicine? _____ Antihistamines? _____.

6. Are you using any type of drug? _____ If yes, what? _____ When? _____ Where? _____ With whom? _____ How much? _____.

7. Would you submit to a physical examination to include a blood, urine, saliva and/or breath test(s) by a medical doctor or hospital so we can be sure that you are in good health and able to safely perform your job? _____ If no, reasons for refusal _____.

   a) Check with hospital for satisfactory arrangements.

   b) *Get signed release statement* by employee to have the hospital/physician release information to company (See " Statement: Voluntary Submission for Physical Examination of Drug/Alcohol Testing and the Release of Findings and Information" form). If the employee refuses to sign the Statement for voluntary testing, the employee should be told that he/she is refusing a direct order which constitutes insubordination and that such refusal will be treated as a presumption that the employee is intoxicated or impaired by drugs to the extent of his/her not being able to do his/her job.

8. Would you submit to basic coordination tests? _____.

9. Did you drink alcohol or an alcoholic beverage today? _____
   What did you drink? _____ How much? _____ When did
   you start? _____ When did you stop? _____ Where did
   you drink? _____ With whom did you drink? _____.

Basic On-Site
Coordination Examination

1. Balance:
__ Fair __ Falling __ Swaying __ Staggering
__ Sagging knees (eyes closed, one foot and head
                    back, etc.)

2. Walking and Turning:
__ Fair __ Swaying __ Stumbling
__ Arms extended for balance __ Falling
__ Sure footed __ Reaching for support.

3. Finger to Nose:
Right. __ Sure __ Uncertain
Left. __ Sure __ Uncertain

4. Speech:
__ Fair __ Slurred __ Incoherent
__ Confused __ Silent __ Whispering.

5. Awareness:
__ Fail __ Confused __ Bewildered
__ Sleepy __ Alert.

Observation Checklist

Directions: Check pertinent items

1. **Walking :**   __ Stumbling __ Staggering __ Falling
   __ Unable to __ Swaying __ Holding on

2. **Standing :**   __ Swaying __ Rigid __ Unable to stand
   __ Feet wide apart __ Staggering
   __ Sagging at knees

3. **Speech:**   __ Shouting __ Silent __ Whispering
   __ Slow __ Rambling __ Mute __ Slurred
   __ Slobbering __ Incoherent

4. **Demeanor:**   __ Cooperative __ Polite __ Calm
   __ Sleepy __ Crying __ Silent __ Talkative
   __ Excited __ Sarcastic __ Fighting.

5. **Actions:**   __ Resisting communications __ Fighting
   __ Threatening __ Calm __ Drowsy
   __ Profanity __ Hyperactive __ Hostile
   __ Erratic.

6. **Eyes:**   __ Bloodshot __ Watery __ Dilated
   __ Glassy __ Droopy __ Closed.

7. **Face:**   __ Flushed __ Pale __ Sweaty.

8. **Appearance &**
   Clothing: __ Unruly __ Messy __ Dirty
   __ Partially dressed __ Neat __ Having odor
   __ Stains on clothing __ Bodily excrement stains

9. **Breath:**   __ Alcoholic Odor __ Faint alcoholic odor
   __ No alcoholic odor.

10. **Movements:**   __ Fumbling __ Jerky __ Slow
    __ Normal __ Nervous __ Hyperactive.

11. **Eating**   __ Gum __ Candy __ Mints
    __ Other, specify _____.

12. **Other observations:** _____

_____.

Opinion Based On Observations

A. Under influence of alcohol _____

B. Under influence of drugs _____

C. When not sure, which one of either alcohol or drugs or both _____

D. Unfit to operate machinery or to perform safely in workplace _____

E. Unfit for work for other reason (List) _____

F. Recommended for physical examination _____

G. Does not appear to be under influence of alcohol _____

H. Does not appear to be under the influence of drugs _____

Remarks: _____

Signed _____ Date _____

Witnessed by : _____ Date _____

STATEMENT

Voluntary Submission for Physical Examination
of Drug/Alcohol Testing
and the Release of Findings and Information

      I, _____, voluntarily agree to take a physical examination which may include blood, breath, saliva and/or urine analysis by a physican, medical center, hospital, or medically qualified personnel. Furthermore, I authorize the release of these tests and examination results to _____ Company or any of its represenatitives. By this authorization, I do hereby release any physician, medical personnel, hospital, medical center, clinic, etc., _____ Company, or any of its representatives from any and all liabilities arising from the release or use of the information derived from or contained in my physical examination and test results.

_____   _____
Witness   Employee

_____   _____
Witness   Date

Inspection and Waiver Agreement

To be signed by job applicant in consideration of being employed

I hereby acknowledge assignment from _____ Company of locker number _____, receipt of one lock serial number _____, and _____ keys which have been provided to me for use only on the assigned locker. The locker, lock and keys have been provided to me without charge. I understand that no keys have been retained by the Company and that it will be my responsibility to return the keys, lock and locker in normal working condition, or to replace them of equal value, upon termination of my employment. If I fail to do so, I hereby authorize _____ Company to deduct the replacement cost form my last pay check.

In consideration of being hired, I have the Company's permission to use a Company locker and to receive a lock for use thereon. I agree that I will not use the locker for any purpose that would constitute a violation of any Company rule. I further agree to permit the Company in the exercise of its discretion to search my vehicle, lunch box, purse, parcels, packages, briefcase, desk or work station or to open the locker and search the contents thereof.

_____   _____
Employee   Company Representative

_____
Date

Conditional Reinstatement Agreement
Employee Assistance Program

The conditional reinstatement agreement was designed to provide a worthy employee the opportunity to go through rehabilitation without undue costs of repeated inpatient rehabilitation stays to the company, since the acute treatment of alcohol or drug withdrawal can cost from $10,000 to 20,000 depending on what is needed and the region of the country. Most employees eligible for this program would be those who sought voluntary help. Thus, there may be some instances where an impaired employee is removed from the job and then offered this program in lieu of being terminated. Circumstances for such company leniency would include willingness of the employee to seek help, evidence that this employee has been a good worker and could be valuable again if the substance abuse problem was corrected, and lack of evidence of any harm or damage to other persons or property during the incident where the employee was identified as having a problem.

Conditional Reinstatement Agreement

The undersigned parties hereby agree as follows:

1. That (*employee's name*) recognizes that the Company was lenient in working with him/her due to (*employee's name*) unexcused absense(s) because of alcohol/drug abuse and letting him/her go through its employee assistance/rehabilitation program to help (*employee's name*) deal with his/her drug/alcohol addiction problem.

2. That the Company will conditionally reinstate (*employee's name*) after he/she successfully completes his/her rehabilitation stay at (*hospital name*). (*Employee's name*) will be conditionally reinstated provided he/she agrees to and performs the following:

Here insert conditions applying to drug rehabilitation treatment

Examples of Alcohol Rehabilitation Program:
   a) Daily use of antabuse 250 mg. h. s.
   b) A minimum of two (2) AA Meetings per week.
   c) Requirements of state board for licensed personnel

3. If within the next three (3) years, (*employee's name*) is unable to perform his job duties at (*employer's name*) due to alcohol/drug abuse or fails to continue this alcohol/drug rehabilitation program and the conditions set forth above as outlined in Item 2 and as required by (*employer's name*), alcohol/drug counselor or physician, he or she will be terminated.

4. (*Employee's name*) understands and agrees that if he has to be admitted to a hospital or rehabilitation center again within the next three (3) years he/she will be terminated.

5. *Statement of Agreement.* This agreement is not an employment contract. The company is not guaranteeing employment to an employee for any term of employment, and may terminate the employee at any time without notice. Likewise, the employee may terminate his/her employment with the company at any time without explanation. Where there is a job available and the employee complies with the terms of the employee assistance program, the employee will be conditionally reinstated for an indefinite term, as long as that reinstatement is consistent with the business needs of the company.

_____ _____ _____
Union Representative   Employee   Company Representative
(if applicable)

                                                    Date: _____

Appendix B, **Sample Alcohol and Drug Policy** is reprinted, with permission, from *Employment Law Update* Copyright © 1989, Rutkowski and Associates, Inc. *Employment Law Update* is a monthly newsletter available (at $85/year, $145/two years) from *Employment Law Update*, Box 15250, Evansville, IN. 47716-0250, 812-476-4520.

Arthur D. Rutkowski, J.D., Legal Editor of *Employment Law Update* is a partner in the law firm of Bowers, Harrison, Kent and Miller. He has represented management in labor and employment law for over 20 years and has successfully directed hundreds of union organizing and decertification campaigns and collective bargaining negotiations for management in the USA and Canada. He is a member of the American Bar Association Labor Law Committee on Labor Arbitration and Collective Bargaining.

Barbara Lang Rutkowski, Ed.D., Managing Editor of *Employment Law Update*, specializes in management consulting, management seminar development and labor relations/employment law. Dr. Rutkowski has been on the faculty of the University of Florida and a manager at the University of Florida and Miami Children's Hospital.

Appendix C

Sample Policy
For State Employers

Pre-employment Screening

Introduction

The Personnel Board has both constitutional and statutory authority for administering the State's Civil Service Merit Selection System. This includes determining what tests of fitness are appropriate to evaluate applicants for State positions. Since drug-induced behavior has the potential to seriously impact job performance, drug screening may be appropriate for applicants for some classifications. The Personnel Board is the agency responsible for regulating such drug testing.

In 1986, the Governor issued an Executive Order directing the Personnel Board to cooperate with the Department of Personnel Administration to develop policies and procedures to help bring about a drug-free State workplace. To achieve this end, the Board held five public hearings before adopting regulations and developing rules governing drug screening.

In developing the regulations, the Board attempted to craft them in a way that would address the major concerns about drug testing, such as credibility of test results, the confidentiality of test result and applicants rights and due process.

The salient features of the regulations are summaried here to illustrate the balance between employer needs and applicant rights.

The regulations do not mandate drug screening of applicants for any classification in State service. Rather, they set forward a framework within which a department may come forward and request to institute an applicant screening program, and they regulate such testing.

The rules only regulate drug screening of applicants at initial entry into a sensitive position and do not apply to applicants for promotion who are already in a sensitive position and they do not apply to testing of current employees for assessing their ability to carry out their jobs safely. These are the purview of the Department of Personnel Administration.

Drug screening of applicants would only be permissible under regulations for jobs where there is a high risk to health and safety as a result of drug-induced behavior. Legal advice indicated that the Board must carefully lay a record that shows that it is not arbitrarily and capriciously identifying a position as sensitive and therefore, as one for which drug testing is job-related. Having departments come in and lay out evidence that proves the position is sensitive is a pro-active measure to minimize exposure to being sued.

Whether a job is sensitive would be determined in a hearing before the Board, a public hearing, at which a department would need to present documentation as to:

(1) The nature of the duties,
(2) The risks to health and safety, and
(3) The sensitivity to drug-induced behavior.

Other parties who are interested should have an opportunity to input, and if the Board concurs that drug testing is in fact job related, then drug screening of applicants would become a requirement in future examinations for that classification. In short, drug screening of applicants for State positions is not universal, but is selective.

The regulations provide for full disclosure to applicants, both before hand, when they're told when a drug screening test will be required, and afterward, when they're entitled to know the results of their individual drug test.

The regulations also set forth standards for the testing laboratories. Only laboratories that are certified by the National Institutie on Drug Abuse, or accredited by the College of American Pathologists and who participate in a quality assurance program may participate in drug testing for the State.

In order to fail the drug test, a sample must fail two separate tests utilizing different methodology. The first, or screening test, must use a form of immunoassay tests, the second or confirmatory test uses gas chromatography/mass spectrometry. Forensic experts in the field have testified before the Board that this represents the "gold standard" in terms of drug testing, drug screening, and is the most defensible way to proceed.

Regulations also require that a department follow strict chain of custody procedures so that samples are not misidentified. Applicants are also required to disclose medications that they have taken during the two weeks prior to the test. This is a protection for applicants against inappropriate disqualification based on a positive drug test that might result from ingesting a legally obtained and legally used substance.

Applicant appeal rights are specified, as is the right of the applicant to have his or her sample retested if they choose to do so at their own cost.

Confidentiality of test results is assured by limiting access severely to test results and ensuring that the test results are used only for the purpose of administering these rules; that is, to determine an individual's eligibility to take State exams where drug testing is required.

Finally, the regulations specify the consequences of failing a drug test. An individual is obviously disqualified for the examination that they're taking. In addition, they're prohibited for a period of one year from competing in any other State examination for which drug testing is required.

In addition, if they test positive for a hard drug — a drug the possession of which would constitute a felony offense — they are prohibited for a period of ten years from competing in any State peace officer examination.

Failing a drug test would not impact an individual's ability to take any other examination for which drug testing has not been deemed job-related.

> Extrapolated from testimoney of Duane Morford
> Chief, Policy Division, Personnel Board, State of California
> Senate Select Committee on Substance Abuse
> Senator John Seymour, Chairman
> October 25, 1988 (238)

213. Pre-employment Testing for Drug Usage.

An appointing power may conduct drug testing of applicants for a class only when:

(a) The appointing power has documented the sensitivity of the class and the consequences of drug-related behavior by showing that:

(1) The duties involve a greater than normal level of trust for, responsibility for or impact on the health and safety of others, and

(2) Errors in judgment, inattentiveness or diminished coordination, dexterity or composure while performing their duties could clearly result in mistakes that would endanger the health and safety of others; and

(3) Employees in these positions work with such independence, or, perform such tasks that it cannot be safely assumed that mistakes such as those described in (2) could be prevented by a supervisor or another employee.

(b) The board concludes after a public hearing that the appointing power has adequately documented the sensitivity of the class and the consequences of drug-related behavior and that drug testing is, therefore, job related for the class; and

(c) As a result of (a) and (b) above, the board approves the inclusion of a requirement for drug testing in the minimum qualifications for the class.

213.1 Notice of Drug Testing in Examination Announcements

Any examination that includes drug testing as provided by Rule 213 shall specify in the examination announcement the type of specimen to be collected and the consequences of failing the drug test.

213.2 Drug Testing of Current Employees and Individuals Reinstating.

An applicant or transferee to a class for which drug testing is required pursuant to Rule 213 who is a current employee or a former permanent or probationary employee with a break in service as defined in Rule 6.4 shall be subject to drug testing pursuant to Rule 312, except that if such employee has a current appointment to a class for which drug testing is required pursuant to Rule 213, he or she shall not be tested. A current or former employee subject to testing under this rule is deemed to be an applicant for purposes of Rules 213.4, 213.5, and 213.6.

213.3 Laboratories Authorized to Conduct Drug Testing.

Drug test samples shall be analyzed by:

(a) A commercial laboratory meeting standards that are the same as those used by the Department of Health and Human Services (DHHS)/ National Institute on Drug Abuse (NIDA) to certify laboratories engaged in urine drug testing for Federal agencies (Mandatory Guidelines for Federal Workplace Drug Testing Program, Federal Register, Vol. 53, No. 69) or those standards used by the College of American Pathologists (CAP) to accredit laboratories for forensic urine drug testing (Standards for Accreditation, Forensic Drug Testing Laboratories, College of American Pathologists); and

(1) Is capable of same site initial screening and confirmatory tests,

(2) Utilizes FDA-approved immunoassay tests, and

(3) Participates in a laboratory proficiency testing program; and

(b) A laboratory which is not a component organization of a State department.

213.4 Required Components for Drug Testing.

Any drug testing or retesting procedure conducted pursuant to Rule 213 or 213.2 must be approved by the executive officer and shall include all of the following:

(a) The drug screening methodology to be used, which shall be a type of immunoassay, except that another may be used if a department can demonstrated that it is equally reliable as immunoassay;

(b) The drugs to be tested which shall include at least the following drugs of abuse:

(1) Amphetamines and Methamphetamines

(2) Cocaine

(3) Marijuana/Cannabinoids (THC)

(4) Opiates (narcotics)

(5) Phencyclidine (PCP)

(c) Cutoff levels for screening tests that will identify positive samples while minimizing false positive test results;

(d) An authorization to test forms which shall include at least the following:

(1) A list of the specific drugs to be tested for, and a description of the consequences of failing, the drug test as specified in Rule 213.5;

(2) A signature block, to be signed by the applicant before the drug test begins, authorizing the test to proceed and authorizing the necessary disclosure of medical information pursuant to Rule 213.4.

(3) A statement that applicants who decline to sign the form or decline to be tested will be disqualified from the examination.

(e)

(1) A requirement that the applicant disclose on a form, separate from the authorization to test form, all drugs and other medications taken, whether prescribed or not, within the 14 days prior to testing. This information shall be examined only by the appointing power and only if the applicant has a positive confirmatory drug test, except that for purposes of administering Rule 213.6, this information may be examined by the board and staff authorized to investigate and/or hear appeals.

(2) A requirement that the appointing power utilize a Medical Review Officer, who shall be a licensed physician with knowledge of substance abuse, to review and interpret positive results of confirmatory tests and the information submitted by the applicant pursuant to Rule 213.4(e)(1), determine whether the result may have been caused for any medically acceptable reason, such as prescribed or over the counter medications, and report to the appointing power his/her opinion as to the cause of the positive drug test. In the process of making this decision, the Medical Review Officer may request the applicant to provide additional information regarding all drugs and other medications taken.

(f) Specimen chain of custody provisions which shall include at least the following:

(1) A procedure to assure that a valid specimen is acquired, the donor is properly identified, and that no tampering or mishandling of the specimen occurs from initial collection to final disposition.

(2) A written log in which is recorded the name, signature, time of receipt, and time of release of each person handling, testing or storing each specimen, and reporting test results.

(3) Collection of specimen samples in a clinical setting such as a laboratory collection station, doctor's office, hospital or clinic, or in another setting approved by the executive officer on the basis that it provides an equally secure and professional collection process.

(g) Procedure for confirmation of positive screening test results utilizing gas chromatography/mass spectrometry (GS/MS);

(h) Notes to the applicant which shall be written and based on the following:

(1) If the screening test result is negative, the test is concluded and the applicant has passed the drug test.

(2) If the necessary confirmatory test result is negative, the test is concluded and the applicant has passed the drug test.

(3) If both the screening test and the confirmatory test results are positive and the Medical Review Officer's opinion is that the positive test results are not because of prescribed or over the counter medication or for any other medically acceptable reasons, the applicant has failed the drug test.

(i) Specimen retention and retesting procedure which shall include at least the following:

(1) Retention of all confirmed positive specimens and related records by the testing laboratory in secure frozen storage for at least one year following the test or until all appeals or litigation are concluded, whichever is longer.

(2) Provisions for retesting of confirmed positive specimens by any laboratory authorized to conduct drug testing pursuant to Rule 213.3, at the request of an applicant and at the applicant's expense, provided that the request is received within 30 days of notifying the applicant of his/her disqualification. Retesting shall correspond exactly with the initial methods and procedures.

(j) Provisions for maintaining the confidentiality of test results, which shall included at least the following:

(1) The results of any test conducted pursuant to Rules 213, 213.2 or 213.4 (i) (2) shall be given only to the applicant who was tested, the appointing power or the executive officer, and cannot be revealed to any other party without the written authorization of the applicant except that for the purposes of administering

(A) Rule 213.5, the executive officer shall reveal a failed drug test to other State appointing powers who administer an examination for which drug testing is required and for which the individual is an applicant; or
(B) Rule 213.6, the executive officer may reveal a failed drug test and other relevant information to the board and staff authorized to investigate and/or hear appeals.

(2) The results of any test conducted pursuant to Rule 213.2 shall not be used in any adverse action proceedings.
(3) The information disclosed by the applicant pursuant to Rule 213.4(e) (1) shall be examined only be the appointing power and only if the applicant has a positive confirmatory drug test, except that for purposes of administering Rule 213.6, this information may be examined by the board and staff authorized to investigate and/or hear appeals.
(4) Drug test results which are positive shall be purged from all records one year from the date the drug test specimen is given except as follows:

(A) The retention period for drug test results which are positive for a drug as specified in Rule 213.5 (b) shall be ten years from the date the drug test specimen is given;
(B) If a disqualification from an examination as the result of a positive test is appealed or litigated, the drug test results shall be retained until the appeal or litigation is resolved.

213.5 Consequences of Failing the Drug Test.

(a) Applicants who fail the drug test pursuant to Rule 213.4(h), will be disqualified from the examination in which they are competing and, except as provided by Rule 213.5(d), shall not be eligible to take any State civil service examination for a class for which drug testing is required until one years has elapsed from the date the drug test specimen is given.

(b) Except as provided by Rule 213.5(d), applicants who fail the drug test because of drug for which possession would constitute a felony offense under Health and Safety Code Section 11350 shall not be eligible to take any State civil service examination for a peace officer until ten years have elapsed from the date the drug test specimen is given.

(c) Any applicant for a State civil service examination for a peace officer class who discloses or whose background investigation reveals use of a drug for which possession would constitute a felony offense under Health and Safety Code Section 11350, subsequent to his or her eighteenth birthday shall be disqualified from the examination in which he or she is competing unless 10 years have elapsed from the date of the disclosed use of the drug; and shall not be eligible to take any State civil service examination for a peace officer class until 10 years have elapsed from the date of the disclosed use.

(d) Any applicant who is disqualified from taking any subsequent examination as specified in this rule may, upon request and with the consent of the executive officer, be permitted to take the specified examination. In acting on the request, the executive officer shall consider evidence submitted by the person of rehabilitation from drug abuse and/or extenuating circumstances regarding the drug use.

Persons denied permission to take a subsequent examination within the specified one- and ten-year periods may appeal in writing to the Board within 30 days of notification.

213.6 Appeal of a Disqualification Resulting From a Failed Drug Test of Background Investigation Report

(a) This rule pertains to and outlines administrative appeal rights only. An applicant appealing under this rule shall follow the procedures in Rules 63 through 74, inclusive.

(b) An applicant disqualified as the result of failing the drug test may only appeal the disqualification on the grounds that the drug was obtained legally, or there has been a violation of test protocol or chain of custody procedures, or other irregularity that invalidates the test result. A disqualified applicant may have his/her drug test specimen retested at his/her own expense as provided in Rule 213.4(i)(2) and include the results of the retesting in his/her appeal.

(c) An applicant disqualified or withheld from certification as a result of disclosure of drug use or whose background investigation reveals use of a drug pursuant to Rule 213.5(c) may appeal the disqualification or the withholding from certification on any grounds allowable by law.

(d) An applicant who prevails upon appeal under this rule will be restored to eligibility in the examination from which disqualified or restored to the eligible list from which withheld.

California State Personnel Board, Title 2, Register 89, No. 18, 5-6-89

Substance Abuse Policy

Introduction

The State Department of Personnel is charged with implementing the Governor's Executive Order D-58-86, which calls for a drug-free State workplace.

To achieve this the Department of Personnel Administration established a program under which employees serving in sensitive positions in State service are subject to drug and/or alcohol testing when there is reasonable suspicion that they are under the influence while at work or on standby.

The program supplements measures previously in place to deal with employee substance abuse, such as employee assistance and discipline programs.

Employee constitutional privacy rights must be considered before implementing substance testing. The State's need to test must be balanced with the employee's normal entitlement to be protected from such action under search and seizure and privacy provisions. This end is achieved by focusing testing on sensitive positions in which:

(1) Impaired performance could clearly endanger the health and safety of others; and
(2) Less intrusive measures could not reliably deal with this problem.

Sensitive positions were specifically identified in such fields as law enforcement, correcitons, fire fighting, health care, and heavy truck and equipment operations, among others.

Whether testing should be random, periodic, or for cause was considered. Again, there was a need to balance the State's interests with employee rights. Legal advice indicated that random is still in some legal dispute, where there is solid legal support for testing based on reasonable suspicion.

A review of State agencies indicated that the majority of State employees perform their work without being under the influence of drugs or alcohol. In view of this, testing based on reasonable suspicion was elected.

With these policy issues decided, the issues surrounding the technical accuracy of drug testing was considered. Extensive technical safeguards were included to avoid the pitfalls of high error rates, questional sample collection practices, easy ways to beat the tests and improper interpretation of test results.

Employees expressed apprehension concerning supervisor harassment, test accuracy, invasion of privacy and due process. In response, the following employee rights were included in the provisions:

(1) Employees and unions are notified and given an opportunity to respond before positions are designated sensitive and become subject to the policy;

(2) Before an employee can be sent for a drug test, the initial determination of reasonable suspicion must be confirmed by a second supervisor or manager who is specifically trained in the testing policy and the detection of reasonable suspicion;

(3) Employees have the right to representation in any interviews that could lead to a decison to take action against them;

(4) At their own expense, employees have the opportunity to have their sample retested at a lab of their choice;

(5) Employees receive copies of all test results and related documentation;

(6) Confidentiality is maintained with test results being released only on a need-to-know basis;

(7) A licensed physician reviews all positive results and considers any medical reasons provided by employees for any positive results that may come back on them.

Imput was solicited from employee unions concerning the policy and how it could impact on their employees. The impact the policies have upon employees is subject to collective bargaining.

Extrapolated from testimoney
Peter Strom, Manager, Policy Development Section
Department of Personnel Administration, State of California,
Senate Select Committee on Substance Abuse,
Senator John Seymour, Chairman, October 25, 1988 (238).

599.960 General Policy

(a) It is the purpose of this article to help ensure that the State workplace is free from the effects of drug and alcohol abuse. These provisions shall be in addition to and shall not be construed as a required prerequisite to or as replacing, limiting or setting standards for any other types of provisions available under law to serve this purpose, including employee assistance, adverse action and medical examination.

(b) Consistent with Government Code Section 19572 and Governor's Executive Order D-58-86, no State employee who is on duty or on standby for duty shall:

    (1) Use, possess, or be under the influence of illegal or unauthorized drugs or other illegal mind-altering substances; or

    (2) Use of be under the influence of alcohol to any extent that would impede the employee's ability to perform his or her duties safely and effectively.

(c) Employees serving in sensitive positions shall be subject to drug and alcohol testing, hereinafter referred to as substance testing, as provided in this Article when there is reasonable suspicion that the employee has violated subsection (b). In addition, when such an employee has already been found in violation of subsection (b) through the adverse action or medical examination processes under the Civil Service Act (Government Code Section 19253.5; Government Code Sections 19570-19593), as a result of substance testing under this article, or by the employee's own admission, the employee may be required to submit to periodic substance testing as a condition of remaining in or returning to State employment. Unless otherwise provided in the settlement of an adverse action the period for this testing shall not exceed one year.

(d) No employee shall perform duties which, because of drugs taken under a legal prescription, the employee cannot perform without posing a threat to the health and safety of the employee or others. Employees whose job performance is so restricted may be subject to reassignment, medical examinations or other actions specified by applicable statues and regulations.

599.961 Sensitive Positions

(a) For the purposes of this Article, sensitive positions are peace officer positions, as defined by Section 830 of the Penal Code, and other positions in which drug or alcohol affected performance could clearly endanger the health and safety of others. These other positions have the following general characteristics:

(1) Their duties involve a greater than normal level of trust, responsibility for or impact on the health and safety of others; and

(2) Errors in judgment, inattentiveness or diminished coordination, dexterity or composure while performing their duties could clearly result in mistakes that would endanger the health and safety of others; and

(3) Employees in these positions work with such independence, or, perform such tasks that it cannot be safely assumed that mistakes such as those described in (2) could be prevented by a supervisor or another employee.

(b) Filled positions shall be identified as sensitive through the following process:

(1) Subject to Department of Personnel Administration approval, each appointing power shall identify the positions under his/her jurisdiction that meet the standards in (a).

(2) The employees serving in the identified positions and, where applicable, their union representatives, shall receive an initial notice that the position has been identified as sensitive and shall be given 30 days to respond.

(3) After considering responses to the initial notice and meeting with employee representatives as required by the Ralph C. Dills Act (Government Code Sections 3512-3524), the Department of Personnel Administration shall issue a final notice to the employees serving in the positions that have been identified as sensitive. This notice shall include a description of the provisions of this Article. Existing practices in this area shall not change for any positions until 60 days after the final notice concerning it is issued.

(c) Vacant positions shall be identified as sensitive through the procedures specified in (b), including those procedures involving employee organizations, except that the employee notification provisions as sated in (b) (2) and (b) (3) shall not apply.

(d) Once a position has been designated sensitive, the appointing power shall take measures to reasonably and likely ensure that future appointees to it are aware that it is sensitive and are informed of the provisions of this Article.

599.962 Reasonable Suspicion

(a) Reasonable suspicion is the good faith belief based on specific articulable facts or evidence that an employee may have violated the policy prescribed in section 599.960(b) and that substance testing could reveal evidence related to that violation.

(b) For the purposes of this Article, reasonable suspicion will exist only after the appointing power or his/her designee has considered the fact and/or evidence in the particular case and agrees that they constitute a finding of reasonable suspicion. A designee shall be an individual other than the suspected employee's immediate supervisor and other than the person who made the initial observation leading to the question of reasonable suspicion. The designee shall be a person who is authorized to act for the appointing power in carrying out this Article and who is thoroughly familiar with its provisions and procedures.

(c) After it has been confirmed by the designee the facts and/or evidence upon which the reasonable suspicion is based shall be documented in writing. A copy of this shall be given to the affected employee.

599.963 Testing Process and Standards

Substance testing under this Article shall comply with the following standards and procedures.

(a) The drug testing process shall be one that is scientifically proven to be at least as accurate and valid as urinalysis using an immunoassay screening test, with all positive screening results being confirmed utilizing gas chromatography/mass spectrometry before a sample is considered positive. The alcohol testing process shall be one that is scientifically proven to be at least accurate and valid as

(1) Urinalysis using enzymatic assay screening test, with all positive screening results being confirmed using gas chromatography before a sample is considered positive or
(2) Breath sample testing using breath alcohol analyzing instruments which meet the State Department of Health Services standard specified in Title 17, Group 8, Article 7 of the California Code of Regulations.

(b) Substances to be tested for shall include the following:

(1) Amphetamines and Methamphetamines
(2) Cocaine
(3) Marijuana/Cannabinoids (THC)
(4) Opiates (narcotics)
(5) Phencyclidine (PCP)
(6) Barbiturates
(7) Benzodiazepines
(8) Methaqualone
(9) Alcohol
(10) In addition, with the approval of the department testing may be conducted for other controlled substances when the appointing power reasonably suspects the use of other substances.

(c) After consulting with expert staff of the laboratory or laboratories selected to perform the testing under this Article, the department shall set test cutoff level that will identify positive test samples while minimizing false positive test results.

(d) Test samples will be collected in a clinical setting such as a laboratory collection station, doctor's office, hospital or clinic or in another setting approved by the department on the basis that it provides for at least an equally secure and professional collection process. The department shall specify procedures to ensure that true samples are obtained.

(e) The department shall specify measures to ensure that a strict chain of custody is maintained for the sample from the time it is taken, through the testing process, to its final disposition.

(f) Drug tests shall be performed by a commercial laboratory selected based on its meeting standards that are the same as those used by the National Institute on Drug Abuse (NIDA) to certify laboratories engaged in urine drug testing for Federal agencies (Mandatory Guidelines for Federal Workplace Drug Testing Program, Federal Register, Vol. 53, No. 69) or those used by the College of American Pathologists (CAP) to accredit laboratories for forensic urine drug testing (Standards for Accreditation, Forensic Drug Testing Laboratories, College of American Pathologists).

599.964 Employee Rights

(a) Employees suspected of violating the policy prescribed in section 599.960 shall be entitled to representation during any interrogative interviews with the affected employee that could lead to a decision by the appointing power to take adverse action against the employee, regardless of whether these interviews occur before or after the sample is taken. Employees shall also be entitled to representation in any discussions with the Medical Review Officer that occur under section 599.965.

(b) The sample collection process shall include the opportunity for the employee to provide information about factors other than illegal drug use, such as taking legally prescribed medication, that could cause a positive test result. At the employee's option, this information may be submitted in a sealed envelope to be opened only be the Medical Review Officer if the test results is positive.

(c) The employee shall receive a full copy of any test results and related documentation of the testing process.

(d) All confirmed positive samples shall be retained by the testing laboratory in secure frozen storage for one year following the test or until the sample is no longer needed for appeal proceedings or litigation, whichever is longer. At employee's request and expense the sample may be retested by that laboratory or another laboratory of the employee's choice.

599.965 Medical Review Officer

Each appointing power shall designate one or more Medical Review Officers, who shall be licensed physicians, to receive test results from the laboratory. Upon receiving results, the Medical Review Officer shall:

(a) Review the results and determine if the standards and procedures required by this Article have been followed.

(b) For positive results, interview the affected employee to determine if factors other than illegal drug use may have caused the result.

(c) Consider any assertions by the affected employee of irregularities in the sample collection and testing process.

(d) Based on the above, provide a written explanation of the test results to the appointing power or his/her designee. The employee shall also receive a copy of this explanation.

599.966 Records; Confidentiality

As prescribed by the director, each appointing power shall maintain records of the circumstances and results of any employee under this Article. These records, and any other information pertaining to an employee's drug or alcohol test, shall be considered confidential and shall be released only to:

(a) The employee who was tested or other individuals designated in writing by that employee.

(b) The appointing power's Medical Review Officer.

(c) The Department of Personnel Administration as needed for the effective administration of the Article.

(d) Individuals who need the records or information to:

(1) Properly supervise or assign employee.
(2) Determine, or assist in determining, what action the appointing power should take in response to the test results.
(3) Respond to appeals or litigation arising from the drug test or related actions.

Department of Personnel, State of California, Title 2, Register 89, No. 37, 9/16/89.

Author's note: Authors express appreciation to Peter J. Strom, Manager, Policy Development Section, Department of Personnel Administration, State of California, Sacramento and Chuck Flacks, aid to Senator Lockyear, Hayward, California, for their assistance in providing this and other material.

Appendix D

PharmChem Detection Times

Drug	Detection Period
Amphetamines	
Amphetamine	2-4 days
Methamphetamine	2-4 days
Barbiturates	
Amobarbital	2-4 days
Butalbital	2-4 days
Pentibarbital	2-4 days
Phenobarbital	2-4 days
Secobarbital	Up to 30 days

Drug	Detection Period
Benzodiazepines	
Valium (Diazepam)	Up to 30 days
Librium (Chlordiazepoxide)	Up to 30 days
Cocaine	
Benzoylecgonine	12-72 hours
Cannabinoids (Marijuana)	
Casual use	2-7 days
Chronic use	Up to 30 days
Ethanol (Alcohol)	12-24 hours
Opiates	
Codine	2-4 days
Hydromorphone (Dilaudid)	2-4 days
Morphine (Heroin)	2-4 days
Methaqualone (Quaalude)	2-4 days
Phencyclidine (PCP)	
Casual use	2-7 days
Chronic use	Up to 30 days

Pharmchem Newsletter, Volumn 17, No. 2.

Bibliography

1. Clare, Anthony W., Drugs Are Big Business, *World Health*, Jun. 1986, pg. 18-19.
2. Mithers, Carol Lynn, High on the Job, *Glamour*, Aug. 1986, pg. 252.
3. Quayle, Dan, American Productivity: The Devastating Effect of Alcoholism and Drug Abuse, *American Psychologist*, Apr. 1983, pg. 454.
4. Nelson, M.B.A., Jack E., Drug Abusers on the Job, *Occupational Medicine*, Jun. 1981, v. 23, no. 6, pg. 403-408.
5. Newcomb, Ph.D., Michael D., Ebrahim Maddahian, Ph.D., and P. M. Bentler, Ph.D., Risk Factors for Drug Use Among Adolescents: Concurrent and Longitudinal Analyses, *AJPH*, May 1986, v. 76, no. 5, pg. 525-531.
6. Dezelsky, T. L., J. V. Toohey, and R. S. Shaw, Non-Medical Drug Use Behaviour at Five United States Universities: A 15-Year Study, *Bulletin on Narcotics*, 1985, v. 37, no. 2-3, pg. 49-53.
7. Associated Press Staff Writers, THC in Pot Eats Away at Brain Cells, Study Says, *San Francisco Examiner*, Sep. 25, 1986, pg. A-11.
8. Goldstein, Richard, Getting Real About Getting High, *Voice*, Sep. 30, 1986, pg. 21.
9. Kaye, Elizabeth, Drugless in L.A., *This World*, May 11, 1986, pg. 10.
10. Findlay, Steven, Kids May Be Catching Adults' Cocaine Habit, *USA Today*, May 23, 1986.
11. Callen, Kate, How Cocaine Kills - Even in Tiny Doses, *San Francisco Examiner*, Sep. 25, 1986, pg. A-12.
13a. Adler, Jerry, Pamela Abramson, Susan Katz, and Mary Hager, Getting High on "Ecstasy," *Newsweek*, Apr. 15, 1985, pg. 96.

13b.   Shafer, Jack, MDMA: Psychedelic Drug Faces Regulation, *Psychology Today*, May 1985, pg. 68

13c.   Flinn, John "Ecstasy" Causes Agony for Doctors, Government, *San Francisco Examiner*, May 19, 1985, pg. A3.

13d.   Klein, Joe, The New Drug They Call Ecstasy, *This World*, Jun. 23, 1985, pg. 10-11.

14.   Staff Writers, The War on Drugs, *The Coming Revolution*, pg.32

15.   Brinkley, Joel, U.S. Illegal Drugs at Record Levels, *Oakland Tribune*, Jun. 2, 1986, pg. A-1.

16.   Cook, Stephen C., Cocaine Crack: Quick, Convenient — and Deadly, *San Francisco Examiner*, Jul. 6, 1986, pg. A-1.

17.   Siegel, Ronald K., Animal Intoxication, *This World*, Apr. 6, 1986, pg, 9.

18.   Lieber, James, Coping With Cocaine, The Atlantic, Jan. 1986, pg. 39-48.

19.   Thomas, Evan, America's Crusade: What is Behind the Latest War on Drugs, *Time*, Sep. 15, 1986, pg. 60.

20.   Danner, Mark D., M. Kleiman, A. Trebach, R. Stutman, R. Giuliani, L. Garcia, L. Grinspoon, E. Van Den Haag, and H. London, What is America's Drug Problem?, *Harper's Magazine*, Dec. 1985, pg. 39.

21.   Martz, Larry, M. Miller, B. Cohn, G. Raine, and G. Carroll, Trying to Say "No," *Newsweek*, Aug. 11, 1986, pg. 14.

22.   Wilde, James, Crashing on Cocaine, Time, Apr. 11, 1983, pg. 22.

23.   White, Raymond S., The Let's Party Syndrome, *Street Pharmacologist*, Dec. 1982, v. V, no. 12, pg. 1.

24.   Siegel, Ronald K., Jungle Revelers, *Omni*, pg. 71.

25.   Lempinen, Edward W., and Tim Schriener, Bay Area Cuts Drug Use — But Still Leads the U.S., *San Francisco Chronicle*, 1986, pg.1

26.   Clark, Matt, and Karen Springen, Docs and Drugs, *Newsweek*, Oct. 6, 1986, pg. 28.

27.   Smith, M.D., David E., and Donald R. Wesson, Substance Abuse in Industry: Identification, Intervention, Treatment and Prevention, *Substance Abuse in the Workplace*, Haight-Ashbury Publications, San Francisco: 1984, pg. 5.

28.   Latimer, Dean, Reliability of Drug Tests, *High Times Magazine*, Oct. 1986, pg. 56-59.

29.   Montague, Mary W., Bosses Strike Back at Sample-Salting, *High Times Magazine*, Oct. 1986, pg. 15.

30.   Willette, Robert E., Development of Assays for Drugs of Abuse, *Controlled Clinical Trials*, 1984, v. 5, pg. 466-471.

31.   Latimer, Dean, Drug Test Shocker: Alka Seltzer Scores as Dope! *High Times Magazine*, Sept. 1986, pg. 15.

32.   Vu Duc, T., EMIT Tests for Drugs of Abuse: Interference by Liquid Soap Preparations, *Clinical Chemistry*, 1985, v. 81, no. 4, pg. 658-659.

33.   Morgan, M.D., John P., Problems of Mass Urine Screening for Misused Drugs, *Substance Abuse in the Workplace*, Haight-Ashbury Publications, San Francisco: 1984, pg. 21

34.   Elahi, Nasik, Encapsulated XAD-2 Extraction Technique for a Rapid Screening of Drugs of Abuse in Urine, *J. Analytical Toxicology*, Jan./Feb. 1980, v. 4, pg. 26-30.

35.   Miller, M.A., Laurence, Neuropsychological Assessment of Substance

Abusers: Review and Recommendations, *J. Substance Abuse Treatment*, 1985, v. 2, pg. 5-17.

36. Gold, M.D., Mark S., and Charles A. Dackis, M.D., Role of the Laboratory in the Evaluation of Suspected Drug Abuse, *J. Clinical Psychiatry*, Jan. 1986, v. 47, no. 1, pg. 17-23.

38. Center for Disease Control, The Results of Unregulated Testing, *JAMA*, Apr. 26, 1985.

39. Christophersen, Asbjorg S., Tetrahydrocannabinol Stability in Whole Blood: Plastic Versus Glass Containers, *J. Analytical Toxicology*, Jul./Aug. 1986, v. 10, pg. 129-131.

40. Abercrombie, Marsha L., and John S. Jewell, Evaluation of EMIT and RIA High Volume Test Procedures for THC Metabolites in Urine Utilizing GC/MS Confirmation, *J. Analytical Toxicology*, Sept./Oct. 1986, v. 10, pg. 178-180.

41. McBurney, L. J., B. A. Bobbie, and L. A. Sepp, GC/MS and EMIT Analysis for Delta 9-Tetrahydrocannabinol Metabolites in Plasma and Urine of Human Subjects, *J. Analytical Toxicology*, Mar./Apr. 1986, v. 10, pg. 56-64.

42. Alrazi, J., M. Lehrer, S. J. Mule, and K. Verebey, One Hundred EMIT Positive Cannabinoid Urine Samples Confirmed by BPA/TLC, RIA, and GC/MS, *J. Analytical Toxicology*, Mar./Apr. 1986, v. 10, pg. 79.

43. Gottheil, M.D., Ph.D., Edward, Glenn R. Caddy, Ph.D., and Deborah L. Austin, Fallibility of Urine Drug Screens in Monitoring Methadone Programs, *JAMA*, Aug. 30, 1976, v. 236, no. 9, pg. 1035-1038.

44a. Verebey, K., D. Jukofsky, and S. J. Mule, Evaluation of a New TLC Confirmation Technique for Positive EMIT Cannabinoid Urine Samples, *Res. Common. Subtance Abuse*, 1985, v. 6, no. 1, pg. 1-9.

44b. Cais, M., S. Dani, and M. Shimoni, A Novel Non-Centrifugation Radioimmunoassay for Cannabinoids, *Isr. Arch. Toxicology*, 1983, v. 53, suppl. 6, pg. 105-113.

44c. Baselt, R. C., Stability of Cocaine in Biological Fluids, *J. Chromatography*, 1983, v. 268, no. 3, pg. 502-505.

44d. Stafford, D. T., H. S. Nichols, and W. H. Anderson, Efficiency of Capillary Column Gas Chromatography in Separating Lysergic Acid Diethylamide (LSD) and Lysergic Acid Methylpropylamide (LAMPA), *J. Forensic Science*, 1984, v. 29, no. 1, pg. 291-298.

44e. Smith, R. M., Arylhydroxy Metabolites of Cocaine in the Urine of Cocaine Users, *J. Analytical Toxicology*, 1984, v. 8, no. 1, pg. 35-37.

44f. Hennegerg, M., I. Wozniak, D. Brodzinska, and K. Wencel, An Original 'Street Test' for Urine Screening for Morphine and Its Evaluation, Med. Cent. Grad. Educ., Bydgoszcz Pol, *Alcohol Alcohol*, 1984, v. 19, no. 4, pg. 311-317.

44g. Law, B., P.A. Mason, and A.C. Moffat, Forensic Aspects of the Metabolism and Excretion of Cannabinoids Following Oral Ingestion of Cannabis Resin, *J. Phamaceutical Pharmacology*, 1984, v. 36, no. 5, pg. 289-294.

44h. Law, B., P. A. Mason, A. C. Moffat, and L. J. King, A Novel 125-I Radioimmunoassay for the Analysis of Delta-9 Tetrahydrocannabinol and its Metabolites in Human Body Fluids, *J. Analytical Toxicology*, 1984, v. 8, no. 1, pg. 14-18.

44i.   Law, B., P. A. Mason, A. C. Moffat, and L. J. King, Confirmation of
        Cannnabis Use by the Analysis of Delta-9 Tetrahydrocannabinol
        Metabolites in Blood and Urine by Combined HPLC and RIA, *J. Ana-
        lytical Toxicology*, 1984, v. 8, no. 1, pg. 19-22.

44j.   Ferslew, K. E., J. E. Manno, and B. R. Manno, Determination of Urinary
        Cannabinoid Metabolites Following Incidental Exposure to Marijuana
        Smoke, *Res. Common. Substance Abuse*, 1983, v. 4, no. 4, pg. 289-300.

44K.   Ray, L., Problems of Substance Abuse: Exploitation and Control, *Soc.
        Sci. Med.*, 1985, v. 20, no. 12, pg. 1225-1233.

44l.   Jones, A. B., H. N. ElSohly, E. S. Arafat, and M. A. ElSohly, Analysis of
        the Major Metabolite of Delta-9 Tetrahydrocannabinol in Urine. IV. A
        Comparison of Five Methods. *J. Analytical Toxicology*, 1984, v. 8, no. 6,
        pg. 249-251.

44m.   Lurie, I. S., Problems in Using High Performance Liquid Chromatogra-
        phy for Drug Analysis, *J. Forensic Science*, 1984, v. 29, no. 2, pg.
        607-610.

44n.   Rajananda, V., N. K. Nair, and V. Navaratnam, An Evaluation of TLC
        Systems for Opiate Analysis, *Bulletin of Narcotics*, 1985, v. 37, no. 1,
        pg. 35-47.

44o.   Sutheimer, C. A., R. Yarborough, B. R. Hepler and I. Sunshine, Detection
        and Confirmation of Urinary Cannabinoids, *J. of Analytical Toxicology*,
        1985, v. 9, no. 4, pg. 156-160.

44p.   Erickson, P. G., Cannabis Legislation Reforms in the USA, an Unfinished
        Job, *Psychotropes*, 1985, v. 2, no. 1, pg. 96-98.

44q.   Von Meyer, L., Detection of Cannabinoids in Blood and Urine by EMIT
        Confirmation by TLC, *Z. Rechtsmed.*, 1985, v. 94, no. 3, pg. 219-225.

44r.   Dutt, M. C., Laboratory Diagnosis of Opiate Drugs, *Ann. Acad. Med.
        Singapore*, 1984, v. 13, no. 1, pg. 53-65.

44s.   Gupta, R. N., Drug Level Monitoring: Sedative Hypnotics, *J. Chromatogr.
        Biomed. Appl.*, 1985, v. 340, pg. 139-172.

45.   NORMAL, Urine Testing for Marijuana & Other Drugs, *Common Sense
        for America*, 1986, pg. 30-31.

46.   Angarola, Robert A., Drug Detection Programs in Industry, *PharmChem
        Newsletter*, Jul./Aug. 1984, v. 13, no. 4, pg. 1-3.

47.   Willette, Dr. Robert E., Formal Policy, Urinalysis Deters Drug Abuse in
        the Workplace, *PharmChem Newsletter*, Jul./Aug. 1984, v. 13, no. 4,
        pg. 4.

48.   PharmChem Laboratories, PharmChem Product Brochure, PharmChem
        Laboratories, Inc., Menlo Park, CA.

49.   PharmChem Laboratories, Drug Panel (1000) and Methodology, Pharm-
        Chem Product Brochure, PharmChem Laboratories, Inc., Menlo
        Park, CA.

50.   Jones, Donald W., D. Adams, P. Martel, and R. Rousseau, Drug Popula-
        tion in 1000 Geographically Distributed Urine Specimens, *J. Analytical
        Toxicology*, May/Jun. 1985, v. 9, pg. 125-130.

51.   Hansen, H. J., S. P. Caudill, and D. J. Boone, Crisis in Drug Testing,
        JAMA, 1985, v. 253, no. 16, pg. 2382-2387.

52.   McKinney, Debbie, When it Comes to Drug Tests, How Accurate is Posi-
        tive?, *Anchorage Daily News*, Oct. 6, 1986.

53. Adams, William F., and Cynthia L. Remmers, Drugs and Alcohol in the Workplace: Technology, Law and Policy, Santa Clara Computer and High-*Technology Law Journal*, Apr. 1986, v. 2, no. 2.

54. Miller, Ph.D., John G., Enzyme Immunoassay, *Lab 78: Lab Med. for Practicing Physicians*, Sep./Oct. 1978, pg. 45-49.

55. Burton, Ann, and Syva Company, Syva Product Literature Syva Company, Palo Alto, CA., August 30, 1983.

56. Kim, Hyum J., and Eugene Cerceo, Interference by NaCl With the EMIT Method of Analysis for Drugs of Abuse, *Clinical Chemistry*, 1976, v. 22, no. 11, pg. 1935.

57. Walbrecher, David, A Disposable Lifesaver, *Time*, Jul. 14, 1986, pg. 50.

58. Kerr, Peter, Anatomy of an Issue: Drugs, the Evidence, the Reaction, *The New York Times*, Nov. 17, 1986, pg. 1.

59. McCarron, M.D., Margaret M., Phencyclidine Intoxication, *PharmChem Newsletter*, May/Jun. 1986, v. 15, no. 3, pg. 1-8.

60a. Goldberg, Jeff, and Dean Latimer, Future Drugs - They're All in Your Head, *High Times*, October, 1987.

60b. X, Richard Weed vs. the Writer, *This World*, August 3,1986, pg. 9.

61. Guinn, Ph.D., Bobby, Job Satisfaction, Counterproductive Behavior and Circumstantial Drug Use Among Long-Distance Truckers, *J. Psychoactive Drugs*, Jul./Sep. 1983, v. 15, no. 3, pg. 185-188.

62. Parker, Ph.D., D., E. Parker, Ph.D., J. Brody, M.D., and R. Schoenberg, Ph.D., Alcohol Use and Cognitive Loss Among Employed Men and Women, *AJPH*, 1983, v. 73, pg. 521-526.

63. Goodman, M.D., Richard A., Alcohol Use and Homicide, *PharmChem Newsletter*, Mar./Apr. 1986, v. 15, no. 2, pg. 1-9.

64. Crane, Richard, Legal Issues in Employee Drug Detection Programs, Syva Product Literature, Syva Co., Palo Alto, Ca., 1987.

65. Williams, Lena, Reagan Drug Testing Plan to Start Despite Court Rulings Opposing It, *New York Times*, Nov. 29, 1986, pg. 1.

66. Klehs, Johan, Statement by Assemblyman Johan Klehs - Interim Hearings on Drug Testing, Assembly Bill 4242, Oct. 2, 1986

67. McDougald, George S., U.S. Postal Service Notice, U.S. Postal Service, Jun. 26, 1986.

68. Collins, William C., Urine Testing and the Workplace: Some Legal Considerations, Syva Company, Palo Alto, Ca.,1986, pg. 1-20.

69. Sachs, Stephen H., Jack Schwartz, and Gail Smith, Maryland Attorney General Letter, Office of the Attorney General, Oct. 22, 1986, pg. 1-30.

70. Macklin, Daphne, ACLU Case List, American Civil Liberties Union, California Legislative Office, Sacramento, CA, Dec. 3,1986.

71. United States, The Bill of Rights, American Civil Liberties Union, Sacramento, CA.

72. Collins, Robert, U.S. District Judge, Perspectives Quote, *Newsweek*, Nov. 24, 1986, pg. 29.

73. Wessner, Laura, ABC News — Nightline Show #1386, Transcription, Journal Graphics, Inc., New York, Sep. 15, 1986, pg. 1-6.

74. Staff Writers, Drug-Test Rules Belie Reagan's Assurances, *San Francisco Chronicle*, Nov. 28, 1986.

75. Pear, Robert, Testing Plan Indicates Reagan's "Outrage" Over Drug Abuse, *New York Times*, November 18. 1987.

76. American Civil Liberties Union, What ACLU Has to Say About ... Drug
     Testing in the Workplace, American Civil Liberties Union, New
     York, 1986.
77. Takas, Marianne They Want Your Body: Can Your Boss Test You for
     Drug Use?, *Vogue*, Apr. 1986, v. 176, pg. 156.
78. Singleton, Jill, Worker Sues for $2 Million Over a Forced Blood Test, *San
     Francisco Chronicle*, Oct. 10, 1986, pg. 28.
79. Kopp, Quentin, San Francisco Drug-Test Law Impinges on Employers'
     Rights, *San Francisco Business Times*, Oct. 20, 1986, pg. 6.
80. Staff, Fight Illegal Drugs; Don't Test Everybody, *USA Today*, 1986.
81. O'Conner, Colleen, and Mark Miller, The Military Says "No," *Newsweek*,
     Nov. 10, 1986, pg. 26.
82. Waldholz, Michael, Drug Testing in the Workplace: Whose Rights Take
     Precedence?, *The Wall Street Journal*, November 11, 1986.
83. Milstein, Susan, State Court Limits Polygraph Use, *San Francisco Chron-
     icle*, Jun. 26, 1986, pg. 6.
84. Verrey, Janice A., NBC News — Case Histories, NBC Network, Sep. 30,
     1986, v. 1, no. 14, pg. 1-12.
85. Bloch, Jeff, So What? Everybody's Doing It, *Forbes*, Aug. 11, 1986, pg. 102.
86. Rutkowski and Associates, *Employment Law Update*, Sep. 1986, v. 1, no. 1,
     pg. 1-8.
87. San Francisco City. Part II, Chapter VIII, Article 33A. San Francisco Mu-
     nicipal Code
88a. Visclosky, Peter J., and Anne Marie O'Keefe, When Testing Violates the
     Constitution, *The Washington Post*, Sep. 14, 1986.
88b. Rowan, Carl T., The Rush to Draconian Measures, *The Washington Post*,
     Sep. 14, 1986.
88c. Marx, Gary T., Drug Foes Aren't High on Civil Liberties, *The New York
     Times*, Feb. 24, 1986.
88d. Kirp, David L., Taking Uncivil Liberties: Mass Drug Testing, *Christian
     Science Magazine*, Mar. 25, 1986.
88e. Wicker, Tom, Civil Rights on Trial, *San Francisco Chronicle*, Mar. 14, 1986.
88f. Safire, William, Frisking Each Other, *New York Times*, Mar. 14, 1986.
88g. Editorial Staff, Drug Tests Aren't the American Way, *Marin Independent
     Journal*, Mar. 8, 1986.
88h. Editorial Staff City's Landmark Privacy Ordinance, *Marin Independent
     Journal*, Dec. 2, 1985.
89. Marine, Craig, Hercules Drug Test in Court, *San Francisco Chronicle*, Oct.
     12, 1986.
90. Weir, Jeff, Bill Calls for Drug Testing of Workers, *Los Angeles Times*, Apr.
     8, 1986.
91. Weiss, Philip, Watch Out: Urine Trouble, *Harper's Magazine*, June 1986,
     pg. 56.
92. Beggs, Charles E., Move to Legalize Pot on Oregon Ballot, Associated
     Press, 1986.
93. Castro, Janice, Telltale Hair, *Time Magazine*, Mar. 17, 1986, pg. 55.
94. Lacayo, Richard, Putting Them All to the Test, *Time* , Oct. 21, 1985, pg. 61.
95. Staff, The Test that Failed, *The Nation*, Jan. 4, 1986, V. 241, pg. 697.
96. Gordon, Bill, Judge Halts Drug Tests at East Bay Refinery, *San
     Francisco Chronicle*

97. Morganthau, Tom, Mary Hager, Mark Miller, Kim Willenson, Karen
     Springen, and Andrew Murr, A Question of Privacy, *Newsweek*, Sep.
     29, 1986, pg. 18.

98. Staff Writer, First the Lie Detector, Then the Chemicals, *Newsweek*, Jan.
     27, 1986.

99. Staff Writers, Anti-Drug Bill Passed By Congress, *San Francisco Chronicle*,
     Oct. 18, 1986.

100. Staff Writer, Can You Pass the Job Test? *Newsweek*, May 5, 1986, pg. 46.

101. Angarola, Robert T., and Judith R. Brunton, Legal Implications for Cor-
     porate Actions, *Substance Abuse in the Workplace*, Haight-Ashbury
     Publications, San Francisco: April 1985, pg. 35-42.

102. Peters, Tom, Tom Peters On Defense, Drugs, Education, *Bay Area
     Business*, pg. 23.

103. Talbott, M.D., G. Douglas, Essential Elements of a Model Employee As-
     sistance Program, *Substance Abuse in the Workplace*, Haight-Ashbury
     Publications, San Francisco: April 1985, pg. 55-56.

104. American Civil Liberties Union, Drug Tests Halted, *ACLU News*, Oct./
     Nov. 1986.

105. Boone, Ph.D., D. Joe, Obtaining and Maintaining Reliable Drug Testing
     Services, Centers for Disease Control, Public Health Service, U.S.
     Dept. of Health and Human Services, pg. 1-8.

106. Burmaster, David R., Employee Drug Use Creates Losses But Proper
     Policies Can Control It, *Occupational Health and Safety*, Dec. 1985,
     pg. 39.

107. Presnall, Lewis F., Folklore and Facts About Employees With Alcohol-
     ism, *J. Occupational Medicine*, 1967, v. 9, pg. 187-192.

108. Lewy, M.D., M.P.H., Robert, Preemployment Qualitative Urine Toxicol-
     ogy Screening, *J. Occupational Medicine*, Aug. 1983, v. 25, no. 8, pg.
     579-580.

109. Steele, Paul D., Labor Perceptions of Drug Use and Drug Programs in
     the Workplace, *J. Drug Issues*, Summer 1981, pg. 279-292.

110. Editorial Staff, Exclusive Report: Drug Abuse in the Printing Industries,
     Printing Impressions, Aug. 1986, pg. 6.

111. Klein, Alfred, Employees Under the Influence - Outside the Law?
     Personnel J., Sep. 1986, pg. 57-71.

112. Diegelman, Robert, Substance Abuse: The Business Approach, *Substance
     Abuse in the Workplace*, Haight-Ashbury Publications, San Francisco:
     April 1985, pg. 51-54.

114. McClellan, Keith, Work-Based Drug Programs, *Substance Abuse in the
     Workplace*, Haight-Ashbury Publications, San Francisco: April 1985,
     pg. 57-75.

115. Trice, Harrison M., and Mona Schonbrunn, A History of Job-based Alco-
     holism Programs: 1900-1955, *J. Drug Issues*, Spring 1981, pg. 171-197.

116. Nocella, C.P.P., Henry A., Strategic Planning by Security Personnel, *Sub-
     stance Abuse in the Workplace*, Haight-Ashbury Publications, San
     Francisco: April 1985, pg. 43-46.

117. Mazzone, Lt. Col., Frank, Substance Abuse in the Workplace: The
     Security Perspective, *Substance Abuse in the Workplace*, Haight-Ash-
     bury Publications, San Francisco: April 1985, pg. 47-49.

118. Walsh, Dr. J. Michael, Drugs in the Workplace, PharmChem Product Literature

119. Staff Writers, U.S. to Dye Toilet Water Blue in Testing Workers for Drugs, *San Francisco Chronicle*, Feb. 19, 1987, pg. 13.

120. Hoffman, Abbie, with Jonathan Silvers, *Steal This Urine Test*, Penguin Books, 1987.

121. Trice, Harrison M., and Paul M. Roman, *Spirits and Demons at Work: Alcohol and Other Drugs on the Job*, Cornell University Press, Ithaca, NY: 1978.

122. Berger, Gilda, *Drug Testing*, Impact Books, NY: 1987.

123. Freeman, Robert, How to "Beat" a Drug Test, *High Times*, Aug. 1988, no. 156, pg. 19.

124. Denniston, Lyle, U.S. Issues Guidelines for Fighting Jar Wars, *San Francisco Examiner*, Feb. 20, 1987.

125. Wiltsee, Joe, Your Rights as an Employee, *Business Week Guide to Careers*, 1986, pg. 33.

126. Gieringer, Dale, (ed.) Drug Testing Advice, *California NORML Reports*, Feb. 1988, v. 12, no. 1.

127. Staff Writer, Urine for Fun and Profit, Frontlines, *Mother Jones*, Apr. 1987, pg. 11.

128. Staff Writer, How People Fight Back, *American Health*, Jul./Aug. 1986.

129. Morgan, M.D., John P., Urine Trouble — A Physician Looks at Testing, *Question Authority*, Feb. 1988. (Dr. Morgan is a professor at City University of New York).

130. Jeffrey Nightbyrd, *Conquering The Urine Tests: A Complete Guide To Success In Urine Testing*, Byrd Laboratories, 225 Congress, Box 340, Austin, TX. 78701,1986.

131. Hanners, David, Powdered Urine Seen as Million-Dollar Idea, *The Dallas Morning News*, Dec. 14, 1986.

132. Staff Writer, Texan is Selling Drug-Free Urine to Meet "Unanticipated Demand," *The New York Times*, Nov. 29, 1986.

133. Carlsen, William, Trucker Fights "Zero Tolerance" Seizure of Rig, *San Francisco Chronicle*, Jul. 1988.

134. Washington Post Staff Writers Reagan Says None Exempt From Drugs, *San Francisco Chronicle*, Jul. 1, 1988, pg. A16.

135. Los Angeles Times Staff Writers, Competing Proposals to Fight Drugs, *San Francisco Chronicle*, Jul. 1, 1988.

136. DuPont, M.D., Robert L., The Treatment and Prevention of Substance Abuse in Adolescents, *Directions in Psychiatry*, 1984, v. 4, lesson 33, pg. 1-8.

137. DuPont, M.D., Robert L., *The Drug Epidemic and Related Disasters Getting Tough on Gateway Drugs*, AMA: 1988.

138. DuPont, M.D., Robert L., Marijuana, Alcohol, and Adolescence: A Malignant Synergism, Seminars in Adolescent Medicine, Dec. 1985, v. 1, no. 4, pg. 311.

139. Staff Writer, 'Disease Concept' a Drug Debate Smoke Screen, *The Journal*, Jan. 1, 1985, pg. 9.

140. DuPont, M.D., Robert L., Substance Abuse, *JAMA*, Oct. 25, 1985, v. 254, no. 16, pg. 2335.

141. DuPont, M.D., Robert L., The Treatment and Prevention of Substance Abuse in Adolescents, *Directions in Psychiatry*, 1984, v. 4, lesson 33, pg. 1-8.

142. DuPont, M.D., Robert L., Awash in Alcohol, *Listen*, Oct. 1983, pg. 11.

143. DuPont, M.D., Robert L., Testimony by Robert L. DuPont, M.D. Before the Subcommittee on Health and Safety, Committee on Education and Labor, U.S. House of Rep., Oct. 31, 1985.

145. Garner, Joe, New Railroad Rules on Drugs Take Effect, *Rocky Mountain News*, Jan. 28, 1986.

146. Armbrister, Trevor, We Can Conquer Cocaine, *Reader's Digest*, Feb. 1987, pg. 63-68.

148. Martel, Ph.D., Patricia A., Donald W. Jones, M.D., and Robert J. Rousseau, Ph.D., Application of Toxi-Lab: A Broad Spectrum Drug Detection System in Emergency Toxicology, American Association for Clinical Chemistry, Aug. 1983, v. 2, no. 2, pg. 1.

149. Staff Writer, Ten Years of Legalization in Alaska, *Common Sense for America*, pg. 10-11.

150. Press, Aric, Gerald C. Lubenow, and Martin Kasindorf, Reality Versus Rhetoric, *Newsweek*, Sep. 8, 1986, pg. 60.

152. Neff, Craig, Steroids on Campus: The Boz Flunks Out, *Sports Illustrated*, 1988, pg. 20-25

153. Pauley, Jane, and Boyd Matson, Drugs in Sports: Striking Out? Today Show, Transcript, NBC-TV, Oct. 24, 1985.

155. Bogdanich, Walt, Labs Offering Workplace Drug Screens in New York Have Higher Error Rate, *The Wall Street Journal*, Feb. 2, 1987.

156. Herzfeld, John, Brain Scans on the Job? *American Health*, Jul./Aug. 1986, pg. 72.

157. Walbrecher, David, Information on BreathScan, Prescott Technologies, Inc., Denver, Colorado, Dec. 5, 1986.

158. Wilson, M.S., Frederick, A Rapid Combined Drug-Screening System, Laboratory Management, Jun. 1984.

159. Product Literature, Toxi-Lab Drug Detection Systems Laboratory Price List, Analytical Systems, Div. of Marion Laboratories, Inc., Jul. 1, 1986.

160. Sutheimer, C. A., R. Yarborough, B. R. Hepler, and I. Sunshine, Detection and Confirmation of Urinary Cannabinoids, *J. Analytical Toxicology*, Jul./Aug. 1985, v. 9, pg. 156.

161. Latimer, Dean, "Freedom Chemist" Admits Scam: "Melanin", *High Times*, Apr. 1987, pg. 20.

162. Castro, Janice, Telltale Hair, *Time*, Mar.17, 1986, pg. 55.

163. Product Literature, KDI Quik Test, Brown Boxenbaum, Inc., New York, Dec. 4, 1987.

164. Product Literature, Luckey Simulator, Luckey Laboratories, Inc., San Bernardino, CA, Bulletin no. S69.

165. Product Literature Abuscreen - Radioimmunoassay for Cannabinoids, Roche Diagnostic Systems, New Jersey.

166. Product Literature, Abuscreen - Radioimmunoassay for Morphine, Roche Diagnostic Systems, New Jersey.

167. Frank, James F., and Theodore E. Anderson, Feasibility Assessment of Chemical Testing for Drug-Impaired Driving, National Technical Information Service, Springfield, VA, Sep. 1985.

168. Product Literature, Spot THC Without Instrumentation - Toxi-Lab Cannabinoid (THC) Screen, Analytical Systems, Kansas City, MO.

169. Renauer, Albin, Drug Testing and Privacy Rights at Work, *Nolo News*, Summer 1988, pg. 10.

170. New York Times Staff Writers, No Drug Tests for Customs Agents, *San Francisco Chronicle*, Jan. 17, 1987.

171. Oregon Marijuana Initiative, Drug Test Proposals Spark Debate, *The Marijuana Report*, May 1986, v. 5, no. 1.

172. Staff Writer, Urine Testing for Marijuana & Other Drugs, *The Common Sense for America*, pg. 30-31.

174. Kerr, Peter, Drug Tests Losing Most Court Cases, *The New York Times*, Dec. 11, 1986.

175. Bodovitz, Kathy, Refinery Workers Ask for Drug Test Ban, *San Francisco Chronicle*, Jan. 17, 1987.

177. Dickey, Glenn, NCAA Should Just Say No to Drug Testing, *San Francisco Chronicle*, Mar. 30, 1987, pg. 25.

178. Taylor, Michael, UC Won't Test Workers for Drugs, *San Francisco Chronicle*, Apr. 24, 1987.

180. Sandalow, Marc, BART Sidetracks Drug Tests, *San Francisco Chronicle*, May 5, 1987.

181. Staff Writer, Probe of FAA's Laboratories, *San Francisco Chronicle*, Apr. 24, 1987.

182. Washington Post Staff Writer, What Compromise Drug-Test Program Would Do, *San Francisco Chronicle*, Jun. 5, 1987, pg. 15.

185. Jarvis, Birney, State High Court Halts CHP Plan for Traffic Checkpoints, *San Francisco Chronicle*, Dec. 20, 1986.

186. Miners, PhD, Ian A., Nick Nykodym, Ph.D., and Diane M. Samerdyke-Traband, Put Drug Detection tothe Test, *Personnel J*, Aug. 1987, pg. 91.

187. Manley, Marisa, Employment Lines, *Inc.*, Jun. 1988, pg. 132.

188. Bogdanich, Walt, Medical Labs, Trusted as Largely Error-Free, are Far From Infallible, *The Wall Street Journal*, Feb. 2, 1987.

189. Adams, Marilyn, Drug Tests in View for Truckers, *USA Today*, Jun. 15, 1988.

190. DuPont, M.D., Robert L., Urine Testing in the Workplace, The U.S. *J Drug and Alcohol Dependence*, Jan. 27, 1986.

191. Burrough, Bryan, How GM Began Using Private Eyes in Plants to Fight Drugs, Crime, *The Wall Street Journal*, Feb. 27, 1986.

192. Bennett, John, Tests for Drug Use Predicted to Spread Through Federal Workforce, *Rocky Mountain News*, Mar. 4, 1986.

193. Leib, Jeffrey, 30% of Major Businesses Testing for Drugs, *The Denver Post*, Mar. 23, 1986.

194. Staff, Drug Testing, The Office of Continuing Education, Unversity of Texas, Jan. 22, 1987.

195. Staff, Employee Drug Screening Q & A, National Institute on Drug Abuse,U.S. Dept. of Health and Human Services, 1986, no. (ADM) 86-1442.

196. Staff, Interdisciplinary Approaches to the Problem of Drug Abuse in the Workplace, National Institute on Drug Abuse, U.S. Dept. of Health and Human Services, 1986, no. (ADM) 86-1477.

197. Maltby, Lewis L., Why Drug Testing is a Bad Idea, *Inc.*, Jun. 1987, pg. 152.

198. Hoffman, Joan W., and Ken Jennings, Will Drug Testing in Sports Play for Industry? *Personnel J.*, May 1987, pg. 52.

199. Murphy, Thomas A., Remarks by General Motors Corp. Chairman at the Assoc. of Labor-Management Administrators and Consultants on Alcoholism, Inc., Detroit, MI, Oct. 5, 1979.

200a. Less, Maura, Highwitness News: Piss Patrol Spotlight On: 3M, *High Times Magazine*, Sep. 1988, pg. 20.

200b. Taylor, Jr., Stuart, Justices to Rule on Drug-Testing Plan, *The New York Times*, Mar. 1, 1988.

201. Tessler, Ray, Judge Deals Blow to NCAA Drug Tests, *San Francisco Chronicle*, Aug. 11, 1988, pg. 1.

202. Greenhouse, Linda, Court Backs Tests of Some Workers to Deter Drug Use, *The New York Times*, Mar. 22, 1989.

203. Greenhouse, Linda, Justice Hear Thornburgh Defend Drug-Testing Plan, *The New York Times*, Nov. 3, 1988, pg. A-10.

204. Jacoby, Tamar, Drug Testing in the Dock, *Newsweek Magazine*, Nov. 14, 1988, pg. 66.

205. Staff Writer, The High Court Weighs Drug Tests, *Newsweek Magazine*, Apr. 3, 1989, pg. 8.

206. Washington Post Syndicate. Drug Tests Nab 203 Federal Workers, *San Francisco Chronicle*, Mar. 8, 1989, pg. A-16.

207. Morganthau, Tom, and Mark Miller, The Drug Warrior, *Newsweek Magazine*, Apr. 10, 1989, pg. 20.

208. Staff Writer, Anti-Drug Smuggling Campaign Called Ineffective, *San Francisco Chronicle*, Jun. 9, 1989, Section A.

209. Dodson, Marcida, Drug Testing Comes Home, *San Francisco Chronicle*, Jun. 6, 1989, pg. B-6.

210. Smith, David Urine Testing in the Workplace: Standards of Practice and Evaluation of Results, Proceeding of the Institute for Addiction Studies, Oct. 3, 1986, Oakland, Ca.

211. Staff, Instructions for U-R-Klean, Houston Enterprises, PO Box 27776, Tempe, Az. 85285-7776, (602) 968-0773, (602) 464-8768.

224. Latimer, Dean, Highwitness News: What To Do If You're Fired By A Urine Test, *High Times Magazine*, Nov. 1986, pg. 14.

225. Chen, Edward, M., and John M. True, III, Recent Developments in Employee Drug Testing, *Civil Rights and Attorneys' Fees Annual Handbook*, 1989, Vol. 4.

226. Staff, Urine Tests Are Easily Faked, *Newsweek*, Jul. 31, 1989, pg. 5.

227. Adams, William F., and David S. Rosenbloom, Developments in Drug Testing: The New Federal Standards, *Labor and Employment Law Update*, Apr. 24, 1989, no. 89-4, pg. 1-6, Orrick, Herrington & Sutcliffe, San Francisco.

228. Adams, William F., The Dos, Don'ts and Whys of Drug Testing, *Labor and Employment Law Update*, Apr. 18, 1988, no. 88-3, pg. 1-10, Orrick, Herrington & Sutcliffe, San Francisco.

229. Adams, William F., Controlling Drugs and Alcohol in the Workplace: A Summary of Drug Testing Law and Legislation and Guide to Corporate Policy Development, Institute for Applied Management and Law, San Francisco, Oct. 28, 1988.

230. Sax, Brian M., and William F. Adams, The Continuing Problem of Drug
      and Alcohol Use in the Workplace, Orrick, Herrington & Sutcliffe,
      Seventh Annual Seminar for Employers, San Francisco.

237. Bennett, William. *National Drug Control Strategy*, U.S. Government
      Printing Office, Sep. 1989.

238. Seymour, Senator John, Interim Hearings on Status of Drug Testing in
      the Workplace, California Legislature Senate Select Committee on
      Substance Abuse. Oct. 25, 1988 in Sacramento, Oct. 26, 1988 in San
      Francisco.

239. California Government Code, State Personnel Board, Title 2, 213, Register
      89, No. 18, May 6, 1989.

240. California Government Code, Department of Personnel
      Administration,Title 2, Article 29, Substance Abuse, Register 89, No.
      37, Sep. 16, 1989.

241. Staff, Court Upholds Drug Tests for Job Applicants, *San Francisco
      Chronicle*, Nov. 18, 1989, pg. 9.

242. Stroock, Anne, Random Drug Test Challenge Upheld, *San Francisco
      Chronicle,*. 23, 1990.

243. Decresce, Robert P., Lifshitz, Mark S., *Drug Testing In The Workplace*,
      American Society of Clinical Pathologists Press and The Bureau of
      National Affairs Books, 1989.

Index

Controlled Substances
Chemical & Legal Guide to Federal Drug Laws
Dr. Alexander Shulgin
448 pp., Tables, $39.95

" Indispensable . . . organizes and compiles disparate information into a comprehensive single reference source"
-American Book Review

"A valuable reference . . . saves a vast amount of time and energy of those who must research"
-Journal of Forensic Sciences

"Makes accessible chemical and legal facts"
- J. Bakalar, Harvard Medical School

Controlled Substances is an essential reference for anyone concerned with controlled substances and maintaining a drug free workplace. It contains:

✧ A 215 page chapter listing every formerly and currently schueduled (illegal) drug, the authority for its inclusion in the law, its exact name, its chemical abstract identification number, and all known symptoms for the drug.

✧ A complete listing of all chemical structures of controlled substances, arranged by structural families.

✧ 46 pages of drug code numbers assigned to drugs, solvents, vitamins, food stuffs, and things recognized.

✧ A complete empirical formula index of all compounds mentioned in the current statutes.

✧ 4 appendices detailing the original Controlled Substance Act (CSA) of 1970, the Designer Drug Act of 1986 and the present form it has taken, the working of the Emergency Scheduling Act, the analogue Enforcement Act, and the current Federal Sentencing Guidelines.

✧ 5 Schedules for controlled sub-stances and their criteria.

✧ Definitions of somewhat vague and misleading terms used in the laws, like "high abuse potential" and "substancially similiar."

Drug Testing at Work
Guide for Employers and Employees
Beverly Potter, Ph.D.
Sebastian Orfall, M.A.
252 pp., Illus., $17.95

"A valuable reference"
-Dr. David Smith

"Balanced . . . very good"
-Dr. Alexander Shulgin

Drug Testing at Work is the first comprehensive guide to drug testing in the workplace. It describes how the tests work, legal issues, how to set up a program and steps employees can take to avoid a false positive.

Drug Testing at Work contains a sample company policy that includes how to handle employees under the influence, questions for suspected substances abusers, observational check list, on-site coordination examination, testing consent and release of information forms, inspections and waiver agreement and conditional reinstatement agreement.

Drug Testing at Work explains what the tests can and can't determine and shows employers how they can maintain a drug-free workplace without violating individual rights.

Drug Testing at Work reveals the dangers employees face in testing. People using over-the-counter medicines, for example, can get positive results (false positives) for narcotics. And tests reveal personal information such as health problems and pregnacy.

Drug Testing at Work reveals techniques drug users have used to beat the test, including adulteration, substitution and flushing, and how employers can fight cheating.

Drug Testing at Work describes the alternatives open to employers who have tested positive, including retesting, asking for employee assistance and the perils of suing.

The Way
of the Ronin
Riding the Waves
of Change at Work
Dr. Beverly Potter
252 pp., Illus., $9.95

"Intelligent and inspiring book"
     -ALA Booklist

"One of the best business books of the year"
     -Library Journal

Ronin (translates "wave-man") were the maverick warriors who lead Japan out of feudalism into the modern world. Used as a metaphor, Ronin are the mavericks and change masters who promise to lead the U.S. out of "corporate feudalism" into a long awaited reniassance.

In *The Way of the Ronin,* Beverly Potter offers a unique and inspiring approach to handling the stress of change and performing excellently under the demands of today's corporate environment.

The Way of the Ronin, first published by The American Management Association, draws upon the wisdom of great philosophers, the findings of trend watchers, the latest research of management experts, and the technology of behavior change to show how to:

◇ Thrive on change
◇ Tell excellence from perfectionism
◇ Turn enemies into allies
◇ Become a workplace warrior
◇ Manage self-starters
◇ Develop maverick career strategies

Maverick as Master
in the Workplace
Audio Cassette
60 Minutes, $9.95

An interview with Dr. Beverly Potter by Michael Toms, host of New Dimensions Radio, featured on over 100 NPR shows. She provides insights to empower the independent minded to rise above corporate feudalism and get ahead while enjoying it more.

Beating
Job Burnout
How to Transform
Work Pressure
into Productivity
Dr. Beverly Potter
256 pp., Illus., $9.95

"Worthwhile"
     -Female Executive

"Must reading for anyone who works"
     -Management Concepts

Beating Job Burnout tells what causes the destruction of motivation and how to refuel enthusiasm for work. It describes eight strategies for beating it by developing personal power including self-management, tailoring the job, changing jobs, building social support, controlling negativity and developing detached concern.

Preventing
Job Burnout
A Workbook
Dr. Beverly Potter
90 pp., illus., $7.95

Preventing Job Burnout is a fun book for busy people, filled with exercises and worksheets and formatted for rapid reading and comprehension. Provides a guide to the eight paths to personal power and beating job burnout. Ideal for training.

Beating Job Burnout
Audio Cassette
45 Minutes, $9.95

A lively and informative interview with Dr. Beverly Potter in which she describes the symptoms and causes of job burnout and what to do to prevent it. Originally produced by Psychology Today Cassette Program.

Turning Around
Keys to Motivation and Productivity
Dr. Beverly Potter
256 pp., Illus., $9.95

"Best book on the topic"
-Personnel Psychology

"Outstanding merit for business people"
-Soundview Executive Summaries

Turning Around explains behavior management and how to apply the techniques to daily supervision situations, including how to:

⬧ Improve performance
⬧ Maintain high motivation
⬧ Conduct job interviews
⬧ Give directives
⬧ Mediate conflicts
⬧ Lead meetings
⬧ Manage yourself

Turning Around takes the mystery out of behavior management and brings it down-to-earth with realistic, practical applications geared to your most pressing needs.

Turning Around, originally published by The American Management Association, provides real-world case studies packed with easy-to-adapt techniques. It is a valuable reference to return to when faced with difficult management questions.

Turning Around shows step-by-step how to assure top performance from yourself and all those on your team. It fully explains even the most complex techniques in down-to-earth terms.

Turning Around focuses strictly on objectives and how to achieve them day-in and day-out. It makes your job easier and your career progress more satisfying.

Self-Leadership Tools

Keynotes & Workshops

An age of constant change, with demands for more innovation, stands before us. The old rules don't work anymore. We must become pathfinders, leading ourselves and others into new frontiers. Dr. Beverly Potter and Sebastian Orfali offer customized training and consultation in using self-leadership tools, including problem discovery, creating a compelling vision, self-starting, developing strategic alliances, generating enthusiasm, gathering cooperation and orchestrating teamplay.

Following are examples of exciting keynote topics and training sessions:

⬧ Drug Testing at Work

⬧ Pathfinding: Tools for Self-Leadership

⬧ Managing Yourself for Excellence

⬧ Beating Job Burnout

⬧ Managing Workstress

⬧ Managing Authority: How to Give Effective Directives

⬧ Secrets of Effective Interviewing

⬧ From Conflict to Cooperation

⬧ Maverick Career Strategies

⬧ The Way of the Ronin: Riding the Waves of Change

For brochure, call 415-540-6278, or write to Post Office Box 1035, Berkeley, Ca 94701

To Order Books:

Indicate the books you want, add up total. California residents add 7.25% sales tax. Add $3 handling per order and $1 per book for UPS or 1st class shipping. Send check, money order, P.O. or Visa/MC (with exp date and signature) and complete shipping instructions to: Ronin Publishing, Inc., P.O. Box 1035, Berkeley, Ca 94701 or call 415-540-6278. Discounts are available for volumn orders.

The Authors

Beverly A. Potter, Ph.D., earned her doctorate in counseling psychology from Stanford University and her masters in vocational rehabilitation counseling from San Francisco State University. She is a member of the Stanford Staff Development Program.

Dr. Potter has had a wide range of experience with law enforcement, the criminal justice system, corporations, associations and colleges. She has trained police officers in "crisis intervention" and been "on the beat." She has seen the problems of substance abuse first hand. As a researcher, she lived on a heroin treatment ward and she worked with inmates in the San Francisco County Jail.

Dr. Potter is a specialist in management psychology and has provided training for Hewlett-Packard, GTE, SUN, Becton Dickinson, IRS, Stanford Medical School, Stanford University, Design Management Institute, Department of Energy and others. She has authored several books (see previous pages).

J. Sebastian Orfali, MA., earned his masters at the University of New Mexico. As publisher of And/Or Press and Ronin Publishing, he has edited and published over 120 books about controlled substances, health, technology and current issues, including *The Holistic Health Handbook, Secrets of Life Extension, Marijuana Botany, The Cocaine Handbook, The Network Revolution* and *Controlled Substances*.

Sebastian Orfali has provided consulting for a variety of organizations and associations, including Pacific Bell, United Way, Institute for the Future, Microsoft Press, and Klett Verlag, A.G. He offers keynotes and workshops on management issues, including drug testing in the workplace.